Hiking Massachusetts

A Guide to the State's Greatest Hiking Adventures

Second Edition

Benjamin B. Ames

FALCONGUIDES

GUILFORD, CONNECTICUT
HELENA, MONTANA
AN IMPRINT OF GLOBE PEQUOT PRESS

For Teddy and Isabel, with love to Shannon and gratitude
to the conservationists and volunteers who preserve our wild places.

To buy books in quantity for corporate use
or incentives, call **(800) 962-0973**
or e-mail **premiums@GlobePequot.com.**

FALCONGUIDES®

FalconGuides is an imprint of Globe Pequot Press.
Falcon, FalconGuides, and Outfit Your Mind are registered trademarks of Morris Book Publishing, LLC.

Photos by Benjamin B. Ames, except author photo by Annie Branch.

Maps: Alena Joy Pearce © Morris Book Publishing, LLC

Project editor: Julie Marsh
Layout: Casey Shain

Library of Congress Cataloging-in-Publication Data
Ames, Benjamin B.
  Hiking Massachusetts : a guide to the state's greatest hiking adventures / Benjamin B. Ames. – Second Edition
    pages cm. – (State hiking guides series)
  Summary: "Sample 39 of the finest trails Massachusetts has to offer. This hiker's paradise offers routes to mountaintop vistas, historic landmarks, and pristine seashore. Hike along cranberry bogs in Massasoit State Park, overlook the Merrimack River in Maudslay State Park, follow the Appalachian Trail over Becket and Walling Mountains in October Mountain State Forest, or walk the state from Rhode Island to New Hampshire on the Midstate Trail."—Provided by publisher.
  ISBN 978-0-7627-8480-6 (pbk.)
  1. Hiking—Massachusetts—Guidebooks. 2. Massachusetts—Guidebooks. I. Title.
  GV199.42.M4A48 2014
  796.5109744-dc23
                                                                                    2014004123
Printed in the United States of America

Contents

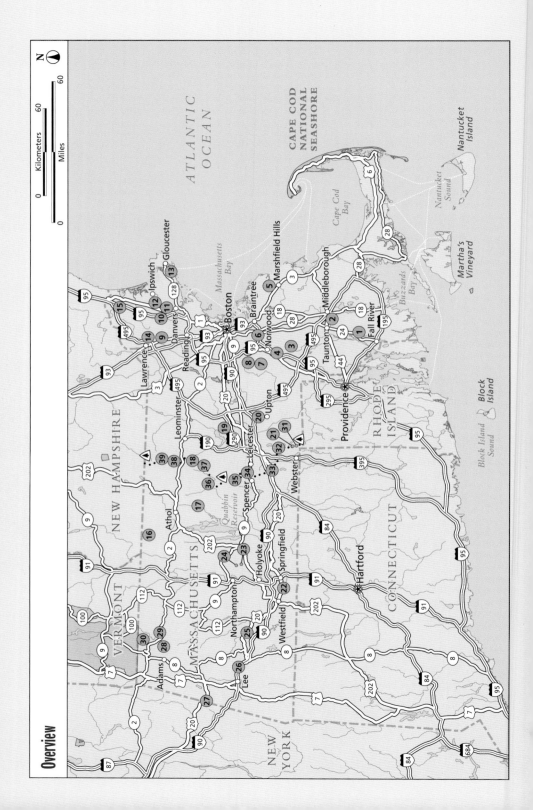

Introduction

Among natural regions in the United States, Massachusetts ranks near the top on just about anybody's list of places to enjoy outdoor recreation and wilderness exploration. Even better, centuries of human history in New England have opened these wild acres to easy access via miles of ancient hiking trails, logging roads, footpaths, and dirt roads. With a free day to roam the state, hikers can easily discover places they've never been, from riverbank to rocky ledge, from open field to shaded forest.

Massachusetts hosts 15 national parks, 143 state parks, 70 state forests, and hundreds of additional acres managed by watershed management and fish and wildlife agencies. Additionally private groups such as Mass Audubon and the Trustees of Reservations oversee large swaths of town conservation land and dozens of animal sanctuaries.

For this book, the author chose an assortment of the region's best pathways, including some of the state's greatest hits, a handful of hidden gems, and a 92-mile trail that spans the state from Connecticut to New Hampshire. The list features thirty loops and out-and-back trails in every corner of the state, as well as a nine-chapter description of the long-distance Midstate Trail.

None of these wild areas would exist in their pristine conditions without the tireless efforts of conservation professionals, state conservation and recreation workers, and all the donors and volunteers who support them. Many thanks for their dedication to the natural resources of the region. Be safe and enjoy!

Massachusetts Weather

I left Cambridge on a sunny March day, congratulating myself on being a careful hiker—I'd packed a sweater and long pants, and thrown my winter hat in the pack for good measure. Arriving at a trailhead near the Barre Falls Dam after a short drive, I immediately walked into the woods and gasped.

With each step snow flew up my pant legs, packing around my boot cuffs. After 50 yards I was wading knee-deep. And after 75 yards I realized my dog was getting nowhere at all—the snow was so deep that it packed under his belly so his legs couldn't reach the ground!

You'd think I would learn a lesson from that experience, but the next weekend I ventured toward North Andover, an even shorter drive from my sunny, urban block. Sure enough, I traipsed into the woods, and got a little farther—perhaps 200 yards—before returning to the car.

That's Massachusetts weather. And it's one of your most important challenges, even on short day hikes in the state. Generally speaking there are three bands of weather in the state: the cape and eastern seashore tend to have moderate weather,

◁ *Despite the pavement, Massasoit Park Road is a quiet, winding trail (hike 2).*

with little snow; but when it rains in the east, it snows in the central plains and Connecticut River Valley; and the autumn foliage comes earliest of all in the western, mountainous Berkshires.

Another crucial detail for any hiker is how much daylight he or she has. Massachusetts's sunrise varies from 5 a.m. in June to 7:15 a.m. in December, and sunset varies from 4:15 p.m. in January to 8:30 p.m. in June.

Average monthly temperatures in Boston range from 28 degrees Fahrenheit in January to 72 degrees Fahrenheit in July. But beware: The extremes can reach 40 degrees on either side of those numbers. Seasonally, nighttime frosts begin in late September and end by early May. Boston's average annual precipitation (including both snow and rain) is 44.23 inches.

Flora and Fauna

Why are birch trees white and laurels green?
Can animals smell fragrant plants like sweet fern and bayberry, as people can?
And wait a minute—look, a polar bear, a tarantula, a python!

Okay, so there are no polar bears walking wild in Massachusetts, but the state has a little bit of almost everything else. One of the best ways to learn all about it is at the EcoTarium, a natural history museum in Worcester (www.ecotarium.org).

Choose from three floors of exhibits, an observatory, and a planetarium. Then head outside, riding the Explorer Express Train or walking along nature trails through 60 acres of ecosystems, with interpretive signs along the Lower Pond Trail, Timescape Trail, and Meadow Trail. Had enough time with your feet on the ground? Head for the Tree Canopy Walkway, suspended 40 feet up in a grove of oak and hickory, with visitors harnessed to safety cables as they traverse swinging bridges spanning up to 150 feet. There's also a small zoo—with that polar bear—and snakes, opossums, and more. And at day's end EcoTarium features "jazz at sunset."

The nature of modern Massachusetts has been hugely impacted by modern civilization and industry. Today it's the third most densely populated state in the country, but it boasts the nation's eighth-largest forest and park system, according to the Massachusetts Association of Professional Foresters (www.massforesters.org). Put another way, it's the thirteenth most populous state overall, but ranks just forty-fifth in size.

On the rebound from the age of agriculture, the state is changing fast. After farmers cleared most of the land, Massachusetts was about 30 percent forested in 1900. Today it has grown back to 64 percent forested, with 3.2 million forested acres, 84 percent of which (2.5 million acres) is privately owned. The remaining 16 percent is split between municipal forests (300,000 acres), the state's Department of Conservation and Recreation (264,000 acres), private NPOs (130,000 acres), the Metropolitan District Commission's Division of Watershed Management (100,000 acres), and the Division of Fisheries and Wildlife (50,000 acres).

The Skyline Trail climbs quickly up Tucker Hill (hike 6).

Massachusetts is a state of small farms, with the number of farms growing from 5,258 to 6,100 from 1992 to 2000. The amount of farmland couldn't keep up, growing merely from 526,440 to 570,000 acres. This lowered the average farm size from 100 to just 93 acres—both minuscule by Midwestern standards. But those Massachusetts farmers are busy! By national rank the state is second for cranberries, ninth for maple syrup, thirteenth for sweet corn, fifteenth for apples, and eighteenth for tomatoes.

Did I mention cranberries? It's one of the state's claims to fame, with Massachusetts's 14,400 acres delivering fully 37 percent of the US cranberry crop. Only Wisconsin makes more, with New Jersey in third, then Oregon and Washington.

Along with blueberries and grapes, the cranberry is one of the few fruits native to North America. Its name was originally "crane berry," thanks to early settlers who recognized the shape of its flowers, which last just ten to twelve days each spring. Full of vitamin C, it was often brought on long ship voyages to fight scurvy, and Native Americans used it with deer venison and fat to make long-lasting "pemmican." But the berries are rather stingy with their juice—at a weight of 440 cranberries per pound, it takes about 10 pounds of berries to make a gallon of juice. And despite the beautiful photos of berry harvests, they do not actually grow in water, but in sandy bogs or marshes. Farmers flood these fields for easy harvest, because the berries float.

Also keep an eye out for the black-capped chickadee (state bird), mayflower (state flower—remember the Pilgrims' boat), and American elm (state tree—now very rare because of Dutch elm disease). Of course the state's beverage is cranberry juice, and the state berry is the cranberry.

Wilderness Restrictions and Regulations

No hunting is allowed on Sunday in Massachusetts. But always use your judgment when heading into the woods in the fall. Think twice about hiking if you see hunters walking the paths at your trailhead. And think three times before bringing an unleashed dog into the autumn woods.

The crucial thing for hikers to know is that shotgun deer season runs for two weeks beginning the Monday after Thanksgiving. The rules allow hunting from a half hour before sunrise to a half hour after sunset. The archery deer season starts earlier but draws fewer hunters into the woods. It runs from October 21 to November 30. Other seasons include pheasant and quail from Columbus Day to Thanksgiving, and turkey seasons in October and May. Check the Division of Fisheries and Wildlife site for updates, www.masswildlife.org.

Wild game animals in Massachusetts are accustomed to living near people. Despite the dense human population, the state boasts a steady count of some 90,000 resident deer, state figures show. That translates to about 10 deer per square mile in northwestern Massachusetts, and a whopping 50 per square mile on Martha's Vineyard and Nantucket islands.

Other wild animals that frequently explore Massachusetts towns and suburbs include skunks, raccoons, gray fox, red fox, coyotes, wild turkey, black bear, and fishers. The quiet forests are home to many more animals, with an estimated sixty land mammal species within the borders of the state. Common trail sightings include moose, beaver, woodchuck, opossum, and porcupine.

Wildlife spotted on the trails of this book range far beyond mammals, although the author did startle a grazing moose at Monroe State Forest. Other sightings were a great horned owl at Robinson State Park, cormorants at Norris Reservation, a great blue heron at Wachusett Meadow Wildlife Sanctuary, a northern water snake at Noanet Woodlands Reservation, a northern black racer snake at Bradley Palmer State Park, and, nearly everywhere, hosts of frogs, toads, red eft newts, and garter snakes.

How to Use This Guide

Take a close enough look and you'll find that this little guide contains just about everything you'll ever need to choose, plan for, enjoy, and survive a hike in Massachusetts. We've done everything but load your pack and tie up your bootlaces. Stuffed with more than 200 pages of useful Massachusetts-specific information, *Hiking Massachusetts* features thirty-nine mapped and cued hikes and everything from advice on getting into shape to tips on getting the most out of hiking with your children or your dog. With so much information the only question you may have is: How do I sift through it all? Well, we have an answer for that too.

We've designed this guide to be highly visual, for quick reference and ease-of-use. What this means is that the most pertinent information rises quickly to the top, so you don't have to waste time poring through bulky hike descriptions to get mileage cues or driving directions. They're set aside for you. And yet this guide doesn't read like a laundry list. Take the time to dive into a hike description and you'll realize that this guide is not just a good source of information, but it's a good read too. And so, in the end, you get the best of both worlds: a quick-reference guide and an engaging look at a region. Here's an outline of *Hiking Massachusetts*'s major components.

Water lily

What You'll Find in This Guide

The state is divided into four regions plus the Midstate Trail. Each region begins with a section introduction, where you're given a sweeping look at the lay of the land in that particular region. After this general overview, specific hikes within that region are described. A short summary gives you a taste of the hiking adventure for each hike in the region. You'll learn about the trail terrain and what surprises each route has to offer.

Next you'll find the quick, nitty-gritty details of the hike: where the trailhead is located, the nearest town, hike length, approximate hiking time, difficulty rating, best hiking season, type of trail terrain, and what other trail users you may encounter. Our Finding the trailhead section gives you dependable directions from a nearby city right down to where you'll want to park. The Hike section is the meat of the chapter. Detailed and honest, it's the author's carefully researched impression of the trail. While it's impossible to cover everything, you can rest assured that we won't miss what's important. In the Miles and Directions section we provide mileage cues to identify all turns and trail name changes, as well as points of interest. Between this and the route map, you simply can't get lost. Finally, the Hike Information box is a hodgepodge of information. For most hikes, it offers trail hotlines (for updates on trail conditions) and local outdoor retailers (for emergency trail supplies), as well as where to stay, what to eat, and what else to see while you're hiking in the area.

Hike Specs

Overview. This short description of each hike includes those special natural features for which it was chosen as well as any other aspects that make the trail outstanding.

Start. This is where the hike begins, the trailhead.

Distance. This figure gives the total distance hiked and the geometry of the trail. Hikes fall into the following categories: "Loop trails" start and finish at the same trailhead with at least a portion of the route not retracing its steps on the return route. A loop includes shapes such as a figure eight or a lollipop. Completing a loop may require a short walk on a dirt road to get back to the trailhead. An "out and back" hike is a trail where you travel the identical route coming and going.

The distance of a loop hike is simply the perimeter of the trails described, while an out-and-back hike is twice the length of the trail. Since the advent of GPS devices, measuring trail distances has become fairly accurate and all primary trail routes described in this book include GPS distances and coordinates. Most wilderness trail signs do not include distances, and when they do, they are often just somebody's best guess. Because of the accuracy of GPS readings, the text may give mileages that differ from trail signs.

Hiking time. This is an estimate of how long it will take to hike the trail. Note that this is just an estimate and can vary widely according to hiking pace and stops along

A red eft looks for food in a puddle near Muddy Pond (hike 38).

the way. Most hikers average about 2 miles per hour, although a steep 2-mile climb on rocky tread can take longer than a 4-mile stroll through a gentle river valley.

Difficulty. This is a subjective opinion made by the author of the difficulty of the hike. Hikes are classified as easy, moderate, or difficult. Difficulty ratings are inherently flawed. What's easy for you might be difficult for someone else. Still, such ratings offer a useful approximation of a hike's challenge. Remember to factor in your own fitness level when interpreting the rating and planning your trip.

Trail surface. This indicates what type of surface you will be hiking on, such as dirt trail, boardwalk, paved path, etc. These details have a large impact on hiking time and difficulty, as hikers navigate the challenges of each distinct trail. Massachusetts is a four-season state, so a broad, sandy path can be an easy cruise in the summer, a tricky trail when autumn leaves obscure its rocks and roots, or a real workout when snow drifts linger into spring.

Best season. A suggested best time of year in which to hike the trail is listed here Use this section to balance challenges such as mosquito swarms in spring and hunting season in fall with rewards like awesome autumn views and summer swimming holes.

Land status. This indicates who owns or manages the land on which the trail passes, for example, state forest or wildlife sanctuary.

Nearest town. The closest city or town with basic amenities is listed here.

Other trail users. This section tells you if you should expect to see other trail users during your hike, such as hunters, mountain bikers, horseback riders, etc.

Canine compatibility. This tells you if it is legal to bring your dog on the trail.

Schedule. This tells you what hours the trail and visitor centers, offices, etc. are open to the public, and what times trails open and close. Important winter information is also included.

Fees and permits. This tells you if you need to carry any money with you for park entrance fees, parking fees, or tolls. Specific amounts are not listed as they can change faster than the book can be printed; check the website or call the trail contact for updated fee amounts.

Maps. This section provides a listing of maps particular to the hike. Maps listed will include park maps and USGS 1:24,000 quad maps. (A detailed map is provided for each hike, showing trailheads, parking, trails, peaks, and other landmarks. These maps are not, however, meant for orienteering or compass work.)

Trail contact(s). This is the direct phone number and website for the local land manager(s) in charge of all the trails within the selected hike. Use this hotline to call ahead for trail access information, or after your visit if you see problems with trail erosion, damage, or misuse.

Finding the trailhead. Directions to the trailhead are provided here. Often two or more sets of directions are listed to get you to different trailheads or to guide you from different starting points. This information should be used in conjunction with the maps in this guide, USGS maps, and state road maps.

Hike Information

Local information. Contact information for the local convention and visitor bureau or similar organization.

Local events/attractions. Information about other hiking or non-hiking events or attractions in the area.

Accommodations: This section lists campsites and hotels near the trailhead.

Organizations. Local nonprofit or "friends" groups affiliated with the destination.

Other resources: Helpful stuff to know as you explore new trails, towns, and regions.

Local outdoor retailers: Find the closest outdoor gear shop for those days when you left a water bottle at home or snapped a shoelace while lacing up your boots.

Wetland scenes are common on the Stone Bridge Trail (hike 11). ▷

Trail Finder

Listed from easiest to hardest within each category

Best Hikes with Great Views
19 Mount Pisgah Conservation Area
15 Maudslay State Park
9   Ward Reservation
4   Moose Hill Wildlife Sanctuary
13 Ravenswood Park
29 Mohawk Trail State Forest
6   Blue Hills Reservation
16 Mount Grace State Forest
18 Wachusett Mountain State
    Reservation
30 Monroe State Forest

23 Rattlesnake Knob
24 Skinner State Park

Best Hikes with Kids
14 Weir Hill Reservation
22 Robinson State Park
2   Massasoit State Park
3   Borderland State Park
5   Norris Reservation
11 Ipswich River Wildlife Sanctuary
12 Bradley Palmer State Park
29 Mohawk Trail State Forest

Best Hikes for Solitude

19   Mount Pisgah Conservation Area
12   Bradley Palmer State Park
10   Boxford State Forest
29   Mohawk Trail State Forest
13   Ravenswood Park
17   Brooks Woodland Preserve

Best Flat Hikes

22   Robinson State Park
2   Massasoit State Park
19   Mount Pisgah Conservation Area
5   Norris Reservation
3   Borderland State Park
12   Bradley Palmer State Park
11   Ipswich River Wildlife Sanctuary
1   Freetown/Fall River State Forest
10   Boxford State Forest
21   Douglas State Forest

Best Steep Hikes

16   Mount Grace State Forest
29   Mohawk Trail State Forest
6   Blue Hills Reservation
18   Wachusett Mountain State
     Reservation
23   Rattlesnake Knob
24   Skinner State Park
25   Chester-Blandford State Forest

Best Short Hikes

5   Norris Reservation
14   Weir Hill Reservation
19   Mount Pisgah Conservation Area
27   Pittsfield State Forest
29   Mohawk Trail State Forest

Best Hikes for Nature Watching

5   Norris Reservation
7   Rocky Woods Reservation
11   Ipswich River Wildlife Sanctuary
8   Noanet Woodlands Reservation
13   Ravenswood Park

Best Hikes along Rivers

22   Robinson State Park
5   Norris Reservation
12   Bradley Palmer State Park
15   Maudslay State Park
17   Brooks Woodland Preserve

Best Hikes on Long-Distance Trails

10   Boxford State Forest
27   Pittsfield State Forest
16   Mount Grace State Forest
24   Skinner State Park
26   October Mountain State Forest
31–39   Midstate Trail

Best Hikes with Waterfalls

25   Chester-Blandford State Forest
28   Savoy Mountain State Forest

Best Hikes to Ponds

2   Massasoit State Park
14   Weir Hill Reservation
3   Borderland State Park
7   Rocky Woods Reservation
8   Noanet Woodlands Reservation
27   Pittsfield State Forest
20   Upton State Forest
21   Douglas State Forest
26   October Mountain State Forest

Legend

Interstate Highway		Cattle Guard	
US Highway		Cemetery	
State Highway		Church	
County/Local Road		Dam	
Unpaved Road		Inn/Lodging	
Railroad		Fire Tower	
Utility/Power Line		Fishing Area	
Featured Trail		Gate	
Trail		Horseback Riding	
Midstate Trail		Mileage Marker/Intersection	
Boardwalk/Steps		Parking	
Ferry Route		Peak/Summit	
State Line		Picnic Area	
Small River/Creek		Quarry	
Marsh/Swamp		Radio Tower	
Body of Water		Ranger Station/Headquarters	
National/State Forest/Park		Restrooms	
National Management/Wildlife/Reservation Area		Scenic View/Viewpoint	
		Shelter	
State/County Park		Spring	
Airport		Swimming	
Bench		Telephone	
Boat Ramp		Town	
Bridge		Trailer Service	
Building/Point of Interest		Trailhead	
Campground		Visitor/Information Center	
Campsite		Waterfall	
Capitol		Wildlife Refuge	

Southeast Massachusetts

For a small state in a moderate climate, you'd think Massachusetts would have a consistent seashore. But it takes just a few steps for hikers to tell the difference between rocky, exposed Cape Ann to the north and sandy, marshy Cape Cod to the south.

For classic examples, take a walk at Borderland State Park, Douglas State Forest, Freetown/Fall River State Forest, or Massasoit State Park. In each place the dry soil is sandy under your boots, with low shrubs spread over a flat, broad landscape. One hike at Ravenswood or Maudslay State Park will show the difference, as you scramble over the steep and stony trails of the north shore.

This soil determines plants and animals too. Split by Boston in the center, the capes are like grumpy siblings who look alike but can't stand to look at each other. The family began 25,000 years ago, when the most recent glacier stalled in this neighborhood. But northern snows kept pushing, and like a conveyor belt the glacier sent rocky deposits to the state, dropping them as it melted. By 10,000 years ago the glacier was completely gone, and the state looked entirely different.

The face-lift included terminal moraines formed of this glacial till, molding the hills and ridges of modern-day Cape Cod and the islands. It also dropped random boulders, called glacial erratics, plopped down as if airmailed from hundreds of miles away. And in some places, chunks of the glacier stuck in the earth like terrestrial icebergs, melting until they created ponds with no inlet or outlet, fed only by groundwater—kettle ponds.

The region changed very slowly, as the sea's erosion made dunes and barrier beaches. But change accelerated in the mid-seventeenth century when European settlers arrived, clear-cutting southern Massachusetts by 1800, and watching much of the topsoil wash away with the wind and rain. Today you can tell southeastern Massachusetts by its flat, sandy ground filled with plants that love the acidic soil—blueberries, cranberries, and pine barrens.

◄ *The quiet Whitetail Loop is a good place to find deer tracks in the sandy soil (hike 1).*

1 Freetown / Fall River State Forest

This sprawling, flat, sandy park is a typical Massachusetts coastal forest, filled with deer, pheasants, and freshwater fish, and surrounded by nearby cranberry farms. The hike offers a tour of this sand–plain ecosystem, with sandy soil, scrub oak, white pine, and thick laurel undergrowth. Unfortunately, it is also a favorite of dirt bike riders, but this loop sticks to a part of the forest largely avoided by motorized vehicles.

Start: From the dirt parking lot off High Street, just south of its intersection with Copicut Road
Distance: 5.6-mile loop
Hiking time: About 2.5 hours
Difficulty: Easy, with broad trails and little elevation change
Trail surface: Broad, sandy trails
Best season: Spring
Land status: MA Department of Conservation and Recreation
Nearest town: Fall River

Other trail users: Mountain bikers, dirt bike and ATV riders, equestrians, hunters (in season), dogsledders, snowmobilers
Canine compatibility: Dogs permitted
Schedule: Open half hour before sunrise to half hour after sunset
Fees and permits: None
Maps: USGS Somerset, MA
Trail contact: Freetown/Fall River State Forest, Assonet; (508) 644-5522; www.mass.gov/eea/agencies/dcr/massparks/region-south/freetown-fall-river-state-forest.html

Finding the trailhead: From Taunton, take MA 24 south to exit 10, for North Main Street, Assonet, and Freetown. Turn left off the exit to head south on North Main Street. At 0.8 mile, cross through an intersection onto MA 79 South. Ignoring all signs for state park entrances, turn left onto High Street at 1.2 miles. Cross an intersection at 2.6 miles with Copicut Road. At 3.3 miles, turn right into a gated dirt parking lot located just before the paved road changes to dirt. *DeLorme: Massachusetts Atlas & Gazetteer:* Page 57 O21. GPS: N41 45.553' / W71 04.310'

The Hike

The forest's 5,441 acres yield some fascinating finds, like fuzzy, neon–green caterpillars and anthills the size of TV sets. The sandy soil holds deer prints, horseshoe prints, tire tracks, and boot prints. And the woods are full of deer and pheasants.

In the 1930s the Civilian Conservation Corps (CCC) built dozens of stone-lined pits here, to hold water from streams and provide pumping sources for fire engines. Today they are numbered with signs—useful as landmarks—marked on forest maps. The park also includes the 227-acre Watuppa Reservation, which belongs to the Wampanoag Nation and is the site for their annual tribal meeting. The profile of the famous Wampanoag leader, Chief Massasoit, can be seen in Profile Rock, a 50-foot outcropping.

The trailhead parking lot is a favorite place for motorbike and ATV riders to park their trucks. Their noise and fumes can be noxious, but they generally do not ride on

Keep an eye open for natural highlights on the Whitetail Trail, from towering anthills to bright orange fungus.

the loop you'll be hiking. Also, the park is closed completely to motorized vehicles between the last Sunday of November and May 1. The forest is a popular site for mountain bikers too, who often race on the trails. However, like the motorbike riders, they seldom ride east of High Street.

The forest's wildlife management area (WMA) is stocked with pheasants to prepare for hunting season, which begins here in mid-October. Together the Acushnet and Freetown/Fall River State Forest WMAs are 355 acres. The trails are littered with shotgun shells, but there is no hunting allowed on Sunday at any time of year in Massachusetts. Likewise, the state stocks Rattlesnake Brook with brook trout each spring, and anglers flock in season. There are restrooms and free maps at park headquarters.

The land is also part of the 13,600-acre Southeastern Massachusetts Bioreserve, a chain of unfragmented woodland stretching from the state forest southward toward Dartmouth and Westport. Although it's located just 10 miles from a major population center, the combined land encompasses a mosaic of ecologies, including three types of water bodies, thirteen kinds of freshwater uplands, and twelve kinds of upland communities. Just the forty-seventh such bioreserve in the country when it was founded in 2002, it comprises the 3,800-acre former Acushnet Sawmill Property (once used as a woodlot for furniture and firewood), a combined 10,200 acres of state forest and wildlife management land, some city-owned watershed land, and 2,000 acres of water surface in Fall River's two reservoirs. The Trustees of Reservations maintain a

Gateway Center to the bioreserve in the 516-acre Copicut Woods section, introducing visitors to this complex ecosystem of forests, streams, and cedar swamps.

Among Fall River's many historic sights and sites, one stands out:

Lizzie Borden took an axe
gave her mother forty whacks
when she saw what she had done
she gave her father forty one.

Yes, this is the city where the famous crime occurred. On Fall River's Second Street lived the Borden family: Lizzie, her sister Emma, their father, Andrew Jackson Borden, and stepmother, Abby Durfee Gray Borden. On August 4, 1892, the parents were found killed by hatchet blows to their heads. Lizzie was acquitted in the ensuing trial, but was still ostracized by the community. Today there is a bed-and-breakfast museum, where you can sleep in the same rooms where family members lived (and died), and even eat the same breakfast meal they did on that fateful day—bananas, johnnycakes, sugar cookies, and coffee.

Miles and Directions

0.0 Start at the dirt lot and turn right onto High Street, heading south.

0.1 Pass a sign for Haskell Path, and soon pass Water Hole 14. Cross the town line from Freetown into Fall River and immediately turn left, onto the dirt, blue-blazed Whitetail Loop.

1.0 Turn right at an intersection to stay on the Whitetail Loop.

1.4 Turn left at a fork, leaving the Whitetail Loop and heading north on the sandy, two-track Grinnell Path. Stay on this main trail as smaller paths branch off to the right.

2.0 Pass through a brown metal gate into a dirt parking lot, called Hunters Lot C. Cross through the lot and turn right onto the rough, dirt Copicut Road, heading south.

2.2 Pass by Cedar Swamp Road on your left.

2.5 Turn right onto the narrow Bridle Path Trail, marked by two roadside boulders, leaving the dirt road.

3.2 Turn right at a T intersection, heading west on Clark Field Path.

3.6 Cross another trail at a four-way intersection, continuing on a narrower path.

3.8 Go right at a fork, then immediately right again, picking up the blue-blazed Whitetail Loop heading north. On maps, this intersection is just north of Water Hole 28.

4.2 Pass Water Hole 29 on your left.

4.3 Go left at a fork. You are now retracing your original steps on the Whitetail Loop.

4.7 Go left at an intersection to continue following blue blazes.

5.4 Pass by a grassy trail on your left.

5.5 Turn right onto paved High Street, immediately crossing the town line from Fall River into Freetown. Soon pass Water Hole 14 on your left and then the Haskell Path.

5.6 Turn left into the dirt parking lot and find your car.

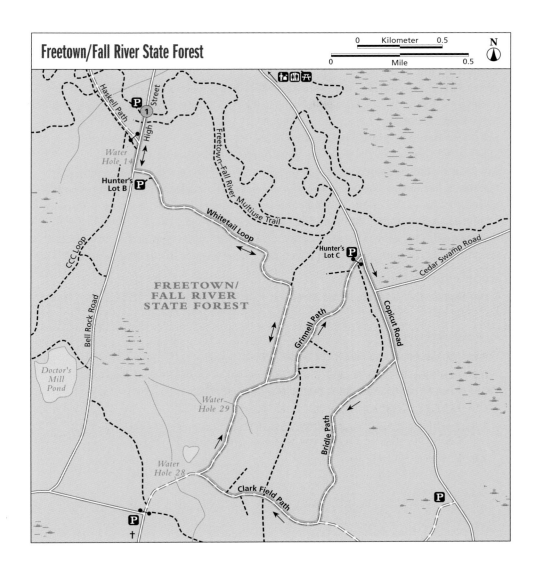

Freetown/Fall River State Forest

Hike Information

Local Information

Fall River city website: www.fallriverma.org

Fall River Police Department: www.frpd.org. The website has some great info about Fall River and its history.

Local Events/Attractions

The Edaville Railroad: Carver; (508) 866-8190; www.edaville.com. This family historical park has a museum and children's train and carousel rides. You can even take a 5.5-mile steam locomotive trip through an 1,800-acre cranberry plantation. The website also lists local hotels and campgrounds.

Battleship Cove: Fall River; (508) 678-1100; www.battleshipcove.com. This museum of Fall River's rich nautical history features ships like the battleship USS *Massachusetts,* destroyer USS *Joseph P. Kennedy Jr.,* submarines, PT boats, captured Japanese boats, helicopters, and more.

Fall River Heritage State Park: Fall River; (508) 675-5759; www.mass.gov/eea/agencies/dcr/massparks/region-south/fall-river-heritage-state-park.html

Fall River Historical Society: Fall River; (508) 679-1071; www.fallriverhistorical.org

Fun Day in the Forest: This annual outdoors celebration is held in early October at the forest. It includes guided trail walks, van tours of the forest, a rock climbing wall, pony and hayrides, music, and refreshments.

Freetown 50: This annual mountain bike race is held in mid-September at the forest. Ask for details of both events at the forest headquarters on Slab Bridge Road.

Accommodations

Lizzie Borden Bed and Breakfast Museum: Fall River; (508) 675-7333; http://lizzie borden.com

Organizations

Friends of the Freetown/Fall River State Forest: Assonet; (508) 995-1335. This conservation group meets every other month at forest headquarters to protect the forest, sponsoring trail work, forest cleanup, and other activities.

Local Outdoor Retailers

Carabiner's Climbing Gym: New Bedford; (508) 984-0808; www.carabiners.com

2 Massasoit State Park

Located on the northern edge of Massachusetts's coastal sand plain, this park marks a transition from the more thickly forested hills of northeastern Massachusetts to the flat, sandy lands of Cape Cod and the coast. The trail touches the edge of Big Bearhole Pond, with wonderful views of this forested lake and the scrub oak and pitch pine growing on its sandy shores. The walk ends as you reach a cranberry bog near the front gate.

Start: From the parking lot at park headquarters
Distance: 3.4-mile loop
Hiking time: About 2 hours
Difficulty: Easy
Trail surface: Flat and sandy paths
Best season: Spring
Land status: MA Department of Conservation and Recreation
Nearest town: Middleborough
Other trail users: Mountain bikers, equestrians, cross-country skiers

Canine compatibility: Dogs permitted
Schedule: Until it regains its funding, the park is closed to overnight camping and vehicle traffic, but its roads are open to pedestrians and bicycle riders.
Fees and permits: None
Maps: USGS Taunton, MA and Bridgewater, MA
Trail contact: Massasoit State Park, East Taunton; (508) 822-7405; www.mass.gov/eea/agencies/dcr/massparks/region-south/massasoit-state-park.html

Finding the trailhead: From Middleborough, take I-495 north to exit 5, for MA 18 South, Lakeville, and New Bedford. Follow MA 18 South for 0.5 mile and turn right at a blinking yellow light onto Taunton Street (this road's name changes to Middleboro Avenue as you cross the county line). At 2.5 miles, turn left at the sign for the park's main entrance. The parking area is 200 yards inside, past several gates. *DeLorme: Massachusetts Atlas & Gazetteer:* Page 57 H26. GPS: N41 52.840' / W70 59.497'

The Hike

The millstone displayed on the trail near Middle Pond was pulled from the water several years ago, when rangers did their annual draining to kill off fast-growing invasive plants. Along with the cranberry bog near the main parking lot, the park thus holds two of the most enduring symbols of the state's agricultural history. But its name predates them both. Massasoit was a Wampanoag Indian chief—one of the tribes that first welcomed the pilgrims upon their arrival at nearby Plymouth Rock, just 20 miles to the west. Massasoit was born around 1590, near present-day Bristol, Rhode Island. He is noted for signing a famed peace treaty with the pilgrims in 1621 that was never once broken throughout the remainder of his life—nearly forty years.

The Peter Adams Trail through this park commemorates a more recent chapter in American history. Adams was a black Revolutionary War soldier buried with his family in Talbots Cemetery, a small plot on nearby Sherwood Avenue. His headstone reads simply, PETER ADAMS, D. 1841, AGED 101 YEARS. A SOLDIER OF THE REVOLUTION. Nearby lies his wife, Margaret, who died in 1844 at the age of 92. An adjacent historical marker reads, PETER ADAMS, A FREE NEGRO MAN AND A SOLDIER OF THE REVOLUTION IS BURIED HERE.

While they were certainly the first to settle the new world, British pilgrims were not the first visitors to arrive in America by boat. There are many signs that Viking explorers reached Cape Cod centuries earlier, and in Middleborough there are signs of even older tenants—an archaic village at the mouth of the Nemasket River that has been radiocarbon-dated to 2,300 BC.

Nearby Lake Assawompsett—the largest natural body of freshwater in Massachusetts—drains into the Nemasket, which feeds the Taunton River and soon reaches the sea. It's a natural magnet for human settlers; Native Americans relied on the Nemasket for food and water, and Pilgrims built gristmills, furnaces, and forges here. They later built cotton mills and shovel works as the local economy expanded. In 1871 Big Bearhole Pond was known as Dean Factory Pond, the site of a sawmill, cooper's shop, and shoe store.

Despite its rich history, the park lost its state funding in 2011, so many of its bathrooms and campsites are shuttered. But the land is still beautiful, from the trails popular with dog walkers and mountain bikers to the ponds bustling with herons, ducks, and geese.

The sandy soil, seagulls, and clam shells are clues that you're near the ocean. And for proof that this acidic earth is perfect for cranberry crops, you need only look to the nearby corporate headquarters of Ocean Spray, the fruit and juice producer.

Miles and Directions

0.0   Start in the parking lot and follow paved Massasoit Park Road past the welcome station and stop sign.

0.2   Turn right through a metal gate with a sign for No MOTORIZED VEHICLES, leaving the pavement for a wide, sandy path.

0.3   Cross straight through a clearing in the woods, passing stacks of picnic tables on your left and a trail branching off to your right.

0.6   Cross a boardwalk over a small stream.

0.7   Turn right onto the paved Massasoit Park Road.

0.8   Continue straight on the main paved road headed toward the Bridle Trail, passing the "E Road" campsite access road to your right.

1.2   Continue straight again as you pass a right fork where "H Road" leads to campsites. Your path is now known as Bearhole Road.

1.5   Continue straight through a metal gate, passing Fisherman's Landing on your left and a historic mill site on your right. Cross the dam where Big Bearhole Pond on your left flows into Middle Pond on your right.

1.6   Turn right at a fork about 50 yards after the pavement ends. Stay straight on this wide Bridle Trail, close by the shore of Middle Pond on your right, as a succession of smaller footpaths branch off.

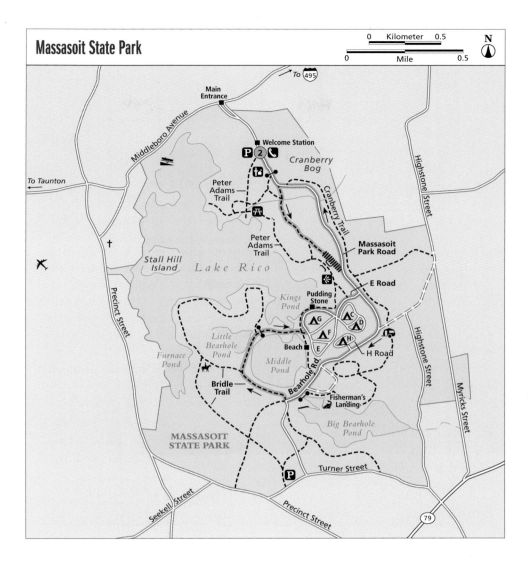

Massasoit State Park

To (495)

Main Entrance

Welcome Station

P 2

Cranberry Bog

To Taunton

Peter Adams Trail

Peter Adams Trail

Massasoit Park Road

Stall Hill Island

Lake Rico

E Road

Middleboro Avenue

Highstone Street

Precinct Street

Kings Pond

Pudding Stone

A G

A C

A D

A F

A H

Little Bearhole Pond

Beach

E

H Road

Furnace Pond

Middle Pond

Bridle Trail

Bearhole Rd.

Fisherman's Landing

Big Bearhole Pond

Highstone Street

Myricks Street

MASSASOIT STATE PARK

Turner Street

P

Seekell Street

Precinct Street

79

1.8 Turn right at a four-way crossroads and soon cross an earthen dike between Little Bear-hole Pond on your left and Middle Pond on your right.

1.9 Turn right through a metal gate to continue circling Middle Pond on your right.

2.2 Reach a large concrete building with bathrooms and showers for the nearby beach, and turn left onto the paved "G Road," passing by campsites.

2.4 Turn left at another bathhouse, then left again onto the paved "E Road."

2.6 Turn left at a junction and retrace your steps along the main, paved Massasoit Park Road back to your car.

3.4 Arrive back at the parking lot.

The trees around Middle Pond are full of herons looking for fish.

Hike Information

Local Information

Old Colony Historical Society Museum and Library: Taunton; (508) 822-1622; www.old colonyhistoricalsociety.org. A fee is charged for adults.

3 Borderland State Park

This wet, sandy land is a typical southeastern Massachusetts ecosystem, with the acidic soil beloved by cranberry bogs and cedar swamps. The park's many ponds were formed by damming its streams, first to spin waterwheels for a nineteenth-century furnace, and later for fishing, boating, and skating. The broad carriage paths that encircle Leach Pond and Upper Leach Pond are filled with baby carriages, mountain bikes, horses, and joggers on a beautiful spring day, while the footpaths that twist around the park's northern half are narrow, rocky, and quiet. This loop is a combination of the two, just scratching the surface of the park's four-season variety.

Start: From the visitor center off Massapoag Avenue

Distance: 4.0-mile loop

Hiking time: About 2.5 to 3 hours

Difficulty: Easy, thanks to broad flat trails and minimal elevation change

Trail surface: Packed dirt trails, with some sections scrambling over bare rock

Best season: Summer

Land status: MA Department of Conservation and Recreation

Nearest town: Sharon

Other trail users: Mountain bikers, cross-country skiers, equestrians

Canine compatibility: Dogs permitted (must be kept on leash around visitor center)

Schedule: Open year-round, until 6:30 p.m.; summer hours 8 a.m. to 7:30 p.m.

Fees and permits: Visitor center lot charges a small parking fee

Maps: USGS Brockton, MA

Trail contacts: Borderland State Park, North Easton; (508) 238-6566; www.mass.gov/eea/agencies/dcr/massparks/region-south/borderland-state-park-generic.html. Friends of Borderland, North Easton; (508) 238-6566; http://friendsofborderland.org

Finding the trailhead: From Boston, drive south on I-95 to exit 8 and turn left onto South Main Street toward Sharon, soon passing Ward's Berry Farm. At 3.3 miles, turn right at the light in Sharon Center onto Billings Street and immediately go right again, onto Pond Street. At 4.2 miles, reach the rotary at Lake Massapoag and continue straight on Massapoag Avenue along its shore, following signs for the park. At 7.7 miles, turn left at the park sign and immediately left again for the visitor center parking lot. *DeLorme: Massachusetts Atlas & Gazetteer:* Page 53 L16. GPS: N42 03.745' / W71 09.883'

The Hike

Borderland was tailored for outdoor recreation, earning its name when the Ames family purchased a series of farms that straddled the town lines of Sharon and Easton. The family's four young children spent years fishing and boating on the estate's ponds, and scouted many of its trails. My grandfather was one of those children, born on the grounds and raised in the great stone mansion built in 1910 by his parents, Harvard University botany professor Oakes Ames and artist and suffragette Blanche Ames.

This hike begins at the visitor center, with restrooms, free maps, historical photographs, and natural history displays. Walk south along a broad carriage road toward the mansion, encircling Leach Pond (named for General Shepherd Leach, who built it in 1825 to power his furnace). This carriage road winds through swampland, where the sound of mating frogs can be deafening even at noon on a spring day. You circle the pond, home to mallards and ringed by bluebird boxes, continuing on this easy pathway until it reaches Mountain Street, just north of the Upper Leach Pond. Trace the pond's northern shore along Tisdale Road until you pick up the Granite Hills Trail. Head north on this narrow footpath to experience the park's wilder side, leaving the crowds behind as you scramble over boulders and twist between tall trees. This loop rejoins the broad carriage loop on Leach Pond's northern shore, soon passing the stone lodge where the Ames family used to build fires for warmth after a day of ice skating. The pond is fed by Poquanticut Brook and kept by Ollie's Dam, named for my grandfather's elder brother, Oliver, who loved to work on it. The broad carriage trail soon returns to the visitor center.

The excellent park staff organizes year-round events that concentrate on natural history. The grounds are also used for everything from dog shows and Civil War reenactments to art exhibits and fishing derbies. Additional events include outdoor concerts, a weekly morning walk, Halloween ghost stories, mushroom hunts, insect walks, and free hayrides. Phone the park for more details.

After your walk, be sure to explore the mansion, which is open for tours every month (except in winter) on the third Friday (from 10 a.m. to noon) and third Sunday (from 1 to 3 p.m.). The decorations and furnishings in its twenty rooms have been preserved from the family's residence here, so you can see Oakes's library and Blanche's paintings, political cartoons, and inventions such as the color wheel, a standardized gradation of painting tones. This extraordinary woman also cofounded the Birth Control League of Massachusetts in 1916. The rooms are stocked with historic mementos of the family's political history, such as a 1910-era Star Spangled Banner, which had thirteen stripes and forty-six stars.

A monument recently installed by the Easton Historical Commission sums up the story well:

> Borderland. The former estate of two remarkable people, Oakes and Blanche Ames. Within this park are the sites of several eighteenth- and nineteenth-century industries: a bog iron operation, a reservoir for Easton furnace industries, early Easton homes, and a stone mansion.

Miles and Directions

0.0 Start at the visitor center and walk south along the broad carriage road that skims the field and approaches the Ames Mansion.

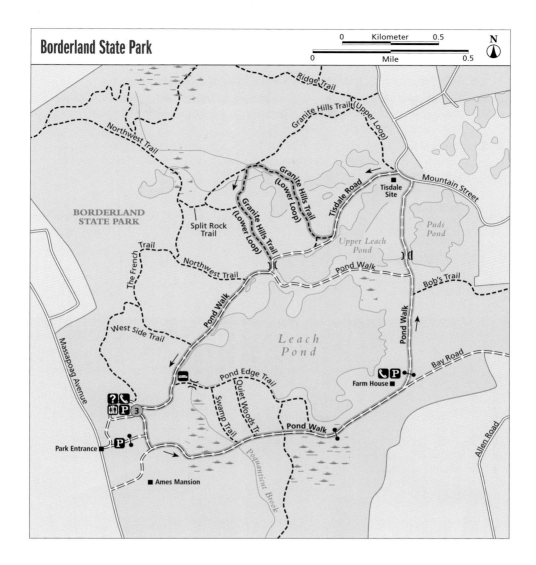

Borderland State Park

0 — Kilometer — 0.5

0 — Mile — 0.5

N

BORDERLAND STATE PARK

Ridge Trail

Granite Hills Trail (Upper Loop)

Northwest Trail

Granite Hills Trail (Lower Loop)

Granite Hills Trail (Lower Loop)

Tisdale Road

Tisdale Site

Mountain Street

Split Rock Trail

Puds Pond

The French Trail

Northwest Trail

Upper Leach Pond

Pond Walk

Bob's Trail

Pond Walk

West Side Trail

Pond Walk

Leach Pond

Pond Walk

Bay Road

Massapoag Avenue

Pond Edge Trail

Quiet Woods Tr.

Swamp Trail

Farm House

Pond Walk

Allen Road

Park Entrance

Pond Walk

Poquantia Brook

■ Ames Mansion

0.2 Branch left at a fork in the road, just before reaching the mansion's looped driveway. Stay on this main Pond Walk path as you pass signs for the smaller Swamp Trail and Quiet Woods Trail.

0.8 Reach the shore of Leach Pond on your left, skirting its edge as you continue on the broad path, soon passing the wooden boxes of a bluebird nesting area.

1.1 Turn left at a junction just past a white farmhouse (a private residence), following a sign for Pond Trail Walk, Upper Leach Pond, and Puds Pond. Continue straight along this two-track path, ignoring a footpath that forks left in the middle of a clearing.

1.5 At the end of this clearing, cross a cement dam, where Puds Pond (on your right) drains into Upper Leach Pond (visible through trees to your left). Cross a wooden footbridge and continue straight, keeping the shore of Puds Pond close on your right.

1.8 Pass through a metal gate and turn left onto a paved road, Mountain Street.

1.9 Turn left again, leaving the pavement and reaching the Tisdale ("Old Homestead") Site at the northern tip of Upper Leach Pond. Continue along a broad carriage path called Tisdale Road, keeping the pond on your left.

2.4 Turn right onto the narrow Granite Hills Trail (Lower Loop), crossing an open meadow to a boardwalk through the trees. (***Bailout:*** Continue straight along the gentle Tisdale Road for a more direct return to the visitor center.)

2.8 Turn left at a junction to continue on the Granite Hills Trail, soon crossing two more boardwalks.

3.0 Pass by a sign for the Split Rock Trail as you scramble through boulder fields and over stony ridges.

3.2 Turn right onto the broad, groomed Tisdale Road.

The stone lodge building was built as a warming hut for ice skaters on Leach Pond.

3.3 Turn right onto the Pond Walk trail where a wooden footbridge crosses Upper Leach Pond to your left, and follow this main path back toward the visitor center.

3.8 Pass by the stone lodge building on your left and follow the white-blazed, broad path back to the visitor center.

4.0 Arrive back at your car.

Hike Information

Local information

Get Outdoors New England: www.gonewengland.org

Local Events/Attractions

The park organizes seasonal events, such as bird watching in the woodcock-mating season, stargazing on clear nights, storytelling for adults, and tours of the Ames Mansion. Check at the visitor center for details.

Restaurants

Pizzigando: Sharon; (781) 784-8161. Pizza and sandwich shop.
Ward's Berry Farm: Sharon; (781) 784-3600; www.wardsberryfarm.com. Farm stand with fresh fruits, vegetables, and baked goods.

Hike Tours

Check at the visitor center.

Local Outdoor Retailers

City Sports: Boston; (617) 782-5121; www.citysports.com
Eastern Mountain Sports (EMS): Boston; (617) 254-4250; www.emsonline.com
Hilton's Tent City: Boston; (800) 362-8368; www.hiltonstentcity.com
Patagonia: Boston; (617) 424-1776; www.patagonia.com

4 Moose Hill Wildlife Sanctuary

This loop begins with a quick walk through reclaimed pastures, then settles in for a flat, sweeping stroll through the woods. At the park's southwestern edge, you get terrific views from Allen Ledge and Bluff Head, where granite cliffs drop off steeply. Look around you—the park is so diverse it has twelve of the state's twenty-three habitats spanning forest, field, and wetland ecosystems set in a 2,200-acre wildlife preserve.

Start: From the visitor center off Moose Hill Street

Distance: 3.9-mile loop

Hiking time: About 2 hours

Difficulty: Moderate, due to length and one steep section

Trail surface: Primarily broad, flat dirt trails, with one steep section and one rocky section

Best season: Fall

Land status: Massachusetts Audubon Society

Nearest town: Sharon

Other trail users: Hikers only; Massachusetts Audubon does not allow dogs, bicycles, or horses

Canine compatibility: Dogs not permitted

Schedule: Open year-round, sunrise to sunset, closed Monday; nature center open 9 a.m. to 5 p.m., closed Monday

Fees and permits: Day-use fee for adults; free with Audubon membership

Maps: USGS Norwood, MA and Brockton, MA

Trail contact: Moose Hill Wildlife Sanctuary, Sharon; (781) 784-5691; www.massaudubon .org/Nature_Connection/Sanctuaries/ Moose_Hill

Finding the trailhead: From Norwood, take I-95 south to exit 10, for Coney Street, Walpole, and Sharon. Turn left off the exit onto MA 27 North, turning right in 0.3 mile to stay on this road. At 0.9 mile, turn left onto Moose Hill Street. At 2.2 miles, turn left onto Moose Hill Parkway and immediately enter the sanctuary parking lot. *DeLorme: Massachusetts Atlas & Gazetteer:* Page 52 H13. GPS: N42 07.435' / W71 12.418'

The Hike

The red oak forest of the moist flatlands changes quickly to white pine stands as you ramble along the elevated ledges of the sanctuary's western border. They are separated by a sea of knee-high ferns along the Forest Trail, providing great variety for a 4-mile hike. Since these are mixed wetlands and forests, the trails can be quite wet in spring, so be sure to wear good boots. Following a shady loop on the Forest Trail, you move on to sweeping views from Allens Ledge on the Bluff Trail. After your comfortable, flat stroll, it feels like cheating to get such a great view without climbing, but your guilt won't last long as you gaze westward off these bare granite cliffs. A stone chimney stands alone at cliff's edge, the last remnant of a cabin once perched here.

Continuing the loop, you'll soon reach the old stone cistern. It once held water collected from the wetlands to the west, which was used at one point to feed an orchard that is now lost to the woods you see to the east, and used later for the town of Sharon's drinking water. The modern wooden ramp is a safety measure so clumsy animals (and people) can escape the steep walls.

Like all Audubon lands, trails leading away from the visitor center are blazed blue, and those leading back are blazed yellow. The long-distance Warner Trail passes through the sanctuary on its way from Canton, Massachusetts, to Rhode Island. The nature center is stocked with helpful books and guides to these woods, as well as maps and restrooms. In the fields around Billings Barn (just west of the nature center), many of the trees are labeled by species. This 2,200-acre sanctuary was founded by Massachusetts Audubon in 1916, the first of its kind in the state.

Stately trees line the meadows around the Billings Barn.

Moose Hill has an active schedule of speakers, classes, and workshops. You can learn how to attract birds to your backyard, identify wildflowers, study owl behavior, delve into forest or wetland ecology, and plant the best kinds of flowers in your yard to attract butterflies and hummingbirds. You can also learn maple sugaring in February and March and do a summer solstice hayride in June. Keep an eye open year-round for new exhibits in the art gallery at the visitor center.

On warm, drizzly days in early spring, watch for Moose Hill's migrating amphibians. They're a little subtler than thundering herds of buffalo, but just as predictable. Each spring, frogs and salamanders awake from their hibernation in the leaf litter of the forest floor and crawl, hop, or slither to the nearest vernal pool, a fish-free puddle that's safe for breeding. Some of them, like the spotted salamander, even return to the puddle of their birth, like anadromous fish heading upriver from the sea. On average they make a trip of about 100 meters, but some go nearly half a mile. Moose Hill holds an annual "Frog and Sally Rally" to protect the commuting critters from cars and other traffic.

SWIMMING NEAR MOOSE HILL

For a chance to cool down after walking nearly 4 miles of trails at Moose Hill, you can head for a freshwater swim at Lake Massapoag. Historians say the lake draws its name from the Algonquin term for "large water," a fitting label for this 353-acre natural resource. Locals use the lake for fishing, boating, swimming, sailing, and windsurfing, and many others visit for its yacht club, summer camps, and outdoor concerts.

Historically, nineteenth-century workers chopped hefty chunks of ice from the frozen lake and stored them in a huge, wooden icehouse, ready to be packed in sawdust and shipped around the world. After a fire leveled the building in 1903, the town converted the site to a popular summer swimming spot called Memorial Park Beach, open only to Sharon residents.

Bathers from out of town can enter the water at Community Center Beach, open from 10 a.m. to 5 p.m. from Memorial Day to Labor Day each summer. The site offers lifeguards, picnic tables, and restrooms, with day passes sold in the parking lot. Located on the lake's southern shore, the beach is on Dubinsky Drive, not far from the Sharon Community Center (219 Massapoag Ave.).

Miles and Directions

0.0 Start at the nature center and head west across Moose Hill Street to pick up the Billings Loop, a broad, gravel carriage path that begins at the intersection of Moose Hill Street and Moose Hill Parkway.

0.3 Turn right—and then quickly left—to zigzag onto the Old Pasture Trail, marked by a stone wall on its left shoulder. (*FYI:* A wooden bench at this intersection bears the brass plaque BE AT PEACE.)

0.6 Bear left at a three-way intersection (with the Summit and Moose Hill Trails) to stay on the Old Pasture Trail.

0.8 Turn right onto the Turkey Trail.

0.9 Turn right onto the Forest Trail, a peaceful loop through a flat, fern-carpeted glen of trees.

1.3 Follow the trail through a hairpin left turn.

1.5 Follow the trail in another hairpin left, at a sign for the sanctuary boundary.

1.8 Turn right to rejoin the Turkey Trail.

2.1 Turn right onto the white-blazed Bluff Trail.

2.3 Turn left to continue on the Bluff Trail, climbing quickly to Allens Ledge Chimney, a gorgeous overlook marked by a towering stonework fire pit. Then continue along the ridge on the wooded, white-blazed Bluff Trail.

2.6 Reach a second terrific vista (*FYI:* Gillette Stadium football arena is often visible to the southwest), and pass over the bare rock to follow the white blazes along a steep cliff to your right.

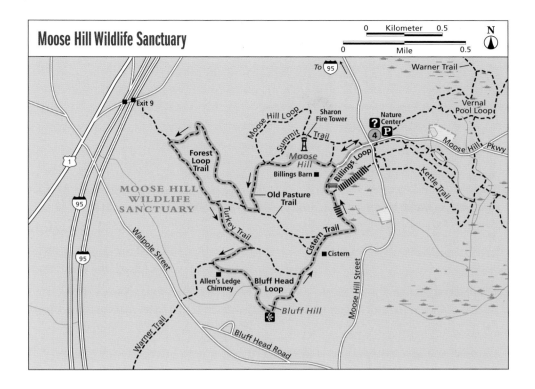

Moose Hill Wildlife Sanctuary

2.9 Fork right to continue the Bluff Trail (a left turn would put you back on the Turkey Trail).

3.0 Continue straight along the Bluff Trail, passing a junction with the Old Pasture Trail on your left, and soon pass an old stone cistern.

3.3 Follow the trail through a hairpin left turn, then along a boardwalk.

3.4 Turn left onto the Billings Farm Loop as you cross a broad meadow. (*FYI:* A wooden bench here is marked Soar.)

3.5 Bear right at a barn (*FYI:* The wooden bench here says Connect), then fork right again to rejoin the Billings Farm Loop.

3.9 Cross the paved Moose Hill Street and reach your car.

Hike Information

Local Events/Attractions

Year-round wilderness photography exhibits, nocturnal wildlife viewing at Halloween Prowl, maple sugaring in February and March, Bird-A-Thon Fundraiser and Mother's Day nature walk in May, summer solstice hayride in June

Local Outdoor Retailers

Eastern Mountain Sports (EMS): Dedham; (781) 461-0160; www.emsonline.com

5 Norris Reservation

This is not a complex or challenging hike, but for its proximity to Boston, it offers amazing views and a unique up-close tour of a salt marsh and the North River. The loop winds through wooded marshes in the North River watershed.

Start: From the parking lot at the intersection of West and Dover Streets
Distance: 2.0-mile loop
Hiking time: About 1 hour
Difficulty: Easy, with broad, flat trails
Trail surface: Wide, wood-chipped trails
Best season: Spring
Land status: The Trustees of Reservations

Nearest town: Norwell
Other trail users: Cross-country skiers
Canine compatibility: Leashed dogs permitted
Schedule: Open year-round, sunrise to sunset
Fees and permits: None
Maps: USGS Weymouth, MA
Trail contact: The Trustees of Reservations, Beverly; (978) 921-1944; www.thetrustees.org

Finding the trailhead: From Braintree, follow MA 3 South to exit 13, for MA 53 and 123, Norwell, and Hanover. Turn left at the light off the exit ramp onto MA 53 North. At 0.6 mile, turn right at a light onto MA 123 East (aka Main Street), following signs for Norwell and Scituate. At 3.5 miles, turn right onto West Street, at the Norwell State Police Station. Go through a stop sign, turn left onto Dover Street, then immediately turn right, pulling into a gravel parking lot opposite a post office. *DeLorme: Massachusetts Atlas & Gazetteer:* Page 54 F8. GPS: N42 09.578' / W70 47.434'

The Hike

The reservation encompasses 117 acres of wooded upland and salt marsh in the watershed bracketed by Second Herring Brook and the North River. The landscape reveals its recent history, as Eleanor's Path is named for Eleanor Norris, who donated her family's farmland to form the original 101-acre grant. The balance of the plot includes an adjacent 16 acres from the McMullan family.

Historically, the Wampanoag caught fish and shellfish from the North River here. When the Europeans arrived, settlers built first a sawmill, then in 1690 a millpond and gristmill. Only rusted farm tools and crumbling stone foundations and millstones provide reminders of this early industry.

The first European settlers had little room to graze their cattle, so they turned to marsh grass, or "salt hay." Using flat-bottomed boats called gundalows, they hauled up to 8 tons of hay per trip, traveling far upriver. This boat-building skill served them well when Britain was running short of lumber and realized that it cost half as much to build a ship in the nascent United States. Norwell settlers looked around at the 200-foot trees that blanketed the northeast, and met the demand by felling trees that had grown unhindered for 150 centuries.

Today's trees include black tupelo, American holly, and red cedar, but the most significant trees for shipbuilding were white oak, walnut, spruce, and pine. Eventually more than a thousand oceangoing vessels were launched into the narrow North River, where they were ferried to the sea. Ships built here were as big as the *Columbia,* a 220-ton schooner that sailed around the globe. Exploring the new west, the ship also served as the namesake for Oregon's Columbia River and Canada's British Columbia.

But poor Norwell has had a series of industrial setbacks. Its shipbuilding era lasted until the newest boats had deeper drafts than the river. The resourceful settlers bought chickens, and poultry farming was soon the town's biggest business. But a terrible virus wiped out all the local flocks, so the farmers were forced to sell their land to devel-

Eleanor's Path crosses a small dam below the old mill pond.

opers. The town changed yet again when returning World War II soldiers used their G.I. Bill loans to spark a residential building boom, and by 1955 they had diversified the Yankee population almost overnight.

Present-day hikers can see long wooden boardwalks that stretch to docks and floats from private homes across the North River. Benches along the west bank of the river allow you to breathe in the boggy smell of the muddy salt marsh, and to catch glimpses of water birds' nests in the overhung banks on the far side. But be sure to wear boots; there can still be snow here on Saint Patrick's Day.

After your hike, check out Norwell's James Library & Center for the Arts, which offers concerts and art exhibits. And stop by the Norwell Town Fair, held at the local high school in mid-June, for sights such as the ox-pulling contest. Or if you prefer to get wet, sign up for the Great River Race, a regatta for human-powered craft held on the North River in early August.

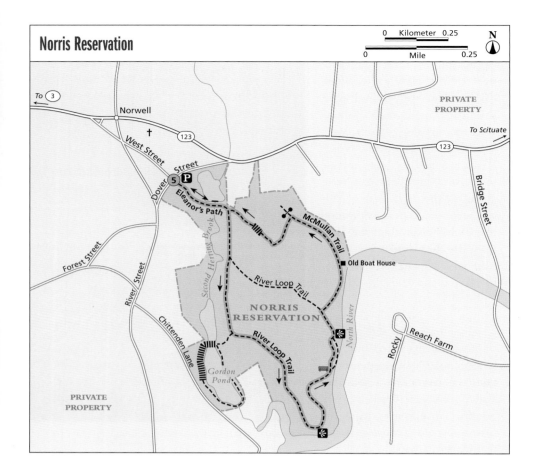

Norris Reservation

Miles and Directions

0.0 Start in the parking lot and enter the woods at a trailhead kiosk with a map display, following Eleanor's Path.

0.2 Turn right just after crossing an earthen dike below a small pond.

0.3 Bear right at a fork and continue to head south as the trail runs parallel to Second Herring Brook, close by on your right.

0.5 Go left at a fork onto the River Loop Trail. A right here would lead to the Gordon Pond Trail.

0.9 Reach a bench with beautiful views of the North River and the private homes on its opposite shore. Continue on, heading north with the river on your right.

1.1 Reach another bench with great views of the river and continue north, either on a smaller path that runs very close to the river or on the main path, a few yards inland; both paths soon reach a third bench.

1.3 Turn right at a fork onto the McMullan Trail. Soon enter the McMullan Woods section of the reservation, cross a concrete culvert in the trail, and reach the Old Boathouse. Its overhanging porch is a great place to stop for lunch.

1.6 Bear left at a metal gate, following the main trail and soon crossing a boardwalk.

1.8 Turn right onto Eleanor's Path, crossing the familiar dam as you keep the pond on your right.

2.0 Arrive back at your car.

Hike Information

Local Information
Norwell website: www.townofnorwell.net

Local Events/Attractions
James Library & Center for the Arts: Norwell; (781) 659-7100; www.firstparishnorwell.org/james.html

Restaurants
Papa Ginos: Norwell; (781) 878-8417
Brueggers: Norwell; (781) 829-6552
Joe's American Bar and Grill: Braintree; (781) 848-0200

Organizations
North and South Rivers Watershed Association: Norwell; (781) 659-8168; www.nsrwa.org. This group sponsors the annual River Cleanup Day, wetlands education, bird watching, dragonfly watching, river tours, and even riverside yoga classes.

6 Blue Hills Reservation

Start at a sea-level pond and bog and, in just 0.5 mile, climb nearly 500 feet to Tucker Hill, passing through three separate ecosystems. Follow the high ridge along the much-loved Skyline Trail to Buck Hill (496 feet) with its views of the Boston skyline, Boston Harbor, and fantastic sunsets. Then return from scattered pine, hemlock, and scrub oak on the rocky ridgeline to lush lily pads, maples, and sandy bogs below.

Start: From the Houghton's Pond parking lot

Distance: 3.8-mile loop

Hiking time: About 2.5 to 3 hours

Difficulty: Moderate, due to steepness and rockiness of the trail

Trail surface: Skyline Trail is well marked but narrow, steep, and rocky; Massachuseuck Trail on the return is broad and flat

Best season: Summer

Land status: MA Department of Conservation and Recreation

Nearest town: Randolph

Other trail users: Mountain bikers, equestrians, cross-country skiers

Canine compatibility: Dogs permitted

Schedule: Open year-round, sunrise to sunset

Fees and permits: None

Maps: USGS Norwood, MA

Trail Contacts: Blue Hills Reservation, (617) 698-1802; www.mass.gov/eea/agencies/dcr/massparks/region-south/blue-hills-reservation.html

Finding the trailhead: From Boston, drive south on I-93 and take exit 3, marked HOUGHTON'S POND/PONKAPOAG TRAIL. Turn right off the exit ramp onto Blue Hill River Road, following signs to Houghton's Pond. In 0.3 mile, turn right again at a stop sign onto Hillside Street. Turn right again at 0.4 mile, into the large parking lot at Houghton's Pond. *DeLorme: Massachusetts Atlas & Gazetteer:* Page 53 C20. GPS: N42 12.601' / W71 05.771'

The Hike

The 10-mile Skyline Trail connects nine peaks through the Blue Hills Reservation and boasts one of the best views of the city's skyline. At 635 feet, Great Blue Hill, the region's flagship peak, is the highest point on the Atlantic coast south of Maine, but this walk features a loop over two less crowded hills with equally broad, panoramic views. The route is a study in contrasts. It begins at a popular swimming beach, then passes quickly along quiet paths that lead you from a sandy bog into a hardwood oak and maple forest. You then hike up through hemlock and pine stands and finally onto a windblown ridgeline, populated only by hardy lowbush blueberry and scrub oak.

The Skyline Trail appears to reach a cliff as you crest Buck Hill. ▶

Begin the hike from the large Houghton's Pond parking lot, with its restrooms, water, and snack bar (open from May to October). On summer weekends the lot is filled with Bostonians wanting a cool swim in this spring-fed "kettle pond." It was formed when mile-high retreating glaciers left a frozen chunk of ice embedded in the landscape. Walk about 300 feet north on the sandy shoulder of Hillside Street and stop at the park's reservation headquarters to pick up a trail map for a small fee. This popular park is riddled with trails, but the loop here has a simple theme: Follow blue blazes over the hills toward the west, then turn and follow red blazes back.

Directly across the street from the park headquarters are the blue blazes of the Skyline Trail. As soon as you enter the woods, you'll leave 99 percent of the crowds behind and progress from the frogs and lily pads of the marshland into stands of red and white oak, Norway maple, and American elm. As you start to climb, the crowd noise fades fast, and the new trail is too narrow and steep for mountain bikes and horses to follow. You soon climb sharply up a rocky slope, stepping over stone walls and crossing several sandy paths.

Suddenly, the extra altitude tips the forest's balance from oak and maple to low sassafras trees, white pine, balsam, and eastern hemlock. As you ascend to the ridge-line, you reach Tucker Hill and receive your first reward: a clear view to the west of the weather observatory on Great Blue Hill and the rolling hills behind it. Around you are an exposed rock cap, scrub oak, and loblolly pine. Follow the Skyline Trail due east, down into a saddle, taking care not to twist your ankles on the loose rock. This small elevation change plunges you back into an open forest again, as you follow the blue blazes across a wider trail. You'll start to climb quickly again, and soon after another intersection, pass several car-size boulders called glacial erratics, another reminder of things left behind by the huge sheets of ice that shaped these hills.

The Blue Hills trail maps feature four-digit numbers at the major intersections, and you soon come to #2141. Follow the blue blazes up a set of steep stone steps, crest the ridgeline to Buck Hill, and bask in the second superb view of this short hike. This is a great place to stop for a drink of water, watch the hawks soar close overhead, and, in July, to nibble on lowbush blueberries. To the north, see the Boston skyline and the landmark candy-striped Boston gas tank, with the Braintree/Randolph reservoir to the south. Follow the blue blazes painted on the rocks at your feet and drop off the hilltop on another set of stone steps.

Near the base, turn right onto the red-blazed Massachuseuck Trail for your return trip. The state of Massachusetts draws its name from this tribe of Native Americans, who fished the kettle ponds and hunted deer on the hills here until they were displaced by colonial settlers. The remainder of the hike is a return to civilization, as you can already hear cars on MA 28. Watch also for mountain bike and horse traffic on this wider, flatter trail. With enough snowfall it is a wonderful cross-country skiing route.

Blue Hills Reservation

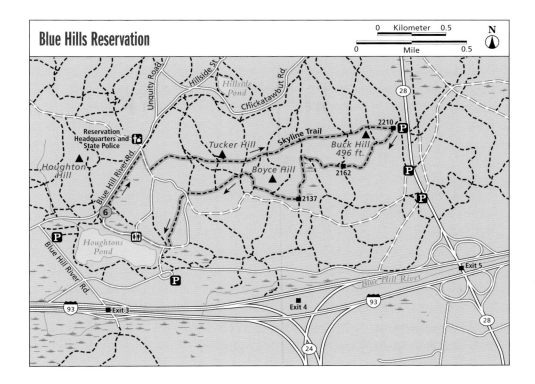

Miles and Directions

0.0   Start at Houghton's Pond parking lot and walk northeast on Hillside Street, away from the visitor center and toward the park's reservation headquarters.

0.3   Turn right onto a dirt road at the trailhead across the street from the park headquarters and state police buildings. Signs here point to the Bugbee Path and Connector Trail to Skyline East.

0.4   Turn left onto the narrow, blue-blazed Skyline Trail at intersection #2054, beginning your climb to Buck Hill.

0.6   Follow the trail through an intersection with the green-blazed Tucker Hill Path at intersection #2072, and begin to climb steeply. (**Note:** Red dots now accompany your blue blazes.)

0.8   Reach Tucker Hill with nice views from its rocky top and keep following the blue blazes eastward into a descent. At the base of the slope, cross the green-blazed Dark Hollow Path, and then cross the white triangle-blazed Forest Path Loop at intersection #2117.

1.2   Cross the Doe Hollow Path at intersection #2141 and begin to climb steeply.

1.5   Reach Buck Hill with its magnificent views, then follow the blue blazes to descend. Continuing eastward, cross the Buck Hill Path at intersection #2181.

1.7   Turn right onto a red-blazed trail at intersection #2210, just before reaching a small parking area on MA 28, and begin your westbound return.

1.8   Bear left at intersection #2183, following red blazes.

2.0 Continue straight through intersections #2162 and #2152, then follow the red blazes through a series of junctions.

2.8 Cross the green-blazed Dark Hollow Path at intersection #2094 and climb gently over one last hilltop.

3.1 Descend a small hill and follow the red blazes through intersection #2071 to cross the green-blazed Tucker Hill Path and a paved utility road. A sign here points you toward the Houghton's Pond main parking lot. Emerge from the woods at intersection #2053 and turn right onto a sandy road, keeping busy Houghton's Pond on your left.

3.8 Arrive back at your car.

Hike Information

Local Information
New England Mountain Biking Association: http://nemba.org. This group sometimes has useful information on the region, such as weather reports and trail conditions.

Local Events/Attractions
Blue Hills Trailside Museum: www.massaudubon.org/get-outdoors/wildlife-sanctuaries/blue-hills. Offers programs, classes, and activities (see sidebar).

Accommodations
Massachusetts website: www.visit-massachusetts.com

Hike Tours
See reservation headquarters.

Organizations
Friends of the Blue Hills: Milton; (781) 828-1805; http://friendsofthebluehills.org. Organizes year-round outdoor activities and workshops.
Blue Hills Trailwatch: (617) 698-1802. Volunteer trail crew.
Appalachian Mountain Club, Boston Chapter: www.amcboston.org
Appalachian Mountain Club, Southeastern Massachusetts Chapter: www.amcsem.org

Local Outdoor Retailers
City Sports: Boston; (617) 782-5121; www.citysports.com
Eastern Mountain Sports (EMS): Boston; (617) 254-4250; www.emsonline.com
Hilton's Tent City: Boston; (800) 362-8368; http://hiltonstentcity.com
Patagonia: Boston; (617) 424-1776; www.patagonia.com
Sports Authority: Braintree; (781) 380-3380; www.sportsauthority.com

Buck Hill offers views in all directions, including the Boston skyline to the north.

TRAILSIDE MUSEUM HOSTS EVENTS AND EXHIBITS

The Blue Hills Trailside Museum, run by the Massachusetts Audubon Society, features cultural, historical, and natural history displays of this 7,000-acre reserve and its 150 miles of trails.

Events at the museum include public service hearings, such as an information session on the West Nile virus. There's the annual honey harvest in October, guided owl-watching walks, wilderness photography workshops, and—for kids—seasonal sessions on migration, hibernation, autumn leaves, and the solstices.

The museum is located at 1904 Canton Ave. in Milton. Hours are from 10 a.m. to 5 p.m., Tuesday through Sunday, and holiday Mondays. Admission fee is required for adults; call (617) 333-0690 or visit www.massaudubon.org/Nature_Connection/Sanctuaries/Blue_Hills/index.php for more information.

To get there, take I-93 to exit 2B (Milton, Route 138 North). Follow the exit ramp to the first set of traffic lights. Go straight through the lights. The parking lot is 0.5 mile ahead on the right. The museum is at the end of the parking lot.

7 Rocky Woods Reservation

This loop tours three small lakes in a loop from Chickering Pond to Notch Pond to Echo Pond. As the path passes Whale Rock, it shows off the park's low swamplands and their bog-loving trees, frogs, and garter snakes. Thanks to this varied ecology, the park comes alive in the early spring—it seems there is a songbird calling high in each hemlock or hickory tree and a snake basking on every other sun-warmed rock.

Start: From the Chickering Pond parking lot, off Hartford Street
Distance: 1.9-mile loop
Hiking time: About 1 hour
Difficulty: Moderate; a short section is steep and rocky, the rest is wide and flat
Trail surface: Mostly flat, packed dirt, with a short section of steep, rocky trail
Best season: Spring
Land status: The Trustees of Reservations
Nearest town: Medfield

Other trail users: Runners, cross-country skiers, mountain bikers
Canine compatibility: Dogs allowed on lead
Schedule: Reservation closes at 6 p.m. daily; mountain bikers prohibited March 1 to April 30
Fees and permits: Day-use fee on weekends and holidays
Maps: USGS Medfield, MA
Trail contact: The Trustees of Reservations, (508) 785-0339; www.thetrustees.org/places-to-visit/greater-boston/rocky-woods.html

Finding the trailhead: From Boston, take I-95/MA 128 south to exit 16B, for MA 109 and Westwood. Drive west on MA 109 for 1.5 miles, then turn right onto Hartford Street. Continue straight through a stop sign. At 3.1 miles, turn right at a sign for the Trustees of Reservations. *DeLorme: Massachusetts Atlas & Gazetteer:* Page 52 C9. GPS: N42 12.417' / W71 16.586'

The Hike

These hills were valuable timberland for New England's early colonists, who cleared them for crops as early as 1640 with a horse and plow. They quarried granite from the ridges and forged farm tools in the 1800s—the adjacent Fork Factory Brook Reservation is named for the pitchfork factory built along Mill Brook in 1839. The work was easier than it could have been, since much of the land was already prepared for farming thanks to the Native American practice of burning the fields every fall. Fresh grasses would grow back first, drawing wild animals in search of grazing food. Thus the Indians restocked their hunting grounds.

The town of Medfield was sacked in February 1676, during King Philip's War, when desperate Native Americans staged a last-gasp assault to push back the European settlers. Eight townsmen were killed and dozens of houses burned, as a force of 1,000 Indians stormed the town. But Philip himself (Metacom was his true name) was killed that August, and the uprising fizzled.

The Chickering Pond Trail circles the reservation's largest lake.

From 1800 until World War II, the town's principal industry was the manufacture of straw hats, which funded factory owners' mansions. But the senior building in Medfield is undoubtedly the Dwight Derby House, built in 1651, and spared in the Indian wars. After careful restoration, the 1651 Shoppe is now open in the old building, stocked with memorabilia commemorating the town's 2001 celebration of its 350th anniversary.

The Rocky Woods Reservation is located at the corner of Medfield, Dover, and Walpole, three woodsy towns that make the park seem larger than its 491 acres. In fact, this hike is all about keeping an eye out for the details: the yellow stripe along the ribs of a garter snake, the stone walls left over from the farming era, and the springtime sound of croaking frogs along the Wilson Swamp Trail, echoing so loudly through the trees they often sound like Canada geese. Rocky Woods hosts a wide variety of geology and plants for its modest size. Featured botany includes the ecology of wood swamps, including forests of white pine, red oak, birch, beech, hemlock, and scattered dogwoods. In the understory, look for pepperbush, swamp honeysuckle, and highbush blueberry. Wildlife loves this diversity of growth, so you find evidence of weasels, red fox, squirrels, raccoons, chipmunks, and skunks, as well as birds like owls, hawks, and kestrels. Keep an eye out for all these creatures as this loop tours three small lakes: Chickering Pond, Notch Pond, and Echo Pond.

Overall, it's a beautiful area despite the existence of an EPA Superfund cleanup site in nearby Walpole. The 30-acre Blackburn and Union Privileges site along the

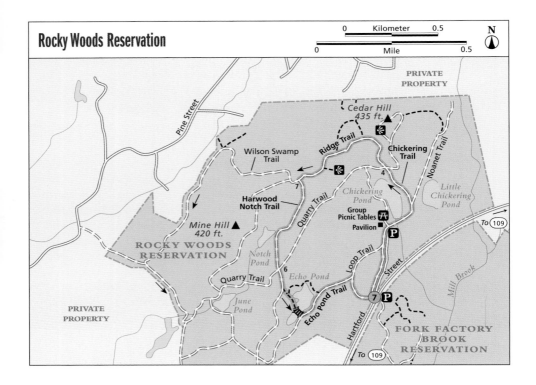

Rocky Woods Reservation

Neponset River was formerly used in manufacturing nails, textiles, asbestos brake linings, and other products. If you have energy after a hike, stop in Medfield's Zullo Gallery, which has painting and sculpture displays, summer classes, and musical performances of jazz, acoustic rock, and folk. In May, stop by the Dover Days Fair, a collection of dancers, dog shows, hayrides, children's games and amusement park rides, and food.

Miles and Directions

0.0 Start at the dirt parking lot and head north toward Chickering Pond on a paved road leading away from Hartford Street. In a few hundred yards, pass by the covered picnic tables and bathrooms used for group events, on your left.

0.3 Walk around the eastern edge of the pond, keeping the water on your left, and begin to follow the red blazes and broad, dirt road of the Chickering Pond Trail.

0.5 Bear right at intersection #4 onto the Ridge Trail and follow its yellow blazes through a number of small junctions.

0.9 Bear left at intersection #7, following the yellow-blazed path now called the Harwood Notch Trail.

1.1 Pass by the small Notch Pond on your right, filled in June with lily pads and bullfrogs.

1.2 Continue straight through intersection #6, staying on the yellow-blazed trail as it narrows and descends toward Echo Pond.

1.4 Cross a boardwalk over the pond and turn left on the other shore to follow the yellow blazes north.

1.6 Turn right at intersection #1 to stay on the yellow-blazed path now called Loop Trail.

1.8 Bear left as you emerge from the woods and begin to hear traffic on Hartford Street.

1.9 Arrive back at your car.

Hike Information

Local Information

Medfield website: www.town.medfield.net
Dover website: www.doverma.org or www.doverrec.com

Local Events/Attractions

Dover Days Fair is held in early May.
Zullo Gallery: Medfield; (508) 359-3711; www.zullogallery.org

Restaurants

There is a cluster of shops at the intersection of Hartford Street and MA 109.

Other Resources

MetroWest Chamber of Commerce: www.metrowest.org. Information on lodging, shopping, and dining.

Local Outdoor Retailers

Eastern Mountain Sports (EMS): Dedham; (781) 461-0160; www.emsonline.com

8 Noanet Woodlands Reservation

Like the nearby, affluent town of Dover, this rolling ramble seems built for comfort. Its broad, well-marked trails with their numbered intersections bring you across a brook and over a scenic vista as a proper introduction before leading up to Noanet Peak. At 371 feet the peak itself offers a peek at the Boston skyline 20 miles to the east. This loop also passes near a historic millpond and stone millworks as it leads through a mature white pine and red oak forest, punctuated with beech and birch trees.

Start: From the ranger station in the parking lot at Caryl Park in Dover
Distance: 3.2-mile loop
Hiking time: About 2 hours
Difficulty: Moderate, due to combination of steep, scrabbly trails and broad, well-marked ones
Trail surface: Dirt path
Best season: Summer
Land status: The Trustees of Reservations
Nearest town: Dover
Other trail users: Equestrians, mountain bikers, Nordic skiers, runners
Canine compatibility: Dogs permitted in Noanet Woodlands, but not in Dover-owned

Caryl Park—the starting point. See Finding the trailhead for alternate, dog-friendly trailheads for this hike.
Schedule: Open year-round, sunrise to sunset
Fees and permits: No fees or permits required for hikers; equestrian and mountain biking permits required
Maps: USGS Medfield, MA
Trail contact: The Trustees of Reservations, (508) 785-0339; www.thetrustees.org/places-to-visit/greater-boston/noanet-woodlands.html

Finding the trailhead: From Boston, take I-95 exit 16B onto MA 109 West (aka High Street). In 0.5 mile, turn right onto Summer Street. At 1.8 miles, turn left onto Westfield Street, following signs to Dover. At 2.4 miles, turn left onto Dedham Street, still following Dover signs. The parking lot for Noanet Woodlands is on the left at 4.2 miles. (**Note:** There's also a parking lot for Caryl Park in another 0.1 mile.)

For hikers with dogs: If you have a dog, you should pick up a trail map at the ranger station in Caryl Park, then continue on to a different trailhead. From Caryl Park, continue 0.4 mile farther on Dedham Street, then turn left at a stop sign, onto Centre Street. Take an immediate left onto Walpole Street at the light, passing a Mobil Station. Your first alternate trailhead is a fire lane in 1 mile on the left. There is another fire lane at 1.6 miles, and a third at 2.1 miles (these small turnoffs fill up quickly with cars on a nice weekend). *DeLorme: Massachusetts Atlas & Gazetteer:* Page 52 A9. GPS: N42 14.867' / W71 16.155'

The Hike

The drive through Dover's farms, horse stables, and tennis courts is a perfect entry to this ramble along well-marked, color-coded, bark-chip trails. The town-owned Caryl Park offers a soda machine and small ranger station, where you can buy a detailed trail

Pass by steeplechase horse jumps along the wooded Caryl Loop.

map. If you have time after the hike, local history is on display at the Benjamin Caryl House, located 100 yards farther along Dedham Road and open from spring to fall on Saturday from 1 to 4 p.m.

Close to the ranger station, the sounds of tennis games, high school playing fields, and a children's playground will follow you into the woods, but the noise fades fast as you press on deeper into the reservation. Its 591 acres of land is bordered by the 1,200-acre Hale Reservation, which gives a feeling of being much farther from Boston than you really are.

This hike stays on wide, well-tended trails, following color-coded plastic disks on the trees. In just 0.5 mile you leave little Caryl Park and cross into Noanet Woodlands. With permit fees for mountain bikers and horseback riders, and a no-riding rule during the muddy spring months, the trails stay flat and unrutted. This hike follows the red-blazed Caryl Loop southward to Upper Mill Pond, then follows the yellow-blazed Noanet Peak Trail to a great vista atop Noanet Peak and then north again home.

Sunday church bells echo through the mature white pine forest as you leave the parking lot far behind. Near the 1-mile mark, you'll pass a huge boulder, dropped there by retreating glaciers, and suddenly realize you have left the sounds of civilization far behind. Come up a rise, and the forest fades from pine to eastern black oak and beech. As you continue to climb, you'll also see scarlet oak and northern red oak. It's a beautiful demonstration of the New England rule that for every 400 feet you gain in elevation, the ecology will change as if you'd gone 100 miles to the north. All these acorns leech tannic acid into the streams. When Native Americans here made acorn cakes, they had to boil the flour in water to remove the bitter taste.

As you climb, be sure also to look down—the loose sandy soil is perfect for amateur tracking. Whether you're with a child or not, it's a fun game to look for prints from dogs, horses, hiking boots, running shoes, and mountain bike tires. Then look up, and on a clear day the sky may be striped with contrails from jets on their way into Logan. There were five wispy, parallel trails at once when I was there. And look around—these stone walls kept cattle and sheep from eating colonial farmers' crops of corn and hay.

You'll have a chance to see some wildlife as you follow the red blazes to Upper Mill Pond—a sleepy northern water snake was coiled by the footbridge there at my last visit. You can also explore the stoneworks and waterfall for the old mill site near here, where the Dover Union Iron Company built its ironworks in 1815. The brook was too small, and the company went out of business in 1830, but landowner Amelia Peabody rebuilt the dam in 1954.

The hike changes quickly as you climb the steep yellow trail to Noanet Peak. As you climb, you'll quickly find yourself walking through eastern red cedar, clinging to the rocky slope. Enjoy the view, then continue north along the ridgeline. Stick with the yellow blazes as they lead you home.

You'll soon hit the intersection where you first entered Noanet Woodlands. Retrace your steps into Caryl Park and back to your car.

Miles and Directions

0.0 Start at the trailhead kiosk immediately behind the ranger station in Caryl Park, marked as intersection #1, and follow the red-blazed Caryl Loop trail southward into the woods. Take a left fork, following red blazes and a sign for Noanet Woodlands.

0.4 Turn left at a T, following another sign for Noanet Woodlands.

0.5 Turn left at intersection #3 (following a sign that announces you are leaving Caryl Park) and left again at intersection #4 (passing a sign for the Dover Union Iron Mill).

0.7 Continue to follow red blazes through intersections #33 and #32.

1.0 Choose the left fork at intersection #29, then follow the red trail straight through intersection #28, passing a huge boulder on your left and beginning to climb.

1.2 Reach Upper Mill Pond and turn right, changing to blue blazes and crossing a footbridge.

1.3 Cross straight through intersection #36, picking up the yellow blazes of the Noanet Peak Trail and climbing steeply.

1.7 Reach a great vista on the bare rock peak, with views of the Boston skyline. Then continue along the yellow-blazed trail.

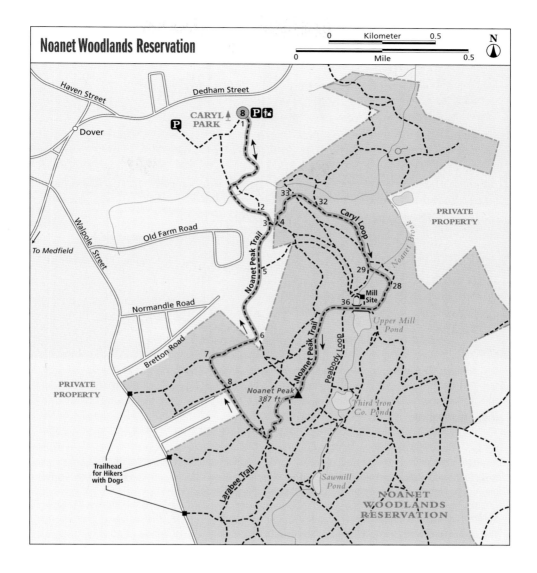

Noanet Woodlands Reservation

Haven Street

Dedham Street

Dover

CARYL PARK ⑧ 🅿️🏠
1

🅿️

Walpole Street

Old Farm Road

To Medfield

33

32

Caryl Loop

PRIVATE PROPERTY

Noanet Brook

2

3 4

Noanet Peak Trail

5

29

28

Normandle Road

Mill Site

36

Upper Mill Pond

6

Bretton Road

Noanet Peak Trail

Peabody Loop

7

PRIVATE PROPERTY

8

Noanet Peak 387 ft.

Third Iron Co. Pond

Trailhead for Hikers with Dogs

Larabee Trail

Sawmill Pond

NOANET WOODLANDS RESERVATION

1.9 Turn right at a T to continue following yellow blazes as you descend from the peak and turn north to head for home.

2.1 Follow the yellow-blazed Noanet Peak Trail through intersection #8, then #7, #6, and #5.

2.7 Bear left at intersection #3 to rejoin the original red-blazed trail; you'll soon pass intersection #2.

2.8 Turn right with the red blazes, following a sign for the parking lot.

3.2 Arrive back at intersection #1 and your car.

Upper Mill Pond offers a final rest before the climb to Noanet Peak.

Hike Information

Local Information

A **ranger station** is on-site, staffed year-round, weekends and holidays, from 9 a.m. to 5 p.m.
New England Mountain Biking Association: www.nemba.org. This group sometimes has useful information on the region, such as weather reports and trail conditions.

Other Resources

The *Dover-Sherborn Press:* www.wickedlocal.com/dover

Local Outdoor Retailers

Eastern Mountain Sports (EMS): Dedham; (781) 461-0160; www.emsonline.com

Northeast Massachusetts

Geologists call the land inside the I-495 loop "the Boston Basin," a flat, low transition between original bedrock to the west, and newer glacial deposits on the cape and islands. Farther seaward, inside the MA 128 loop, there is more evidence of the glaciers' footprints—eskers (long, snaking hills) and drumlins (tear or pear-shaped hills), created when the melting glaciers dropped their earthen loads.

Hikers in the northeast will see more exposed rocky shelves than along the south shore, with taller trees and steeper pitches. Check out Maudslay State Park, Ravenswood, Ward Reservation, and Weir Hill Reservation. At each of these destinations, the very shape of the hiking path under your feet has been shaped by awesome glacial forces.

The Ward Reservation itself contains two such drumlins, known as Boston and Holt Hills, and large enough that they're favored by backcountry skiers. Likewise, Weir Hill itself is a 200-foot-high, two-peaked drumlin. And Ravenswood is a 300-acre moraine, right on the cusp of Gloucester Harbor. With rocky ledges throughout, the soil is marshy, culminating in the Great Magnolia Swamp. Likewise at Rocky Woods, the terrain alternates between granite ridges and frog ponds—the land is wet and flooded between Cedar Hill and Chickering Pond, and between Whale Rock and Notch Pond.

This region has also spawned great diversity of flora and fauna in its wetlands, such as the Ipswich River Wildlife Sanctuary. At Ipswich you will find the Great Wenham Swamp, a huge freshwater wetland bursting with birds (and their predators and prey).

The Stevens Trail rolls through meadows as it drops toward the lake (hike 14).

9 Ward Reservation

The reservation is split evenly by the Andover and North Andover town line, with drumlins on either side: Holt Hill in Andover and Boston and Shrub Hills in North Andover. The Cat Swamp lies between them, ensuring that your loop will feature a contrast of low and high ground.

Start: From the dirt parking lot off Prospect Road
Distance: 4.0-mile loop
Hiking time: About 2 hours
Difficulty: Moderate, with modest elevation change and some narrow footpaths
Trail surface: Mostly two-track dirt paths, with some narrower dirt paths through woods
Best season: Fall
Land status: The Trustees of Reservations
Nearest town: Andover
Other trail users: Cross-country skiers, equestrians

Canine compatibility: Dogs permitted
Schedule: Open year-round; gates close at sunset
Fees and permits: None
Maps: USGS Lawrence, MA
Trail contact: The Trustees of Reservations, Beverly; (978) 682-3580; www.thetrustees .org/places-to-visit/northeast-ma/ward-res ervation.html; Pine Hole Bog Nature Trail pamphlet available from www.thetrustees.org/ assets/documents/places-to-visit/trailmaps/ PineHoleBog.pdf

Finding the trailhead: From Reading, head north on I-93 to exit 41, for MA 125, Andover, and North Andover. Turn right off the exit onto MA 125 North. At 2.1 miles, pass a junction with MA 28, and at 4.8 miles, turn right onto Prospect Road at a flashing yellow light. Turn right into the reservation's dirt parking lot at 5.1 miles. *DeLorme: Massachusetts Atlas & Gazetteer:* Page 29 G19. GPS: N42 38.438' / W71 06.744'

The Hike

At 420 feet, Holt Hill is the highest point in Essex County, with views of the Boston skyline and Blue Hills Reservation on a clear day. Knowing this, local citizens gathered here on June 17, 1775, to watch as Charlestown burned in the Revolutionary War.

Today Holt Hill is better known for the compass-pointing Solstice Stones at its peak. Arranged by Mabel Ward, who donated her family's property for the reservation, the stones point to the compass's cardinal points, and to both pairs of solstices and equinoxes.

Here's when to look. Around March 21 and September 23, the sun rises due east and sets due west—these are the vernal and autumnal equinoxes. Around June 21 the sun will rise in the northeast quadrant of the circle and set to the northwest during the longest day of the year—the summer solstice. And about December 22 the sun will rise in the southeast and set in the southwest quadrant, marking it as the shortest day of the year—the winter solstice. A particular stone in the circle marks each of these points.

Another point of interest is at Holt Hill's feet—Pine Hole Bog, a rare "quaking bog." This phenomenon occurs when a wetland forms across the surface of a shallow pond. Based on a floating mat of entangled mosses, rushes, and shrubs, it typically shimmies and shakes when walked on, and can support botany found nowhere else. Other signs of nature are here for the looking. During one winter visit I stumbled across a pile of turkey feathers in the wooded lowlands, encircled by fox prints in the snow.

Marked by these two drumlins and two wetlands, the reservation is a study in contrast. The Trustees of Reservations maintains a self-guided nature trail along the 700-foot boardwalk that stretches from Holt Hill to the center of the Pine Hole Bog. Numbers that correspond to

A pond along the Ward Trail is full of soaring herons.

a pamphlet titled *Bog Nature Trail* mark the walk. The trails here are poorly blazed, but there are maps at major intersections.

Part of the reason its trails seem to meander at their pleasure is likely due to the haphazard formation of the reservation, which was glued together with pieces from forty-three separate parcels of farm and pasture land. Since they were used for so long as independent businesses, they are uniformly walled-in. According to the Trustees of Reservations, fifteen of the parcels are bordered on all sides by stone walls, twenty-seven are partially bordered, and just one has no walls. That brings the total stone wall distance inside the reservation to 17 miles!

The reservation is also crossed by the white-blazed Bay Circuit Trail. This greenway loop passes through thirty-four towns as it rings Boston on a hiking path that arcs between the MA 128 and I-495 beltways. First proposed in 1929, the ring stretches 200 miles through seventy-nine areas of preserved land, from Plum Island and Ipswich in the north to Duxbury and Kingston on the South Shore.

Be careful when you dress to come here. There is significant snow remaining in the woods in mid-March, requiring snowshoes or cross-country skis. In fact, Boston and Holt Hills are favorite spots for telemarkers and backcountry skiers.

MASSACHUSETTS'S HIGH POINTS

Although it's sovereign of a modest domain, Holt Hill is nonetheless listed on a fascinating website called County Highpointers (http://cohp.org), a guide to climbing the highest point in all 3,141 counties in the United States. They range from Alaska's Mount McKinley (20,320 feet) to a 10-foot-high swamp in Terrebonne Parish, Louisiana. Our own 420-foot Holt Hill occupies a modest, middle rung. Feel free to e-mail the site's creator if you have additions or corrections!

Massachusetts's other high points include:

- 306-foot Pine Hill in Barnstable County
- Three unnamed 390-footers in Bristol County
- An unnamed 311-foot point near Peaked Hill in Dukes County
- 2,841-foot Crum Hill in Franklin County
- 1,794-foot Round Top Hill in Hampden County
- 2,125-foot West Mountain in Hampshire County
- 800-foot Nutting Hill in Middlesex County
- 630-foot Great Blue Hill in Norfolk County
- Two 111-foot regions near Sankaty Head in Nantucket County
- 395-foot Manomet Hill in Plymouth County
- 330-foot Bellevue Hill in Suffolk County
- 2,006-foot Mount Wachusett in Worcester County

Miles and Directions

0.0 Start at the parking lot and turn right to continue uphill, southbound on Prospect Road. In 50 yards, turn left through a metal gate onto a paved road.

0.2 Turn left into the woods onto the narrow, red-blazed Margaret's Trail (part of the Bay Circuit Trail), at intersection #23.

0.5 Turn right onto the red-blazed Ward Trail at intersection #22, passing a frog and heron pond on your left and several smaller footpaths on the right.

1.2 Continue straight through a four-way junction at intersection #18.

1.3 Turn right at a T intersection onto the red-blazed Old Chestnut Street, just before reaching a chain link fence surrounding the humming transformers of a Mass Electric power station. Follow this broad path between Shrub Hill and Boston Hill, passing junctions with the Judy Family Trail (intersection #17) and Sanborn Trail (intersection #16).

1.7 Turn sharp left onto a blue-blazed trail toward Boston Hill at intersection #14, climbing steadily up the Elephant Rock Trail through a series of junctions.

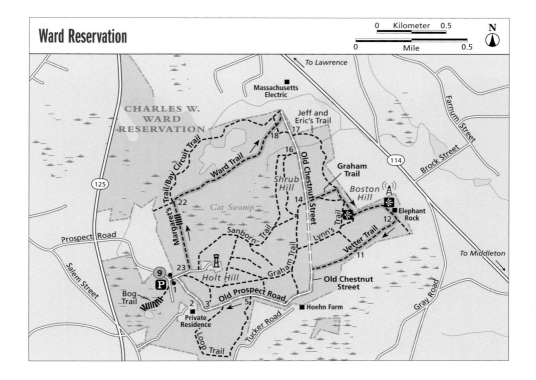

Ward Reservation

0   Kilometer   0.5

0   Mile   0.5

N

2.0   Follow this blue-blazed trail through a sharp left curve as you emerge from the forest and gain terrific views on your right and pass by a fenced antenna tower on the left.

2.2   Reach Elephant Rock—a glacial erratic boulder in a hilltop field—and continue straight past it, following blue blazes gently downhill into the trees.

2.3   Follow the blazes as they bear right onto the Vetter Trail at intersection #12, tracing the treeline at the edge of the meadow.

2.5   At the base of Boston Hill, bear left at intersection #11 to continue with the blue blazes.

2.8   Turn left onto the wide, flat Old Chestnut Street and follow its red blazes for the remainder of the hike.

3.2   Follow the red-blazed trail—now called Old Prospect Road—past the Five Crossings Trail on your left (intersection #5).

3.4   Turn left at a four-way intersection to follow the red blazes onto a smaller path.

3.5   Bear left at intersection #3 and march uphill through an open meadow, close by two private homes on the right. Cross their gravel driveways and pass by intersection #2.

3.8   Pass a steep set of wooden stairs dropping off to the Bog Trail on your left.

3.9   Continue straight ahead with the red blazes past the yellow-blazed Bog Trail to the left (intersection #1) and soon cross a boardwalk.

4.0   Arrive back at your car.

Elephant Rock seems to gaze east from its perch atop Boston Hill.

Hike Information

Local Information
Andover Trails Committee: www.andovertrails.org

Organizations
Bay Circuit Alliance: c/o Appalachian Mountain Club, Boston; (617) 523-0636; http://baycircuit.org/wordpress/
Bay Circuit Trail Information: www.outdoors.org/baycircuittrail/bay-circuit-trail.cfm
Friends of the Ward Reservation: Andover; www.thetrustees.org/places-to-visit/northeast-ma/ward-reservation.html. This group publishes a free, quarterly newsletter.

Other Resources
Geology of the Ward Reservation by George E. Zink

10　Boxford State Forest

This walk through the woods doesn't offer steep climbs or expansive views, but for its proximity to civilization, Boxford State Forest offers quiet trails and glassy ponds, with signs of beaver, deer, and birds all around. The path rambles through boggy lowlands near Crooked Pond, then climbs the gentle Bald Hill before descending for a short stroll on a paved road.

Start: From the Bald Hill trailhead on Middleton Road

Distance: 5.2-mile loop

Hiking time: About 2 hours

Difficulty: Easy, with a combination of flat, broad trails and narrow, twisting paths

Trail surface: Rough dirt

Best season: Fall

Land status: MA Department of Conservation and Recreation

Nearest town: Danvers

Other trail users: Cross-country skiers, snowmobilers, equestrians

Canine compatibility: Dogs permitted

Schedule: Open year-round

Fees and permits: None

Maps: USGS Lawrence, MA

Trail contacts: Department of Conservation and Recreation, Boston; (617) 626-1250; www.mass.gov/eea/docs/dcr/parks/trails/boxford.pdf (online trail map available). Boxford Trails Association/Boxford Open Land Trust (BTA/BOLT), Boxford; (978) 887-7031; www.btabolt.org (also with online trail maps)

Finding the trailhead: From Danvers, head north on I-95 to exit 52, for Topsfield Road, Topsfield, and Boxford. Turn left off the exit onto Topsfield Road, following signs for Boxford. At 1.3 miles, bear left onto Main Street at a three-way intersection, keeping a cluster of small monuments on your right. Reach a stop sign at 1.7 miles and turn left again, onto Middleton Road. At 3.3 miles, turn right into a small, dirt parking lot just south of Lockwood Lane, marked with a kiosk for Bald Hill. *DeLorme: Massachusetts Atlas & Gazetteer:* Page 29 G26. GPS: N42 38.413' / W70 59.458'

The Hike

Hikers will be rewarded here for keeping their eyes open for signs of wildlife—it's easy to find squirrel nests in trees above piles of broken, shelled beech nuts; and deer have left their tracks and scat everywhere, some quite near hunters' deer stands. And the historic Russel-Hooper Farmhouse at the base of Bald Hill—today just a crumbling stone foundation—is a sign of early inhabitants, who cleared the land and built the stone walls.

This loop cruises a nearly 3-mile section of the long-distance Bay Circuit Trail, a 200-mile path that circles Boston from Duxbury on the South Shore to Newburyport in the north. The hike completes its circuit on state forest trails, finally returning to the trailhead via Middleton Road.

Bald Hill itself is part of the Bald Hill Reservation, a 1,624-acre plot split between Boxford State Forest, the Philips Wildlife Sanctuary, and the Essex County Greenbelt (and thus between the towns of Boxford, North Andover, and Middleton). Protected here are ponds, wildflowers, and historic landmarks. Motorized vehicles are banned from the wildlife sanctuary, so the trails are in great shape, although they can be deeply flooded during the spring melt. For more details and trail descriptions, check the *Boxford Bay Circuit Guidebook*.

After your hike, don't miss Boxford's annual Apple Festival each autumn. Held on the third Saturday of September on Elm Street in East Boxford, it features more than a hundred crafters selling their homemade goods. Also, the local historical society sells homemade apple pies. For a complete listing of orchards where you can pick your own apples after a strenuous hike, check out www.mass.gov/agr/massgrown/apple_pyo.htm. For a listing of what to do with all those apples, browse the recipes at http://pickyourown.org/allaboutcanning.htm. You'll find ideas from jam to ice cream.

Heading east on the Towne Loop to return to Middleton Road.

During the holiday season you can cut your own Christmas tree at Herrick Tree Farm. Stop in to choose your favorite tree from a wide range of spruce and fir. (Call ahead for hours.) In the spring, check out the Harlan P. Kelsey Arboretum at 18 Kelsey Road in Boxford. This 4.2-acre plot protects the remnants of a former 500-acre collection of plants imported from North Carolina, and today is managed by the Horticultural Society of Boxford, which is planning a visitor center and parking lot. You can walk along footpaths through this show garden.

Together with Middleton and Topsfield, Boxfield is in a "Tri-Town Area" within Essex County. The town has maintained its rural, agricultural appearance partially through a minimum lot size of 2 acres, unchanged since 1949. Settled in 1645, Boxford hews close to traditional New England small-town form with its two town centers. East Boxford Center boasts the town hall, post office, bank, church, and a country store, while West Boxford is the site of another church and country store, as well as Benson's, a locally famous ice cream shop with homemade flavors like red raspberry.

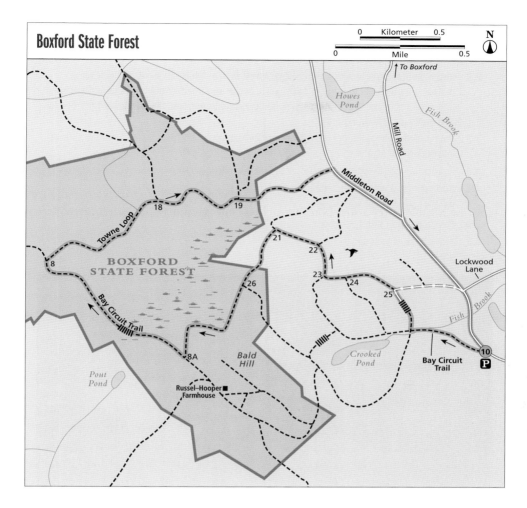

Boxford State Forest

Miles and Directions

0.0 Enter the woods on the white-blazed Bay Circuit Trail from the Bald Hill trailhead on Middleton Road.

0.2 Pass a small pond fed by Fish Brook on the left. (**Note:** This is not Crooked Pond, a larger lake slightly farther west.)

0.3 Turn right onto a narrow, uphill footpath to continue following white blazes (this is marked as intersection #17 on maps).

0.8 Follow the white blazes through a right turn at intersection #24, and soon another right at intersection #23.

1.0 Turn left at a T junction at intersection #22, and soon left again at intersection #21 as the narrow trail twists through quiet woods.

1.5 Follow the white blazes straight past a left turn at intersection #26 to stay on the Bay Circuit Trail.

2.0 Turn right at a T junction onto a broad, two-track dirt trail at intersection #8A, and begin to head north with the white blazes. Soon pass close by a large marsh on your right, which drains into Pout Pond, just visible through trees to your left.

2.8 Turn right at the top of a rise onto a state forest trail, at intersection #8. You now leave the white blazes behind to head east toward Middleton Road. (***Note:*** From here the Bay Circuit Trail continues northward into neighboring North Andover, then on toward the ocean at Ipswich and Newburyport.)

3.3 Continue straight along the main, two-track trail as you pass junctions with narrow trails at intersections #31 and #18.

4.0 Pass by a junction with another small trail at intersection #19.

4.2 Turn right onto paved Middleton Road.

4.6 Pass a junction with Mill Road.

5.0 Pass a junction with Lockwood Lane.

5.2 Arrive back at your car.

The shores of Fish Brook offer great spots of natural color.

Hike Information

Local Information

Mass Audubon: (781) 259-2178 or www.massaudubon.org/Birds_and_Birding/ IBAs/site_summary.php?getsite=55. Provides a great list of birds and wildlife at Bald Hill Reservation.

Haverhill Chamber of Commerce: (978) 373-5663; www.haverhillchamber.com

Haverhill Gazette: www.hgazette.com

Tri-Town Transcript: Danvers; (978) 887-4146; www.wickedlocal.com/boxford. Boxford's newspaper.

Local Events/Attractions

Harlan P. Kelsey Arboretum: Boxford; (978) 462-7310; http://kelseyarboretum.webs .com

Boxford Historical Society: Boxford; (978) 887-5078; http://boxfordhistoricalsociety .com

Herrick Tree Farm: Boxford; (978) 887-5477 or (978) 372-2509; www.herricktree farm.com

Restaurants

Benson's Ice Cream: West Boxford; (978) 352-2911; http://bensonsicecream.com

Hike Tours

Essex County Greenbelt Association: Essex; (978) 768-7241; www.ecga.org/explore _and_engage/view_property/1340-bald_hill_reservation. A land trust focused on preserving open space and ecosystems in Essex County. The group seeks to create continuous open land (greenbelts) of unbroken trails, rivers, and other intact corridors. See website for a schedule of the group's monthly guided walks.

Organizations

Essex National Heritage Area: Salem; (978) 740-0444; www.essexheritage.org/ attractions/bald-hill-reservation-and-boxford-state-forest

Bay Circuit Alliance: Boston; http://baycircuit.org/wordpress/

Andover Trails Committee: Andover; http://andovertrails.org/baycircuit.html

Local Outdoor Retailers

Sports Authority: Danvers; (978) 774-9400

11 Ipswich River Wildlife Sanctuary

At 2,800 acres this is Massachusetts Audubon's largest sanctuary, covering woods, meadows, and wetlands, including the Great Wenham Swamp, the largest freshwater wetland on the north shore. This loop tours the sanctuary's open fields, marshes, and beaver ponds, as well as the thickly wooded Averill's Island, before returning for one more pass through the bustling wildlife neighborhood of the marshland.

Start: From the visitor center at the main parking lot, off Perkins Row
Distance: 2.9-mile loop
Hiking time: About 2 hours
Difficulty: Easy, with flat, rolling trails
Trail surface: Dirt singletrack paths that can get very wet in the spring, even on the boardwalks
Best season: Spring
Land status: Massachusetts Audubon Society
Nearest town: Topsfield
Other trail users: Cross-country skiers. Massachusetts Audubon does not permit dogs, bicycles, horses without permits, or joggers.

Canine compatibility: Dogs not permitted
Schedule: Trails open sunrise to sunset, closed Monday; visitor center open 9 a.m. to 4 p.m. Tuesday through Friday, 9 a.m. to 5 p.m. weekends and Monday holidays May to October, and 10 a.m. to 4 p.m. weekends and Monday holidays November to April
Fees and permits: Day-use fee for adults
Maps: USGS Ipswich, MA
Trail contact: Massachusetts Audubon, Topsfield; (978) 887-9264; www.mass audubon.org/Nature_Connection/ Sanctuaries/Ipswich_River/index.php (maps available at this site)

Finding the trailhead: From Danvers, take I-95 north to exit 50, for Topsfield, and follow US 1 north. At 2.9 miles, turn right onto MA 97 South (aka High Street), following signs for Beverly and Danvers, and at 3.3 miles, turn left onto Perkins Row. At 4.4 miles, turn right at the sanctuary entrance, passing between two stone pillars, and park at the main lot. *DeLorme: Massachusetts Atlas & Gazetteer:* Page 29 H30. GPS: N42 37.906' / W70 55.285'

The Hike

Originally home to the Agawam tribe, this land was part of the original Massachusetts colony in 1643, and the office and visitor center has stood since 1763. Of course, this human history is dwarfed by geologic features such as eskers, kames, and a drumlin, created by a glacier 15,000 years ago. Look for these features as you walk. An *esker* is the sediment left behind as a glacier melts, often in the shape of a winding ridge like a raised railroad bed. A *kame* is similar, since it derives from the sediment dropped by melting glaciers into depressions, which slowly grow into small hills. Today they are often mined for sand and gravel. A *drumlin* is a long, rounded hill that was formed of existing till molded by glaciers as they moved, so they point in a parallel direction to the glacier's path.

The sanctuary trails feature several observation decks perched over marshland.

The variety of ecosystems here is stunning, from freshwater meadows and marshes, to the silver maple floodplain forest along the riverside, and the tall pine-hemlock stands on Averill's Island. This mixture of wetlands and uplands is the perfect mix for birders, and the sanctuary keeps some meadows mowed for bluebird and woodcock habitat (the mailbox-sized birdhouses on posts are for the bluebirds). There is an observation tower for watching waterfowl at Bunker Meadows, and a bench on the boardwalk near Waterfowl Pond that extends deep into the marshes. And although it's not on this loop, the Rockery Trail was designed as an arboretum in the early 1900s, with exotic trees and shrubs planted around enormous glacial boulders.

One point of this sanctuary serves as an epicenter for diversity—the Stone Bridge. An active beaver lodge and dam keep Waterfowl Pond full, while garter snakes slither at your feet, hawks circle over the marsh, and Canada geese feed and fight in the rushes. At some point on your hike, take a minute to stop on the trail, shut your eyes, and just listen. (For a challenge, you can try to count the number of different bird species by their songs.)

Birds aren't the only flying creatures so closely tracked—naturalists have identified more than forty-four species of butterflies here. Check at the visitor center for trail conditions, bird and butterfly sightings, wildlife guidebooks, maps, and restrooms. And the excellent nature center has exhibits of different nests, skeletons, tracks, and photos. As with all Massachusetts Audubon properties, trails that lead away from the visitor center are blazed blue, and those leading back to it are blazed yellow. Remember to check for ticks after warm-weather hikes here.

BIRDING AT IPSWICH

Birders have studied this area for so many years that they have a good idea what to expect in a given season and region. The following information is from the sanctuary's trail map; for the curious, there are far more details available at the nature center.

- The open fields around Bradstreet Hill are nesting and feeding grounds for the tree swallow, eastern bluebird, American kestrel, and bobolink. In the spring and summer, chimney swifts may nest in the chimney of the large house here.
- From the Observation Tower, look over the buttonbush shrub swamp for seasonal visitors: In the spring and fall, blue- and green-winged teals, ring-necked ducks, and hooded mergansers will rest and feed here during their migrations. And in the spring and summer, look for tree and barn swallows, great blue herons, glossy ibises, and great egrets.
- The Great Wenham Swamp may hold rare finds such as the American bittern and pied-billed grebe, as well as more common waterfowl and migrating songbirds.
- The silver maple floodplain forest alongside the Ipswich River is often home to warblers, vireos, and rose-breasted grosbeaks.
- At Waterfowl Pond there are wood ducks nesting in tree holes close to the waters' edge. In spring and fall this is a feeding ground for warblers.
- On the upland wooded trails, there are wood thrushes, pileated woodpeckers, ovenbirds, scarlet tanagers, rose-breasted grosbeaks, and an occasional great horned owl.

If you're here in the fall, make sure to stop at the Topsfield Fair, held during the first week of October. Founded in 1818, the event bills itself as America's Oldest Agricultural Fair. It features giant pumpkins, sand sculptures, a cattle show, and amusement park rides for children. In fact, there's plenty going on at the fairgrounds during the rest of the year too: oriental rug auctions, bridge tournaments, dog and horse shows, car shows, a Native American festival, and antiques and crafts fairs. Check the website for dates.

Miles and Directions

0.0 Start in the parking lot and head east on Bradstreet Lane, the doubletrack dirt road that enters the woods just behind the visitor center.

0.3 Turn left at a T intersection onto the Drumlin Trail and, in 50 yards, bear right at a fork in a beech grove, onto Stone Bridge Trail. This trail passes between the long, low mound of an esker (a glacial hill) on your left and marshland on your right.

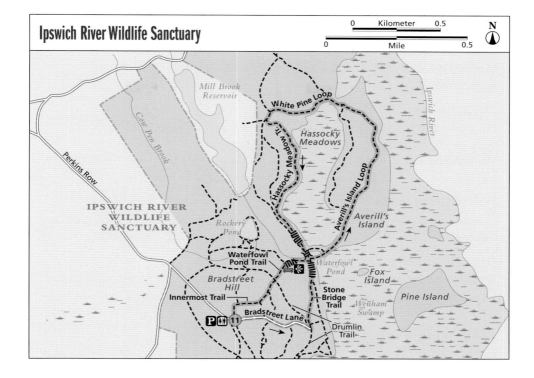

Ipswich River Wildlife Sanctuary

0.6 Cross a small wooden bridge where the South Esker Trail branches off to the right and continue along the Stone Bridge Trail.

0.7 Turn right at a fork and immediately right again just before a stone bridge. Follow the Averill's Island trail along two long, wooden boardwalks tracing Waterfowl Pond on your left.

0.9 Bear right at a fork to begin the eastern leg of the Averill's Island Loop, and soon pass through a grove of impossibly straight, tall white pines and hemlocks.

1.4 Cross a marsh on a wooden boardwalk as you pass a junction with the other leg of the Averill's Island Loop on your left.

1.5 Turn left at the end of the boardwalk onto the western leg of the White Pine Loop.

1.8 Bear left at a junction with the other leg of the White Pine Loop and in 50 yards, turn sharp left again, onto the Hassocky Meadow Trail with its gorgeous views of marshland.

2.2 Turn left at a T intersection onto the North Esker Trail and continue southward along the edge of the marsh on this steep, earthen berm.

2.5 Drop off the esker, cross a boardwalk, and turn left, crossing the Stone Bridge. Immediately over the bridge, turn right onto the Waterfowl Pond Trail.

2.6 Turn left onto the Innermost Trail, treading a long boardwalk through the reeds. (**Side trip:** Take a short detour to stop at the observation bench, thrust far out into the marsh.)

2.7 Continue uphill along the Innermost Trail, crossing intersections with the Drumlin Trail and Ruffed Grouse Trail as you near the visitor center.

2.9 Arrive back at your car.

Hike Information

Local Information

Topsfield website: www.topsfield-ma.gov

Ipswich website: www. ipswichma.com

Local Events/Attractions

Rent canoes from Audubon to paddle on the 8 miles of the Ipswich River that flow through this sanctuary (available May to November).

The Topsfield Fair: Topsfield; (978) 887-5000; www.topsfieldfair.org. Fairgrounds are located on US 1, just south of its intersection with MA 97 (High Street).

Accommodations

Camping is allowed on Perkins Island, located 0.5 mile upriver from the sanctuary headquarters, or you can rent a four-person cabin on sanctuary grounds.

Organizations

Ipswich River Watershed Association: Topsfield; (978) 412-8200; http://ipswichriver .org. The association studies and monitors the river's 45-mile path. They offer maps, current events, natural history, and more.

Other Resources

United States Geological Survey (USGS): http://ipswichriver.org/current-condi tions/. The USGS monitors the river carefully, since conditions were so dry in the summer of 1999 that the river dried up.

12 Bradley Palmer State Park

This loop follows the Ipswich River as it cuts between Bradley Palmer State Park and the adjacent Willowdale State Forest. Together they offer 721 acres and over 20 miles of trails. For a small sample of that variety, this hike leaves the river at the park's edge and emerges from mountain laurel and rhododendron groves as it circles through rolling fields, rises to Blueberry Hill, and returns to the start.

Start: Park headquarters, at main entrance off Asbury Street
Distance: 2.5-mile loop
Hiking time: About 1.5 to 2 hours
Difficulty: Easy, with smooth trails and small hills
Trail surface: Grassy fields and dirt trails
Best season: Summer
Land status: MA Department of Conservation and Recreation and Essex County Greenbelt Association
Nearest town: Topsfield

Other trail users: Mountain bikers, equestrians, cross-country skiers, snowshoers, snowmobilers
Canine compatibility: Dogs permitted
Schedule: Open year-round, sunrise to sunset
Fees and permits: None
Maps: USGS Ipswich, MA. Trail maps are located at the headquarters building.
Trail contact: Bradley Palmer State Park Headquarters, (978) 887-5931; www.mass.gov/eea/agencies/dcr/massparks/region-north/bradley-palmer-state-park.html

Finding the trailhead: From Boston, take I-95 north to exit 50, for Topsfield. Drive north on US 1 for 4 miles, then turn right at the light onto Ipswich Road. At 5.1 miles, turn right onto Asbury Street, and at 5.3 miles, turn left at a stone gate, following signs for the park. Turn right at an intersection and then left into the dirt parking lot. *DeLorme: Massachusetts Atlas & Gazetteer:* Page 30 F1. GPS: N42 39.077' / W70 54.459'

The Hike

Together with Willowdale State Forest, this land was the private estate of Bradley Webster Palmer (1866–1946), a Boston lawyer who represented Sinclair Oil in the Teapot Dome Scandal and President Woodrow Wilson at the Versailles Peace Conference at the end of World War I.

He called the estate Willowdale, and at its peak it contained thirty-two buildings, employed forty people, and spanned 5 square miles, including a full steeplechase course for horse racing. He used the Tudor mansion for enormous parties, but also loved philanthropy; by the time of his death, he had donated all the land to the state. Today it is a busy park for everyone from horseback riders to inline skaters, with free trail maps and restrooms at the park headquarters building. The park's natural history teaches us that wild turkeys were reintroduced here in 1990 after the native birds were nearly hunted to extinction in Massachusetts at the beginning of the last century. You'll also

Canoers launch onto the Ipswich River just above the Willowdale Dam.

find trees, including black cherry, rhododendron, mountain laurel, Scotch pine, Norway spruce, eastern cottonwood, white and red pines, and Canada hemlock. Also keep your eyes open for the three shiny leaves of poison ivy, and for purple loosestrife, an imported plant that is edging out many indigenous species. Your path shadows the southern bank of the Ipswich River for nearly a mile before doubling back through open meadows. You'll step around several equestrian jumps— part of the traditional steeplechase course—before heading uphill to cross a plateau in the center of the land. Dropping back downhill, you follow the bridle paths in a looping trail back to your car.

Long used for hunting and transportation by Native Americans, the Ipswich River has archaeological sites along its banks with Indian artifacts more than 10,000 years old. In its next stage the river was frequently dammed for textile mills, many in the town of Ipswich. Several of these dams still exist, though the river spills over them easily as it makes its way from its headwaters in the town of Wilmington toward the ocean, meeting salt water between Ipswich's Crane Beach and Plum Island. Today it still provides drinking water and recreation to thousands of people, and is a great place for hikers to spot wildlife, from fish to birds to aquatic mammals.

Like any river it occasionally overflows its banks, usually during the spring melt. Seasonal flooding flushes silt off the river bottom and guides anadromous fish back to their freshwater breeding grounds from the ocean. And in this watershed, floods fill another purpose: providing water to the silver maple floodplain forest located in Middleton and Topsfield. Several rare plants here depend entirely on the flooding Ipswich for their survival.

The park's neighbor, Willowdale State Forest, has no developed recreational facilities, but does boast the 100-acre Hood Pond as well as 40 miles of trails. It is split by US 1, with its eastern block abutting Bradley Palmer State Park.

If you're here at holiday time, stop by the Nutter Tree Farm to pick up a handsaw and cut your own Christmas tree. Choose between white spruce and Fraser fir, and pay by the foot for a tree that will fit perfectly in your house. The farm is located at 170 Ipswich Rd., on your left as you drive to the park. Call (978) 887-9835 for details.

Miles and Directions

0.0 Start in the dirt parking lot and follow the paved street you just drove—Bradley Palmer State Park Road—back toward the front gate.

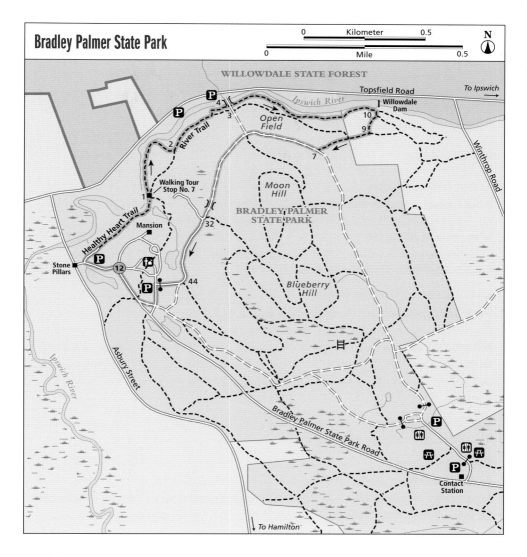

Bradley Palmer State Park

0.2 Turn right onto a paved road just before reaching the stone pillars on Asbury Road, following signs for Accessible Trail and Healthy Heart Trail. Pass a private white house on your left as you leave the pavement and enter the woods on a broad, flat path.

0.4 Cross a long boardwalk close by the banks of the Ipswich River on your left.

0.5 Continue straight on the main path as a smaller trail branches right, soon passing intersections #1 and #2.

0.9 Turn left toward a large wooden bridge at intersection #3, then immediately turn right onto a narrow, blue-blazed path at intersection #4. Continue to follow the river past intersection #6 as you scramble through a thick fir forest with beautiful water views to your left.

1.4 Turn sharp right at the Willowdale Dam (intersection #10), climb a small rise into the woods, and turn right again onto a flat, sandy trail at intersection #9.

1.6 Bear right onto a wide, dirt road at intersection #7 as you emerge into an open field dotted with steeplechase horse jumps.

2.2 Continue straight as the road turns to pavement at intersection #32, and pass by a trail on the right marked NOT OPEN TO GENERAL PUBLIC.

2.4 Stay on the paved road as it curves right at intersection #44, then pass through a metal gate and turn left toward the parking lot.

2.5 Arrive back at your car.

Hike Information

Local Information

Essex County Greenbelt Association: Essex; (978) 768-7241; www.ecga.org. Scheduled hikes and nature walks, local information, education, and more.

Willowdale State Forest: Ipswich; (978) 887-5931; www.mass.gov/eea/agencies/dcr/massparks/region-north/willowdale-state-forest.html

Ipswich River Watershed Association: Ipswich; (978) 356-0418; www.ipswichriver.org

Local Events/Attractions

Foote Brothers Canoe and Kayak Rental: Ipswich; (978) 356-9771; http://footebrothers canoes.com. Rent boats on the river in this park.

Willowdale Estate: located on the park grounds, (978) 887-8211; http://willowdale estate.com. Hosts weddings and parties as well as monthly public tours, movie nights, and tastings.

Accommodations

Visit New England: http://visitnewengland.com/mass/south

Massachusetts vacation website: www.mass-vacation.com/index.shtml

Organizations

Appalachian Mountain Club: Boston Chapter: www.amcboston.org

Appalachian Mountain Club: Southeastern Massachusetts Chapter: www.amcsem.org

Massachusetts's birds website: www.massbird.org. If you're a birder, check it out.

Other Resources

Essex website: www.cape-ann.com/essex. Local maps, lodging, restaurants, shopping directories, and more.

Local Outdoor Retailers

Essex River Basin Adventures: Essex; (978) 768-3722; www.erba.com

Moor & Mountain: Andover; (978) 475-3665

Eastern Mountain Sports (EMS): Peabody; (978) 977-0601; www.emsonline.com

13 Ravenswood Park

Start at the harbor edge of this 600-acre glacial moraine and head north through fields of boulders dropped by the glaciers as they retreated at the end of the last ice age. You'll pass by ocean views over Gloucester Harbor before heading west and dropping through wooded flatlands. Reach the Great Magnolia Swamp and cross a series of boardwalks to return on a broad carriage path to your car.

Start: From the small parking lot at the trailhead off MA 127, just south of Gloucester
Distance: 3.3-mile loop
Hiking time: About 2 hours
Difficulty: Easy, due to broad, flat trails and modest elevation gain
Trail surface: Alternating between marshy flatlands and glacial boulder fields in first 1.5 miles, then broad trails through marshy flatlands, with occasional boardwalks
Best season: Fall
Land status: The Trustees of Reservations and City of Gloucester Watershed
Nearest town: Gloucester

Other trail users: Mountain bikers, cross-country skiers
Canine compatibility: Dogs permitted
Schedule: Open year-round
Fees and permits: None; mountain bikers prohibited from March 1 to April 30 in the park, and barred year-round from the Magnolia Swamp Trail
Maps: USGS Gloucester, MA
Trail contact: The Trustees of Reservations: Northeast Regional Office, Ipswich; (978) 281-8400; www.thetrustees.org/places-to-visit/northeast-ma/ravenswood-park.html

Finding the trailhead: From Beverly, drive north on MA 128 to exit 14, the first Gloucester exit. Follow MA 133 East for 2.8 miles to the edge of Gloucester Harbor, then turn right onto MA 127 South (aka Western Avenue). At 4.8 miles, turn right, into a small parking lot shared with the Cape Ann Discovery Center. *DeLorme: Massachusetts Atlas & Gazetteer:* Page 30 J14. GPS: N42 35.503' / W70 41.908'

The Hike

As you drive along the arm of Cape Ann toward Gloucester, the trip down Route 133 is like touring a museum of the region's modern history. You pass by marinas filled with shrink-wrapped sailboats in dry dock, and cattailed marshes draining into the Atlantic. Tugs, barges, and lobster boats are moored at their piers near the city's State Fort Park. And the curious Hammond Castle stands on the harbor's rocky beach like a monument to the sea.

Ravenswood Park is a more ancient kind of museum. The park itself is a moraine–a long mound of dirt and rock left behind by melting glaciers. Its ponds and swamps were formed when the glaciers left huge chunks of ice stuck in the earth, intersecting the water table and leaving holes full of water and sediment when they melted.

HAMMOND CASTLE

John Hays Hammond Jr., an inventor who worked on guided missiles and radio communications, built Hammond Castle in 1929. After making a fortune in African diamond mines as a mining engineer, he built the structure for the Hammond Research Corp., where he allegedly invented over 800 items, claiming more than 400 patents. One of the most important was remote control, which he tested by sailing empty ships around Gloucester harbor. Today the building houses his collections of medieval art, tiles, and paintings. Check the schedule for chamber music concerts, dinner theater, historical fairs, and Shakespeare productions.

From the trailhead, drive north on MA 127 (aka Western Avenue). In 0.5 mile, turn right onto Hesperus Avenue. In 0.7 mile, turn right into the castle's parking lot at 80 Hesperus Ave. Open 10 a.m. to 4 p.m. on weekends only from November to May, and daily in June, July, and August. Tickets sold for both adults and children.

Fernwood Lake is an example of these *kettle ponds,* and the Great Magnolia Swamp is a glacial bog.

Your hike begins and ends on the Old Salem Road, a broad carriage path that bisects the park. Within a quarter mile, you leave it, following the Ledge Hill Trail as it winds through forest land scattered with boulders and ocean views. There is so much stone in these birch and pine woods that when farmers finished building stone walls, there was enough left over to line the trails, like natural guardrails.

In about 1.4 miles you pass the Hermit's Plaque on Old Salem Road, a marker to Mason Walton, who arrived here in 1884 and lived alone in a cabin in these woods for the next thirty-three years. His book about the experience is in the town library.

Be sure you have good boots, as you follow the muddy Magnolia Swamp Trail that shadows the swampland through rhododendron groves, then crosses through the swamp itself on a chain of wooden boardwalks. When you reach the familiar Old Salem Road, it's less than a quarter mile to your car.

Used since 1623, Gloucester calls itself America's Oldest Seaport, and it has plenty of action to back up the claim. Activities include sea chantey concerts on a retired schooner anchored in the harbor, the Maritime Gloucester Museum on Harbor Loop, and the Essex Shipbuilding Museum. And if you're here in the fall, be sure to check out the Gloucester Schooner Festival, held each Labor Day. Old ships and replicas participate in sailing races, and you can enjoy deck tours, fish fry dinners, and fireworks. Check out www.gloucesterma.com to learn what's happening on the day that you'll be there.

◀ *A flooded quarry holds frogs and lillies.*

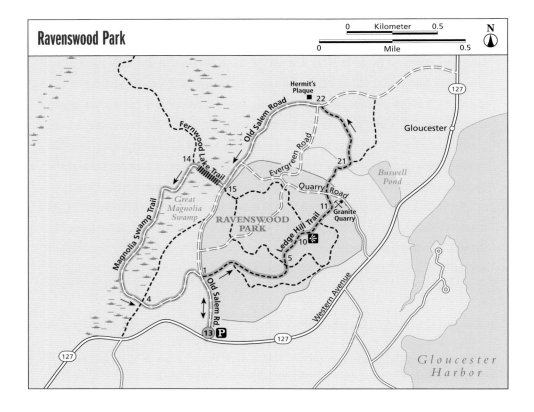

Also don't miss Gloucester's most famous landmark, the one and a half times life-size *Fisherman at the Wheel,* sculpted in 1923 by Leonard Craske. Standing on Stacy Boulevard, it honors the more than 10,000 Gloucester fishermen lost at sea in nearly four centuries. An additional Wall of Remembrance was added in 2000, naming 5,400 of those lost sailors.

Miles and Directions

0.0 Start at the Trustees of Reservations trailhead and walk north on Old Salem Road, a broad, flat path.

0.2 Turn right at a sign for the Ledge Hill Trail, at intersection #1.

0.6 Follow the Ledge Hill Trail through a left turn (at intersection #5) and a right turn (at intersection #6).

0.8 Stay on the Ledge Hill Trail through intersection #10 and reach a gorgeous overlook of Gloucester Harbor, the Atlantic Ocean, and blinking lighthouses to the east. Descend off the hilltop and follow the trail through intersection #9. Passing a small granite quarry on the right, following the Ledge Hill Trail through intersection #11 and then across Quarry Road at intersection #12.

1.1 Follow the trail as it turns left at intersection #21 and climbs through a field of enormous boulders.

1.4 Turn left onto broad, open Old Salem Road as Ledge Hill Trail ends at intersection #22.

1.9 Turn right into the woods onto the narrow Fernwood Lake Trail at intersection #15. (***Bailout:*** Continue south along Old Salem Road for a quicker return to your car.)

2.0 Cross a long boardwalk and turn left onto the Magnolia Swamp Trail at intersection #14. The trail uses extensive boardwalks to ramble south through the wetland.

2.8 Cross an intersection with a small path at intersection #4 to stay on the Magnolia Swamp Trail, and soon pass a balancing rock.

3.1 Turn right onto the broad, flat Old Salem Road at intersection #1.

3.3 Pass through the metal gate at the trailhead and arrive back at your car.

Hike Information

Local Information
Gloucester online: www.cape-ann.com/gloucester.html
City of Gloucester website: www.ci.gloucester.ma.us

Local Events/Attractions
Hammond Castle, Gloucester; (978) 283-7673; www.hammondcastle.org. The museum and home of inventor John Hays Hammond Jr. (see sidebar).
Schooner Adventure, Gloucester; (978) 281-8079; www.schooner-adventure.org
Schooner Sails: *Thomas E. Lannon,* Seven Seas Wharf, Gloucester; (978) 281-6634; www.schooner.org
Maritime Gloucester Museum, http://maritimegloucester.org
Cape Ann Museum, www.capeannmuseum.org

Restaurants
Tony's Magnolia House of Pizza and Italian Cuisine, Magnolia; (978) 525-3030; www.magnoliahouseofpizza.com. From the trailhead, drive north on MA 127 (Western Avenue). In 0.5 mile, turn right onto Hesperus Ave. In another 0.7 mile, pass Hammond Castle and at 1.9 miles, reach the village of Magnolia. Tony's is in Cole Square, at the intersection of Fuller and Norman Streets. Nearby Lexington Avenue is also full of shops, restaurants, and hotels.

Other Resources
Gloucester Daily Times: www.gloucestertimes.com

Local Outdoor Retailers
Eastern Mountain Sports (EMS), Peabody; (978) 977-0601; www.emsonline.com

14 Weir Hill Reservation

Weir Hill is a two-peaked drumlin rising between Stevens Pond and the 2-mile-long Lake Cochichewick. This hike crosses the hilltop meadow, then drops 200 feet to trace the peninsula's perimeter. The town of North Andover has more than 3,000 acres of preserved open space, offering sweeping views and quiet trails.

Start: From the reservation entrance on Stevens Street
Distance: 2.5-mile loop
Hiking time: About 1.5 hours
Difficulty: Easy, with gentle elevation changes and broad trails
Trail surface: Two-track dirt trails and lakeside footpaths
Best season: Summer
Land status: The Trustees of Reservations

Nearest town: North Andover
Other trail users: Cross-country skiers
Canine compatibility: Dogs permitted
Schedule: Open year-round, sunrise to sunset
Fees and permits: None
Maps: USGS Lawrence, MA
Trail contact: The Trustees of Reservations, (978) 682-3580 or (978) 356-4351; www .thetrustees.org/places-to-visit/northeast-ma/ weir-hill.html

Finding the trailhead: From Reading, take I-93 north to exit 41, for Andover/North Andover. Turn right off the exit onto MA 125 North. At 7.1 miles, turn left at a light to merge onto MA 114 and continue on MA 125 North, passing the Merrimack College campus on your left. Turn right at another light to continue on MA 125 North, and at 7.9 miles, turn right at a light onto Andover Street. Fork right at 8.5 miles and drive through the rotary in Old North Andover Center. Cross straight onto Great Pond Road, then turn left onto Stevens Street. Cross between two parts of Stevens Pond and see the reservation entrance on the right at 9.7 miles. *DeLorme: Massachusetts Atlas & Gazetteer:* Page 29 D19. GPS: N42 41.794' / W71 06.638'

The Hike

Settlers first built their homes in nearby North Andover in 1646—originally naming the town after Cochichewick Brook. Likewise, they named this hill after Native Americans' fish weirs in the same waters.

The weirs were underwater fence-like structures made of a woven latticework, supported on wooden stakes. Placed in streams and flowing lakes, water would flow through them while fish would be trapped, speared, or netted. Used by Native Americans across the continent, the woven structures were removed for the winter in colder climes, leaving the stakes or dikes behind. European settlers quickly realized this was a far more efficient way to fish than their own methods, and began to build large-scale, commercial weirs on local rivers.

Those settlers also grazed sheep and cattle on the shoulders of Weir Hill. Then a funny thing happened. Given several centuries to rebound, the forest grew back

A split-rail fence borders the Alewife Trail.

slightly differently on its two exposures. The Trustees of Reservations describes the woodland now as pitch pine and oak on the west side of Weir Hill, and white birch, shagbark hickory, aspen, beech, maple, and white pine on the east side.

This land is in the Merrimack River drainage basin, which covers 279 square miles of eastern Massachusetts. Among the seventy-six lakes and ponds in this region, only Lake Cochichewick—at 592 acres—is larger than 500 acres. The river flows toward Newburyport, where it becomes a tidal estuary for its final 9 miles before emptying into the sea.

To relax after a hike, try a magic or puppet show, or catch some local ventriloquists and musicians. Throughout the summer the town sponsors free events on its common, from a spring sheep shearing festival to the Fourth of July fair.

Another option is to stop by the Stevens-Coolidge Place in North Andover, listed on the National Register of Historic Places. The 92-acre, meticulously landscaped estate is owned by the Trustees of Reservations and is open to the public (see hours in the Hike Information section). The Stevens Estate is another historical attraction. Also in North Andover, the thirty-three-room mansion was built in 1886 by textile magnate Moses T. Stevens in a prime location on Osgood Hill overlooking the lake. Now owned by the town of North Andover, it is rented out as a conference and meeting center. The building also hosts murder mysteries and comedy theater performances.

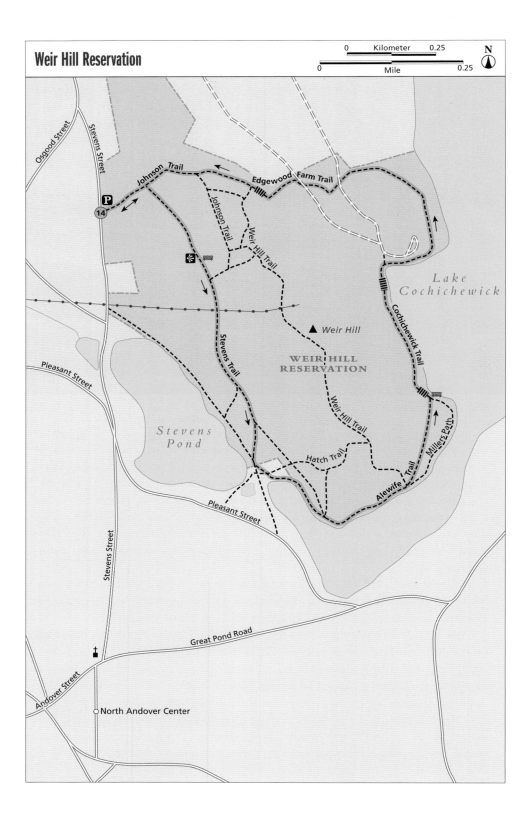

Weir Hill Reservation

0 Kilometer 0.25

0 Mile 0.25

N

Osgood Street

Stevens Street

P
14

Johnson Trail

Edgewood Farm Trail

Johnson Trail

Weir Hill Trail

Lake Cochichewick

Stevens Trail

▲ Weir Hill

WEIR HILL RESERVATION

Cochichewick Trail

Pleasant Street

Stevens Pond

Weir Hill Trail

Hatch Trail

Alewife Trail

Millers Path

Pleasant Street

Stevens Street

Great Pond Road

Andover Street

○ North Andover Center

Although this is a modest hike, be sure to dress with care, since the shore path can be very muddy in early spring. Fortunately all motorized vehicles are prohibited from the reservation, so the trails are in good condition. And like the land's first inhabitants, ice anglers today can be seen dragging their heavy sleds on the ice of Lake Cochichewick, as late in the spring as mid-March. This water body is the sole source of drinking water for North Andover and the largest body of freshwater in Essex County.

Miles and Directions

0.0   Start from the reservation sign, walk uphill through the clearing, and pick up the trail into the woods in the far left corner.

0.1   Turn right at a fork 50 yards into the woods, going steeply uphill on the yellow-blazed Stevens Trail.

0.4   Reach a stone bench in the midst of a clearing on the shoulder of Weir Hill, with beautiful views of the surrounding woods. Continue down the other side, following yellow blazes.

0.8   Follow the Stevens Trail past a map kiosk where a spur trail leads to the Old Railroad Grade and Stevens Pond on your right.

1.0   Stay on the yellow-blazed path—now called Alewife Trail—as you gain views of Lake Cochichewick through a split-rail fence to your right. Soon pass junctions with the northbound Scrub Oak Trail and Weir Hill Trail.

1.3   Follow the yellow blazes in a sweeping turn to the left as the wooden fence ends at a sandy beach with panoramic views of the lake. The trail soon becomes more narrow and rocky as it rambles north through woods and over boardwalks.

1.7   Continue to trace the shore as you pass a junction with the Birch Stand Trail on the left.

1.9   Follow the yellow-blazed path—now called the Edgewood Farm Trail—uphill away from the water.

2.0   Cross a broad path (the other end of the Birch Stand Trail) and follow the yellow blazes as they turn right onto a wider trail.

2.4   Pass by the junction where you began the Stevens Trail, still following yellow blazes.

2.5   Arrive back at your car.

Hike Information

Local Information

North Andover website: www.townofnorthandover.com
Lawrence Eagle Tribune: www.eagletribune.com
Stevens Memorial Library: North Andover; (978) 688-9505; www.stevensmemlib.org
Appalachian Mountain Club's Andover Chapter: http://amcboston.org/andover/

Local Events/Attractions

Stevens-Coolidge Place: North Andover; (978) 682-3580; www.thetrustees.org/places-to-visit/northeast-ma/stevens-coolidge-place.html. Gardens open year-round, sunrise to sunset; check website for house tours.
Stevens Estate: North Andover; (978) 682-7072; www.stevensestate.com

Stop for a view to the west from the shoulder of Weir Hill.

Restaurants

There are several restaurants in the town center, near the North Parish Church.
General Store: North Andover; (978) 688-4116. Sandwiches and drinks.

Organizations

Essex National Heritage Site: www.essexheritage.org. Part of a 500-square-mile area of eastern Massachusetts intended to preserve the historical, cultural, and natural resources of the region.

Andover Village Improvement Society: http://avisandover.org. A local conservation group.

15 Maudslay State Park

This flat loop around a 480-acre park begins with a visit to the ruins of a historic mansion, with commanding views of the Merrimack River and stunning summer flower blooms. The path then traces the edge of a cliff side just above the river's edge—a favorite winter roosting area for bald eagles. After a quick trip to the park's highest point (a modest 150-foot hill), it loops back to the start.

Start: From the ranger station
Distance: 3.9-mile loop
Hiking time: About 1.5 to 2 hours
Difficulty: Easy
Trail surface: Dirt paths
Best season: Summer
Land status: State of Massachusetts
Nearest town: Newburyport
Other trail users: Mountain bikers, equestrians, runners, cross-country skiers

Canine compatibility: Leashed dogs permitted
Schedule: Open year-round, 8 a.m. to sunset daily
Fees and permits: None
Maps: USGS Newburyport, MA
Trail contact: Maudslay State Park Ranger Station, (978) 465-7223; www.mass.gov/eea/agencies/dcr/massparks/region-north/maudslay-state-park.html

Finding the trailhead: From Boston, take I-95 north to exit 57, for West Newbury and Newburyport. Follow MA 113 east for 0.3 mile, then turn left past a cemetery onto Noble Street. At a stop sign, turn left onto Ferry Road and follow it as it bears left at a fork, following signs for the park. The street's name changes to Pine Hill Road and then to Curzon Mill Road—just keep following it, and in a mile you'll see the park entrance on the left (2.1 miles total from I-95). *DeLorme: Massachusetts Atlas & Gazetteer:* Page 19 K20. GPS: N42 49.287' / W70 55.575'

The Hike

Acquired by the state in 1985, and famed for its groves of mountain laurels, this land has a long history. Framed by the Artichoke and Merrimack Rivers, it was a riverfront site for early Native American settlements, then in 1668 it served as a crossing point for the Amesbury-Newbury ferry. It was purchased in 1805 by the wealthy Moseley family when they settled in Newburyport. By 1900 they had bought up surrounding land and named the estate Maudsleigh, after their original home in England. Its mansions included the twenty-two-room gothic wooden Moulton's Castle (razed in 1900), Frederick Moseley's forty-room summer home (razed after his death in 1955), and his daughter Helen's large colonial (burned down in 1978).

The family also had a gift for building gardens, and thankfully for us, these have survived. From the formal gardens and stone bridges to the 16 miles of carriage roads, spring and summer are the time to see blooms on the flowering shrubs, ornamental

Cross an arched stone bridge to head north toward Castle Hill.

trees, azaleas, rhododendrons, and, of course, the laurels. And in the southeast corner, the Theater in the Open features summertime performances for the public.

Pick up a free trail map in the plywood kiosk in the parking lot, then begin your hike by walking west along Curzon Mill Road, past the rangers office. When you turn right, passing through an entranceway in the stone wall, the dirt road leads you through a chute of tall, shady oaks and 20-foot-tall rhododendrons to a flat, open field with a breathtaking view of the Merrimack River. It's easy to see why this was the site for Frederick Moseley's main house. Then pick up the Merrimack River Trail, marked irregularly with small square blazes of the trail's wagon-wheel logo. This trail was conceived as a long-distance path to stretch from Newburyport's Plum Island to Canada, but it currently covers just a fraction of that distance.

This narrow trail scrambles along the steep cliff, with the river on your left supplying views of Newburyport's houses, boats, and marinas. A quick loop takes you up and around Castle Hill, the park's highest point. The trip home is a good place to stretch your legs, as you stroll a smooth, broad trail along the park's edges and back to the parking lot.

FLOWERS PUT ON SUMMER SHOW

Maudslay's botanical offerings are one of the sole remaining vestiges of the once-mighty mansions on the grounds. Visit the park during these times to catch the peak blooming seasons:

April	purple trillium, large flowered trillium, crocus, daffodil
May	1st week—dogwoods begin, hawthorns, crab apple
	2nd week—roses begin, trout lily, wild geranium, jack-in-the-pulpit, royal azalea, lilac
	3rd week—hybrid rhododendrons begin, kaempferi azalea, lady's slipper, apple trees, Carolina rhododendron
	4th week—lily of the valley, bunchberry
June	1st week—ghent/exbury azaleas
	2nd week—roses peak, mountain laurel begins, phlox, coreopsis, foxglove
	3rd week—mountain laurel peaks, rock columbine, ox-eye daisy
	4th week—maximum rhododendron begin
July	1st week—harebells, wood lily
	2nd week—Indian pipe, black-eyed Susan, pipissewa, blueberries
	3rd week—spotted wintergreen
August	goldenrod, pasture thistle, asters

Source: Massachusetts Department of Conservation and Recreation

If you have time after your hike, check out Newburyport, with museums such as the historic Cushing House Museum & Garden, the Custom House Maritime Museum, Massachusetts Audubon's Joppa Flats Education Center and Wildlife Sanctuary, and many more. Or leave the land behind and take a whale-watching cruise out to Stellwagen Bank, a shallow offshore sandbank where the plentiful fish attract humpback, fin, and minke whales.

Miles and Directions

0.0 Start your hike by walking west along paved Curzon Mill Road, passing the ranger office and a junction with Hedge Drive.

0.3 Turn right through a once-grand entranceway in the stone wall onto the wide dirt Main Drive, lined with soaring oaks and elms. (If the gate is closed, follow the small footpath around it.) The trail soon provides a gorgeous overlook of the Merrimack River.

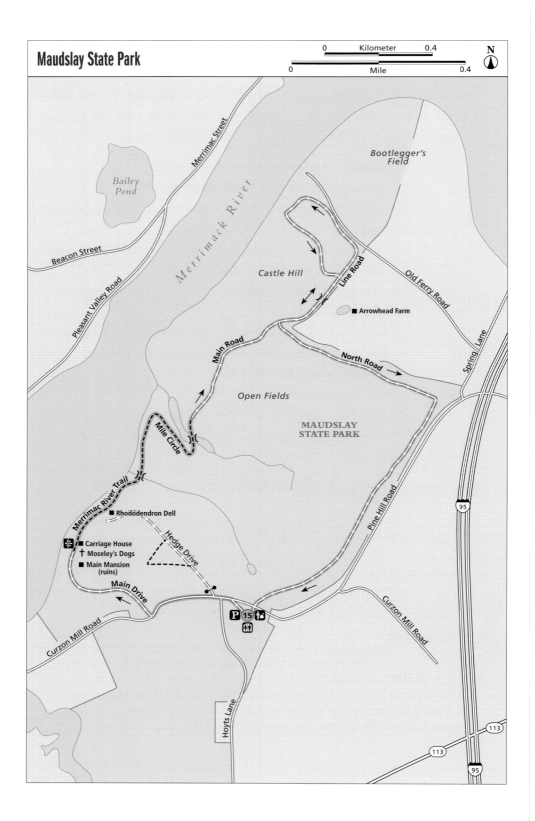

Maudslay State Park

Bailey Pond

Merrimac Street

Beacon Street

Pleasant Valley Road

Merrimack River

Castle Hill

Bootlegger's Field

Line Road

Old Ferry Road

■ Arrowhead Farm

Main Road

North Road

Spring Lane

Open Fields

MAUDSLAY STATE PARK

Mile Circle

Merrimac River Trail

■ Rhododendron Dell

Pine Hill Road

Hedge Drive

■ Carriage House
† Moseley's Dogs
■ Main Mansion (ruins)

Main Drive

Curzon Mill Road

Curzon Mill Road

Hoyts Lane

95

113

113

95

N

0 Kilometer 0.4

0 Mile 0.4

0.5 Turn right onto the Merrimack River Trail at a hedge just past the stone foundation of the original mansion (point #1 on the trail map available at park headquarters). Keep the river on your left, far below a steep bluff, as you pick up this narrow footpath through tall white pines.

0.8 Cross a small wooden bridge over a stream, near point #7 (Rhododendron Dell) on your trail map, and continue on the narrow path as it passes a broader trail on the right.

0.9 Cross a small cement bridge and turn left onto Mile Circle, a sandy, doubletrack main path that continues along the steep riverbank on your left.

1.1 Follow the broad trail as it takes a hairpin turn to the right (passing point #17), and you catch a pretty view of Flowering Pond to your left.

1.2 Turn left onto Main Road, immediately crossing a large stone bridge over the pond (point #16) and forking right on the other side. Follow this wide path through a pine forest, passing several junctions with smaller paths and a restricted bald eagle habitat on your left.

1.6 Bear left at a junction when you step out of the trees, catching sight of the rolling meadows of map point #15 (Open Fields) to your right. Immediately cross through another intersection to begin walking on a bark chip path called Line Road. (The other options here are North Road to your right and Castle Hill Trail to your left.)

1.75 Line Road soon begins to run parallel to a high fence line on your right, the border of Arrowhead Farm.

1.95 Follow the trail in a 90-degree left turn around the base of Castle Hill, then turn left again at the edge of the open field, beginning a gentle climb up the hill.

2.2 Turn left again to head straight for the hilltop, following a wide dirt road to reach the modest peak (point #20) in about 150 yards. Continue along the trail as it descends in a corkscrew down the other side.

2.5 Turn right at the base of the slope onto Line Road, retracing your steps back toward the southwest.

2.7 Turn left onto North Road as you reach the familiar, large intersection near point #15.

3.1 Stay on the broad, flat North Road as Main Road branches sharply to your right, and soon begin walking parallel to the paved Pine Hill Road to your left.

3.3 Pass intersections with Fire Road and Overlook Road, then emerge into an open field.

3.9 Cross the paved Curzon Mill Road and arrive back at your car.

Hike Information

Local Information
New England Mountain Biking Association: www.nemba.org. This group sometimes has useful information on the region, such as weather reports and trail conditions.

Local Events/Attractions
Theater in the Open: (978) 465-2572; http://theaterintheopen.org/content/. A local acting troupe located at the state park. Past productions include plays by Molière and Thornton Wilder, haunted skits at Halloween, and Vermont's famous Circus Smirkus.
Newburyport Whale Watch: Newburyport; (978) 499-0832; www.Newburyport WhaleWatch.com

Main Drive heads toward a stunning bluff above the Merrimack River.

Cushing House Museum & Garden: Newburyport; (978) 462-2681; www.forbeshouse museum.org/CHMG-nw.html

Newburyport Maritime Society's Custom House Maritime Museum: Newburyport; (978) 462-8681; www.customhousemaritimemuseum.org

Joppa Flats Education Center and Wildlife Sanctuary: Massachusetts Audubon Society, Newburyport; (978) 462-9998; www.massaudubon.org/Nature_Connection/Sanc tuaries/Joppa_Flats/index.php

Organizations

Maudslay State Park Association: Newburyport; http://maudslayassociation.org. A nonprofit, tax-exempt organization dedicated to the protection of the park.

Maudslay Projects: http://maudslayprojects.info. A nonprofit group that raises money to restore Flowering Pond.

Other Resources

Greater Newbury Friends of our Trails (FOOT): http://nature.thecompass.com/foot/ trails.html

Local Outdoor Retailers

Eastern Mountain Sports (EMS): Peabody; (978) 977-0601; www.emsonline.com

Central Massachusetts

I magine if the Rockies were located in Worcester.

West of the I-495 belt is the "erosion region," the base of what once were granite mountains 20,000 feet high. Geologists say they were an extension of New Hampshire's White Mountains. But millennia of erosion have carved these peaks down to a series of plateaus 1,000 feet high, laced with river-carved valleys.

Today all that remains of those original giants are Mounts Wachusett and Watatic. This context makes it fun to visit Mount Wachusett, Mount Grace State Forest, or the Midstate Trail, to see these rocky, ancient uplands. Mount Grace is steep enough to have a deserted alpine ski resort on one shoulder. This isolated peak stuck out so clearly from the landscape that the Wampanoag tribe of Native Americans used it as an important landmark. Likewise, the Midstate Trail completes its trip from Rhode Island to New Hampshire by crossing over a succession of peaks, including Mount Wachusett, Brown Hill, Mount Hunger, and finally Mount Watatic.

Gain a great reward for scrambling along the Tyler Trail when you reach the southern overlook (hike 19).

Change here has come more quickly since the arrival of European settlers. The state has over 1,100 lakes and ponds, but the largest two of these are both man-made, and both reside in this region—the Quabbin Reservoir (24,704 acres) and Wachusett Reservoir (4,160 acres) were both created to serve the drinking needs of greater Boston. The land too is changing—once nearly clear-cut, today abandoned farms are quickly giving way to suburbs and young forests.

While hawks migrate over the Berkshires each fall, migratory songbirds prefer the farmland and wooded hills of the central plains and river valley. And the Quabbin Reservoir has hosted several pairs of breeding bald eagles each year since the late 1980s. Visit the Brooks Woodland Preserve and Moose Hill Wildlife Sanctuary to catch more glimpses of this rich tableau.

You can still see erosion in progress—even today the Connecticut River uncovers dinosaur fossils and 300-million-year-old lava flows as it cuts through the state. The mighty river runs quickly through its narrow valley in the north, but spreads out, twisting and lazy, in the south, dropping tons of fertile topsoil there every year.

16 Mount Grace State Forest

With a tall, eight-platform fire tower at its peak and the long-distance Metacomet-Monadnock (M–M) Trail running up its flank, Mount Grace deserves more attention than it gets. But located on the New Hampshire border, far from large towns, the forest is quiet and the steep, wooded trails are usually empty.

Start: From Ohlson Memorial Field, at park headquarters off MA 78
Distance: 4.2-mile loop
Hiking time: About 2 hours
Difficulty: Moderate, due to some steep climbs
Trail surface: Broad dirt paths, with some narrow trails
Best season: Fall
Land status: MA Department of Conservation and Recreation

Nearest town: Warwick
Other trail users: Mountain bikers, cross-country skiers, snowmobilers
Canine compatibility: Dogs permitted
Schedule: Open year-round
Fees and permits: None
Maps: USGS Northfield, MA
Trail contact: Mount Grace State Forest, Warwick; (978) 544-3939; www.mass.gov/ eea/agencies/dcr/massparks/region-central/ mount-grace-state-forest.html

Finding the trailhead: From Greenfield, take MA 2 East to its junction with MA 2A (this intersection is in Erving, between exits 13 and 14). Drive east on MA 2A for 2 miles, turning left onto MA 78 (aka Winchester Road). Go north on MA 78, and at 8.6 miles, park in the large paved lot at Ohlson Memorial Field, adjacent to the park headquarters. *DeLorme: Massachusetts Atlas & Gazetteer:* Page 24 D5. GPS: N42 41.363' / W72 20.469'

The Hike

This loop begins with a gentle descent, heading northward along the valley slope above Mountain Brook and MA 78. After passing the rusting remnants of a ski lift shack, you meet the Metacomet-Monadnock (M–M) Trail and begin a steep climb, leaving the tall white pines of the valley floor and entering a mixed region of hemlock, birch, and beech. The M–M runs 117 miles from the Metacomet Trail (named for a Wampanoag tribal chief) on the Connecticut state line to Mount Monadnock in New Hampshire.

At the summit the unlocked fire tower atop Mount Grace affords clear views of Mount Monadnock to the north, the Berkshires to the west, and the heavily wooded 1,689-acre state forest below. But the stiff breeze cools a sweaty T-shirt so fast that you won't stay up there long. Several mountain biking groups are in the midst of cutting and blazing a Round-the-Mountain Trail that circles the peak, and you pick up these blue blazes on your descent. Pass through a soaring stand of white pines as you return to the picnic tables and restrooms at Ohlson Field.

At 1,621 feet Mount Grace is the state's second highest east of the Connecticut River (Mount Wachusett is 2,006 feet). It was doubtless this altitude that attracted early skiers to hike up its northeastern slope for a schuss down the mile-long Pro Trail or 0.8-mile Novice Trail. In later years a rope tow pulled skiers to the top. However, no one has done any organized skiing here since the 1970s. With the slopes grown in, the lift poles toppled, and the lift engine buried under its collapsed hut, it's a safe bet that no one will try it again anytime soon.

Mount Grace gained its name in grisly fashion when a kidnapped woman buried her infant child here during the colonial era. Mary Rowlandson of Lancaster was kidnapped in 1676 by Wampanoag Indians during King Philip's War. During the group's march toward Canada, the infant baby Grace died, and Mary buried her on the spot.

The nearby town of Warwick was settled in the 1740s and founded in 1763 by tough settlers who ground out a living in these hills just 6 miles east of the Connecticut River, under continuing attacks from the French and Indians. The first established industry here included mid-nineteenth-century sawmills, blacksmith shops, tanneries, and factories that made pails, staves, and axes.

Wind whistles through the girders as you climb the the Warwick Fire Tower's open stairs.

In fact, the tough fiber of these early colonists may persevere today—modern Warwick residents are famed for their longevity. Though the town claimed just 740 residents in the last census, anecdotal evidence suggests that their town's healthy climate will keep them all around for a long time to come.

When you're done with the hike, another local attraction is the Indian Cave, a natural rock formation located north of Stevens Swamp and south of the Old South Road to Northfield. It is said to include a 30-foot tunnel that opens into a 12-square-foot opening.

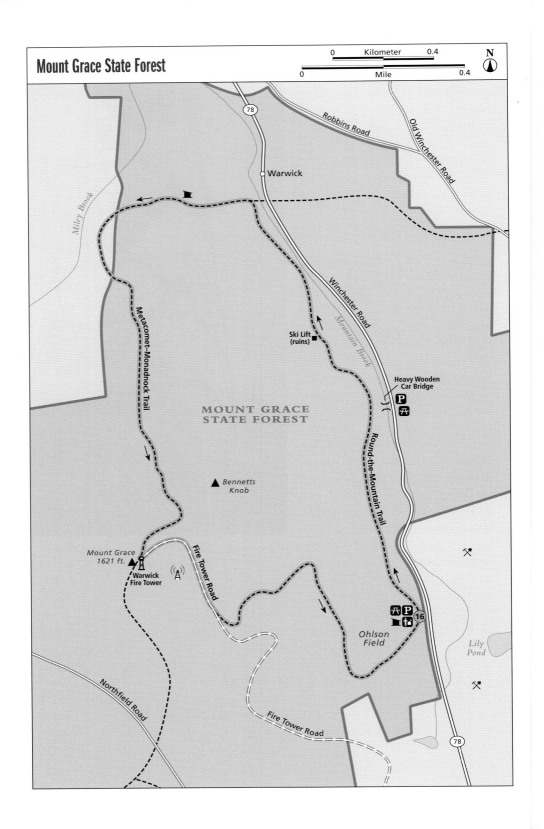

Mount Grace State Forest

0 Kilometer 0.4

0 Mile 0.4

N

78

Robbins Road

Old Winchester Road

Warwick

Miley Brook

Metacomet–Monadnock Trail

Winchester Road

Mountain Brook

Ski Lift (ruins)

Heavy Wooden Car Bridge

P

MOUNT GRACE STATE FOREST

Bennetts Knob

Round-the-Mountain Trail

Mount Grace 1621 ft.

Warwick Fire Tower

Fire Tower Road

Ohlson Field

16

P

Lily Pond

Northfield Road

Fire Tower Road

78

Miles and Directions

0.0 Start in the Ohlson Memorial Field parking lot and walk north along the edge of the open field, with MA 78 on your right. Enter the woods in 100 yards and follow the blue blazes of the Round-the-Mountain Trail.

0.4 Cross a wooden footbridge over a stream.

0.7 Pass by a heavy wooden car bridge (this leads to a dirt road that intersects MA 78 through the trees to your right). Follow the blue blazes as the trail twists uphill.

1.0 Pass by an abandoned ski lift, complete with a rusted engine and series of pulleys stretching uphill through the undergrowth.

1.3 Turn left at a T and head steeply uphill on the broad, white-blazed M-M Trail southbound.

1.5 Pass by an open-faced shelter with picnic tables and fire circles and continue uphill.

1.9 Continue straight with the white-blazed M-M Trail, as the blue-blazed Round-the-Mountain Trail branches off to the right.

2.8 Reach the eight-story Warwick Fire Tower at the peak of Mount Grace. To begin your return to the parking lot, leave the white blazes behind and follow the dirt Fire Tower Road downhill.

3.2 Turn left onto a narrow, blue-blazed footpath at a sign for Ohlson Field.

3.9 Turn left at an intersection at another sign for Ohlson Field and, in 50 yards, turn left again.

4.0 Emerge into the grassy, open Ohlson Field and keep the clearing on your left as you pass another camping shelter.

4.2 Arrive back at your car.

Hike Information

Local Information

Warwick, MA website: www.warwickma.org

New England Lost Ski Areas Project: Mount Grace, Warwick; www.nelsap.org/ma/grace.html. Information on the early ski area here.

Warwick Historical Society: Warwick Center; (978) 544-7545; http://whs.steamkite.com. Photos, furniture, historical diaries, and factory relics. Hours are Sunday from 2 to 4 p.m. during July and August.

Other Resources

Metacomet-Monadnock Trail: http://amcberkshire.org/netmm

Mount Grace Land Conservation Trust: Athol; (978) 248-2043; http://mountgrace.org

17 Brooks Woodland Preserve

This loop begins and ends along the water in the Swift River valley. Following well-marked numbered intersections throughout the hike, you climb into the Harvard Forest with its tall white pine and hemlock trees, then drop back down to the riverside. The trail passes stone cellars that remain from early settlers' homes, and recently chewed tree stumps that show modern beavers are hard at work building their own homes.

Start: From the parking lot on Quaker Drive
Distance: 3.8-mile loop
Hiking time: About 2.5 hours
Difficulty: Moderate, with broad, flat trails that roll up and down the valley hills around the Swift River
Trail surface: Broad, dirt, usually two-track paths
Best season: Fall
Land status: The Trustees of Reservations

Nearest town: Petersham
Other trail users: Cross-country skiers
Canine compatibility: Dogs permitted
Schedule: Open year-round, sunrise to sunset
Fees and permits: None
Maps: USGS Barre, MA
Trail contact: The Trustees of Reservations, (413) 532-1631; www.thetrustees.org/places-to-visit/central-ma/brooks-wood land-preserve.html.

Finding the trailhead: From Leominster, drive west on MA 2 to exit 21, for Templeton and MA 101. Follow MA 101 south for 8.6 miles, then turn left onto MA 32 South. At 10.1 miles, turn left onto MA 32/122 South (aka Barre Road). At 11.6 miles, turn left onto the narrow Quaker Drive, and at 12.1 miles, park at a small dirt lot marked on trail maps as the F. Dudley Cellar Hole. *DeLorme: Massachusetts Atlas & Gazetteer:* Page 37 B16. GPS: N42 28.439' / W72 09.544'

The Hike

The Brooks Woodland Preserve is like a history book, and you can practically hike through the pages of its chapters. It began as home to the Nipmuck Indians, who ground corn and acorns into bread flour using the stone hollows they scraped into large boulders here. You can find many of these today in the northeast part of the property (the Swift River Tract). Petersham was founded in 1754, and the settlement of Europeans ultimately forced the Nipmucks out. European settlers converted the woods to open farmland, built miles of stone walls, and left behind only the stone cellars beneath their homes. Keep your eyes open for a half-dozen of these foundations as you hike. Another colonial remnant is a 10-acre marsh, which was once an open pond feeding water to a downstream mill.

Today the Trustees of Reservations are trying to return the forest to its primeval state. The trees, jumping at the opportunity, are dominating the land with soaring

A wooden footbridge crosses the Swift River ▶
to begin the southbound return.

white pines and hemlocks, scattered with birches, red oak and shagbark hickory, and rhododendron growing underneath. In the spring, drowsy garter snakes wriggle across the trail, while beaver families busily dam the Swift River and Moccasin Brook, creating deep pools and leaving gnawed, pointy stumps along the waters' edge. The reservation also serves as a wildlife sanctuary, supporting a balance of deer, fox, moose, coyotes, porcupines, hawks, owls, bald eagles, wild turkeys, and herons.

The trails are not named or blazed, but they feature numbered intersections that serve as helpful landmarks for this hike. The preserve is bordered by the Harvard Forest (a 2,000-acre woodlands research center managed by Harvard University and founded in 1907), a Massachusetts Audubon Society reservation (the 1,500-acre Rutland Brook Sanctuary), and state-owned lands. It is composed of three sections—the North Common Meadow, Brooks Woodland Preserve, and Swift River Preservation—but this loop stays primarily in the Brooks section, given to the Trustees by the estate of James Willson Brooks, a turn-of-the-twentieth-century lawyer, diplomat, and cofounder of the United Shoe Machinery Company.

A great way to get to know this land is to pitch in on an annual trail-working day. Each spring, volunteers clear fallen trees and overgrowth from the trails. Check the Trustees' website for dates. With 1,200 people, modern-day Petersham boasts an anemic population density of just 21 people per square mile (compare this to Worcester's 4,520 per square mile and Cambridge's 14,899 per square mile). It is listed in the National Register of Historic Places, featuring the town common and about forty-five buildings that were built in the early nineteenth century. In summertime there are frequent band concerts staged at the renovated bandstand.

Despite their proud history in early manufacturing, there is one deed of modern history that residents of central Massachusetts have never forgiven—the flooding of the Quabbin Reservoir. The state's eastern cities had outgrown their local water supplies by the 1920s and began to buy up land around the Swift River, nearly 100 miles inland. One by one these towns were emptied, buildings bulldozed, graveyards dug up, and millions of acres of trees razed. An enormous dam was built in Belchertown in 1939, and by 1946 the central Massachusetts towns of Dana, Enfield, Greenwich, and Prescott were buried beneath almost 40 square miles of water. The reservoir was named for a Native American chief called Nani-Quaben, or "well-watered place."

Miles and Directions

0.0 Start at the trailhead kiosk in the dirt parking lot at the F. Dudley Cellar Hole (intersection #54). Return to the paved Quaker Drive and turn right, walking south back along the road you drove in on.

0.3 Cross a bridge over the Swift River and turn right, passing through a metal gate onto a broad dirt trail. Follow this path north through the Harvard Research Forest, keeping the river on your right.

1.2 Take a hairpin left turn, leaving the river behind to climb a series of steep switchbacks.

1.6 Turn right at a fork shortly after the trail levels off at the top of the climb.

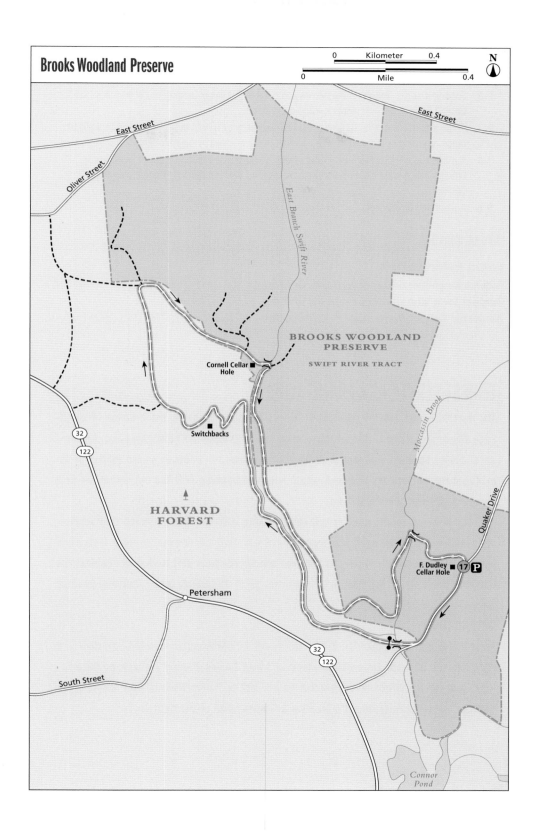

Brooks Woodland Preserve

East Street

East Street

Oliver Street

East Branch Swift River

BROOKS WOODLAND
PRESERVE

SWIFT RIVER TRACT

Moccasin Brook

Cornell Cellar
Hole ■

■ Switchbacks

32
122

HARVARD
FOREST

Quaker Drive

F. Dudley ■ 17 P
Cellar Hole

Petersham

32
122

South Street

*Connor
Pond*

0   Kilometer   0.4
0   Mile   0.4

N

1.9 Turn right at a four-way junction (intersection #30 on the map, but unmarked on the trail), following a stone wall gently downhill.

2.3 Fork right at the bottom of the hill, as you pass a stonework basement called the John Cornell Cellar Hole (intersection #35) on your left.

2.4 Cross a bridge over the Swift River and immediately turn right at a T (intersection #45) to begin returning south toward your car, with the river close by on your right.

3.6 Turn right at a T (intersection #49) to cross a bridge over Moccasin Brook. In 50 yards, emerge into a large clearing and take the second path on the left, marked by a large boulder.

3.8 Arrive back at your car.

Hike Information

Local Information

Petersham online: www.townofpetersham.org

Gardner town site: www.gardner-ma.gov

Worcester County Convention & Visitors Bureau: Worcester; (508) 753-2920; www.worcester.org

FOREST SERVES AS A LIVING MUSEUM

The Harvard Forest, located adjacent to Brooks Woodland Preserve, has a wealth of knowledge about the natural history of this region. Its 3,000 acres are highlighted and explained at the Fisher Museum, designed to display twenty-three 3-D dioramas on the subject of the management and ecology of New England forests, beginning with the era before the first European settlement in Petersham.

The museum and its outdoor self-guided hiking trails are free (although they appreciate donations). They are open year-round from 9 a.m. to 5 p.m. Monday through Friday, and additionally from noon to 4 p.m. on Saturday and Sunday from May to October. Contact the Harvard Forest at 324 N. Main St., Petersham; (978) 724-3302; http://harvardforest.fas.harvard.edu/fisher-museum.

GETTING THERE:

From the east or west, take MA 2, turn off at exit 17 (intersection with MA 32), then turn right onto MA 32 south toward Petersham and travel 3 miles. Harvard Forest is on the left.

From the Worcester area, go north on MA 122 to Petersham and take MA 32 north through the town center; Harvard Forest is 3.5 miles north on the right.

Local Events/Attractions

The Johnny Appleseed Trail Association/Visitor Center: Leominster; (978) 534-2302; www.appleseed.org. Why is this here? The famed Johnny Appleseed of our camp songs was born here in Leominster in 1774, although he was known then as John Chapman.

Organizations

Appalachian Mountain Club: Berkshire Office, Lanesboro; (413) 443-0011

Narragansett Historical Society: Templeton; (978) 939-2303; www.narragansetthistorical society.org

Petersham Memorial Library: Petersham; (978) 724-3405; www.petershamlibrary.net

Other Resources

North Quabbin Woods: Athol; (978) 249-3703; www.northquabbinwoods.org/quest. A local business and conservation group that hosts Quest, a series of riddles and map clues that includes a stop in these woods.

Local Outdoor Retailers

New England Backpacker Inc.: Worcester; (508) 853-9407; www.newenglandback packer.com

18 Wachusett Mountain State Reservation

A ridgeline ascent to the highest point in Massachusetts east of the Berkshires, this hike is located on a state reservation with over 17 miles of trails. The loop passes through a succession of mature hardwood forests and mystical hemlock groves, as well as stone rivers of glacial till. Although its proximity to Boston, paved summit road, and chairlift to the peak can make it quite crowded, it is also famed in the fall as one of the East Coast's premier foliage and hawk-watching spots.

Start: From the reservation headquarters and visitor center off Mountain Road

Distance: 3.9-mile loop

Hiking time: About 3 hours

Difficulty: Moderate, due to steepness

Trail surface: Rocky dirt trails

Best season: Fall

Land status: MA Department of Conservation and Recreation

Nearest town: Princeton

Other trail users: Alpine skiers on northern face of the mountain, but not on trails

Canine compatibility: Dogs permitted

Schedule: Open year-round; visitor center open 9 a.m. to 6 p.m. and parking lot 7 a.m. to dusk

Fees and permits: None

Maps: USGS Sterling, MA

Trail contact: Wachusett Mountain State Reservation, Princeton; (978) 464-2987; www .mass.gov/eea/agencies/dcr/massparks/ region-central/wachusett-mountain-state -reservation.html

Finding the trailhead: From Worcester, drive north on I-190. Take exit 5, for West Boylston and Princeton, to MA 140 North. Turn left onto MA 62 West, toward Princeton, then left again onto MA 31 South. At Princeton Square, turn right onto Mountain Road, passing a gazebo. In 3.1 miles, turn left at the sign for the visitor center. *DeLorme: Massachusetts Atlas & Gazetteer:* Page 38 A2. GPS: N42 29.497' / W71 52.808'

The Hike

Pick up a free trail map at the visitor center, which also has water and restrooms, and a fascinating collection of bird, wildflower, and natural history displays. The Bicentennial Trail begins in the corner of the parking lot and is clearly marked with blue triangles, the same blazes used for all of Wachusett's trails.

Follow Bicentennial for about a mile as it traverses the steep hillside, being careful not to twist your ankles on several hundred meters of glacial till. Continue past the Loop Trail branching uphill to your right (this will be your return path), and enjoy the mature hardwood forest of tall oaks, maples, beech, and hickory. Your traverse ends as you turn onto the Mountain House Trail for a heart-thumping ascent to the ridgeline. This quick elevation gain proves the wisdom of names: Wachusett means "by the great hill" in Algonquin, the same root as the word Massachusett, "people of the great hill."

As you walk the ridge, you'll pass over a series of smooth, pillow-shaped bedrock, polished by the glaciers when they retreated 10,000 years ago. Soon cross the paved Summit Road and reach the towering peak.

Even on a cloudy day, the summit can be crowded, but the view from the 2,006-foot peak is thrilling, with the Boston skyline to the east, Lake Quinsigamond and Worcester to the south, Mount Tom and Greylock to the west, and Mount Monadnock to the north. In September and October this spot is one of the East Coast's premier bird-watching points, directly in a migration route for hawks, ospreys, falcons, and eagles.

For a return route you'll cross the summit and pass the fire observation tower to begin a corkscrew around the shoulders of Mount Wachusett, rejoining your original path near the end. Pass the ski lift and scramble down a series of

Wachusett Lake lies at the foot of a chairlift that crosses the Old Indian Trail.

switchbacks over rock ledges. You'll soon cross the Summit Road again and see some familiar sights: more glacier-polished rock and a thick hemlock grove. Soon you return to the neighborhood of tall, full-canopied oaks. The corkscrew continues as you hold the mountain on your left throughout the descending traverse, and begin to see signs for the visitor center. Soon you'll pick up the Bicentennial Trail and retrace your steps to the visitor center and your car.

Wachusett itself is known geologically as a monadnock, the remnant of a lone peak that once rose high above the surrounding plains, independent of any mountain range. How high? Theory dictates that the peak was once a towering 23,000 feet (Mount Everest in Nepal is 29,035 feet), but was worn down by glaciers and erosion.

If you still have energy left after this hike, there are always events planned by the Reservation and by the ski mountain. Check at the visitor center on Mountain Road for natural history events such as a poetry walk featuring the work of Robert Frost, a hike through old-growth forest, lessons on wind power at Wachusett, a tour of the

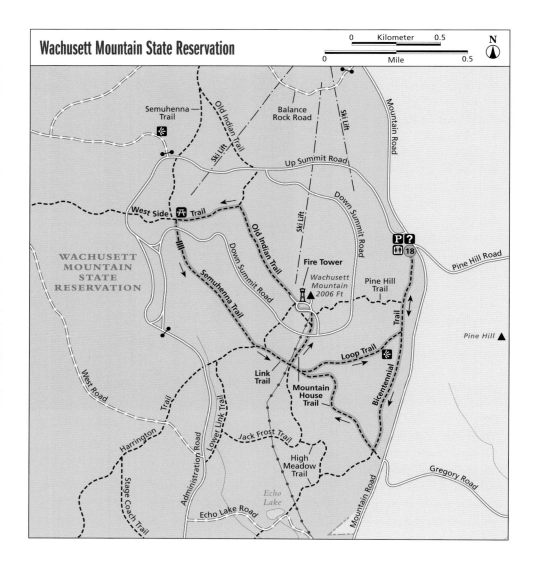

Wachusett Mountain State Reservation

Wachusett watershed, wild animal tracking, and the annual hawk migration watch. This bird migration is a natural wonder, with up to 20,000 birds of prey passing overhead in a single day during the peak of the October-to-November period.

There are 20 miles of marked and named hiking trails in these 2,050 acres—feel free to explore.

Miles and Directions

0.0 Start at the trailhead for the Bicentennial Trail, marked with a sign in the parking lot. Follow this blue-blazed path as it traverses the mountainside, quickly passing junctions leading uphill on your right for the Pine Hill Trail and Loop Trail.

0.8 Turn right onto the Mountain House Trail, a steep, rocky path that is also blue blazed.

1.3 At the top of a pitch, continue straight on the Mountain House Trail, passing junctions with the Loop Trail and Jack Frost Trail.

1.5 Cross the paved Summit Road and follow the Mountain House Trail to its end 50 yards later at the paved summit parking lot. Aim for the fire tower at the peak and pick up the yellow-and-blue-blazed Old Indian Trail just past it, near the top station of a ski lift.

2.1 At the bottom of a steep descent, turn left onto the West Side Trail.

2.4 Cross the paved Summit Road onto the blue-blazed Semuhenna Trail, soon crossing a wooden footbridge.

2.9 Turn left onto the Harrington Trail, cross a wooden boardwalk, and in 50 yards, turn right onto the Link Trail.

3.1 After a short climb, turn right onto the Mountain House Trail, and in 50 yards, turn left onto the blue-blazed Loop Trail to begin your descent.

3.6 Turn left onto the familiar Bicentennial Trail to retrace your original steps toward the visitor center.

3.9 Arrive back at your car.

Hike Information

Local Information

Friends of Wachusett Mountain: Princeton; www.friendsofwachusett.org. Fitness hikes, hawk watches, and full moon walks.

Wachusett online guide: www.wachusett.com

Greater Gardner Chamber of Commerce: Gardner; (978) 632-1780; http://gardnerma .com. Local weather forecasts, shopping, and restaurant and hotel guides.

Local Events/Attractions

The Johnny Appleseed Trail Association: Leominster; (978) 534-2302; www.appleseed .org

Local Outdoor Retailers

Squannacook River Outfitters: Townsend; (800) 577-5332

19 Mount Pisgah Conservation Area

Mount Pisgah is 715 feet above sea level, but is scarcely elevated at all from the trailhead. This flat hike winds through mature white pine and red oak trees and a grid of stone walls, then skirts a steep ridgeline, offering two sweeping views as a reward for very little sweat. It's a great hike for families and kids.

Start: From the trailhead parking lot on Smith Road near its intersection with Green Street, about 4 miles from Northborough town center
Distance: 2.6-mile loop
Hiking time: About 1 to 1.5 hours
Difficulty: Easy; the trail can be rough underfoot, but it is wide and has a flat pitch throughout
Trail surface: Rocky, forested trail
Best season: Summer
Land status: MA Division of Fisheries and Wildlife (MassWildlife)
Nearest town: Northborough

Other trail users: Mountain bikers, equestrians
Canine compatibility: Dogs permitted
Schedule: Open year-round, sunrise to sunset
Fees and permits: None
Maps: USGS Marlborough, MA
Trail contacts: Sudbury Valley Trustees, Sudbury; (978) 443-5588; www.sudburyvalley trustees.org//mount-pisgah-conservation-area (trail maps available). Northborough Conservation Commission, Northborough, (508) 393-5015; www.town.northborough.ma.us/pages/northboroughma_bcomm/conservation/index

Finding the trailhead: From Worcester, drive east on I-290 to exit 24, for Church Street, Boylston, and Northborough. Take a right off the exit ramp, heading north toward Boylston and Clinton, and immediately take another right onto Ball Street, just before you reach the Davidian Brothers Farm and its big red barn. Drive uphill, and at 1.3 miles, pass the Tougas Family Farm on your right. Keep going, and at the end of the road (1.8 miles), turn left at a stop sign onto Green Street. At 2.3 miles, bear right at a fork just before a stone wall onto Smith Road. At 2.5 miles, come to a small gravel parking area and trailhead kiosk on the right. Park here. *DeLorme: Massachusetts Atlas & Gazetteer:* Page 39 I16. GPS: N42 21.580' / W71 40.277'

The Hike

Early New England farmers pulled the thick trunks and heavy rock out of the earth to clear this land and farm it. They left for the cities in the mid-1800s, so their legacy today is a mature, third-generation forest, with stone walls stretching in straight lines for hundreds of yards. There are breaks in the walls where they meet at neat right angles, and as you step through these breaks, it is easy to imagine a farmer driving his team of horses on the same path two centuries ago. (But watch where you step, as there is often fresh dung on the trail from more recent horses.)

The northern overlook offers terrific views of countryside to the east.

The land is still rich for farming, and if you hike here in the fall, be sure to stop by one of the farms as you drive to the trailhead. The Davidian Brothers Farm is right near the highway exit, and the Tougas Family Farm on Ball Street offers apple picking and pumpkin carving until November.

Mount Pisgah is on a plateau, which means you get a lot of views for a little climbing, simply by walking to the edge and peering over. Begin at the trailhead; the path quickly enters a forest of tall white pine, pitch pine, and red oak, punctuated by birches, with some sassafras, beech, and hornbeam understory. This congress of mature trees sharing the sunny canopy is a great example of the long-range effects of agriculture, as the old fields gave all kinds of trees a chance to grow. The ruler-straight stone walls represent a lost art, built without mortar, and withstanding the effects of hundreds of New England winters. When the trail passes close by a stone cellar, you can see that the craft of building in stone was not merely decorative, but formed a strong, enduring foundation for the many labors of these pioneer farmers.

In the leafless autumn the wind whips through these trees, making trunks creak against each other. Many of the older pines have twisted into gnarled wooden shapes. And when woodpeckers knock the trees as you walk, it is easy to imagine the long tale of a tree's life, subjected to weather and bugs and birds and farmers. Farther on, you pass through a thick grove of young white pine saplings—none taller than a man—and the cycle seems complete.

Soon the path pulls parallel to a stone wall, and when you reach its junction with another wall, step through the break and onto an exposed rock ledge for a splendid lookout to the southeast. Retrace your steps to the stone wall corner, turn left, and continue along the plateau edge, walking southwest. The trail starts to roll and pitch as you go, and within a mile you reach the second lookout. It's another bare bedrock shelf, peering southeast. The trail brings you home after a short downhill drop, as you hike northward through a young oak forest mixed with pine. You cross more stone walls, walk through another thick grove of human-size white pines, and follow the blazes to your car.

Mount Pisgah is also the site of one of the almost 600 hidden, waterproof boxes scattered around the country for a little-known competition called letterboxing. Similar to the GPS-based geocaching pursuit, letterboxing invites hikers to follow clues to find small, hidden boxes, then use a rubber stamp to mark their logbook as a prize. Get more information on this fun treasure hunt at www.letterboxing.org.

Miles and Directions

0.0   Start at the trailhead parking lot and walk east on the wide, yellow-blazed Mentzer Trail.

0.2   Bear left at a fork to stay on the Mentzer Trail as the Sparrow Trail branches right, and soon cross an intersection with the Berlin Road Trail.

0.7   Turn right onto the red-blazed Tyler Trail. Continue straight at this junction onto the North Overlook spur trail, which bears left at a T and reaches a terrific vista in 100 yards. After

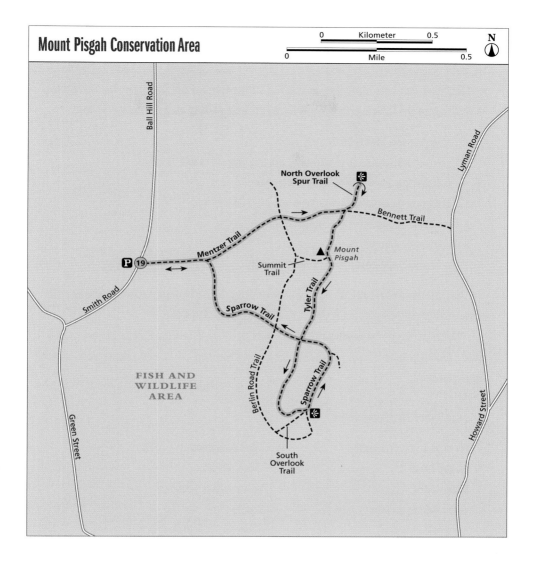

Mount Pisgah Conservation Area

Kilometer

Mile

N

Ball Hill Road

Lyman Road

North Overlook
Spur Trail

Bennett Trail

Mentzer Trail

P 19

Summit
Trail

▲ Mount
Pisgah

Smith Road

Sparrow Trail

Tyler Trail

Berlin Road Trail

FISH AND
WILDLIFE
AREA

Sparrow Trail

Howard Street

Green Street

South
Overlook
Trail

enjoying the view, retrace your steps to the junction. Follow the Tyler Trail south, parallel to the plateau's edge on your left.

1.1 Pass an intersection with the Summit Trail and then the Sparrow Trail.

1.6 Turn toward the left at a T, following yellow blazes for 100 yards to reach the stunning South View Overlook. To continue your hike, head north on the red-blazed Sparrow Trail, with the cliff side on your right.

2.0 Follow the Sparrow Trail through an intersection with the familiar Tyler Trail and then the Berlin Road Trail.

2.4 Continue straight through an intersection onto the familiar, yellow-blazed Mentzer Trail.

2.6 Arrive back at your car.

THE TOUGAS FAMILY FARM

The back roads of Worcester County are full of family farms and roadside stands selling fresh food and pick-your-own fruits and squash. The Tougas Family Farm, located along Ball Street on your way to the trailhead, offers this list of the best picking seasons for the region:

- strawberries: mid-June to early July
- raspberries: late June to mid-July, and late August to mid-October
- blueberries: early July to early September
- blackberries: August to late September
- peaches: August to mid-September
- apples: late August to mid-October
- pumpkins: mid-September through October

See the farm's website at www.tougasfarm.com for more information, or phone their automated picking line for hours and availability at (508) 393-6406.

The University of Massachusetts's Extension Nutrition Education Program offers the following recipe to complement your fresh-picked food. For more, visit http://extension.umass .edu/nutrition/.

Cranberry Pumpkin Muffins

1¼ cups fresh cranberries	1 tsp cinnamon
2 cups flour	½ tsp allspice
1 cup sugar	½ cup butter, softened
½ tsp baking powder	2 eggs
1 tsp baking soda	1⅔ cups cooked pureed
1 tsp salt	pumpkin

Halve cranberries; set aside. Sift together flour, sugar, baking powder, baking soda, salt, cinnamon, and allspice. Add butter, eggs, and pumpkin, and mix together with a pastry blender until just combined. Stir in cranberries. Fill 18 greased muffin cups almost full. Bake in a preheated 350-degree oven for 35 minutes or until a toothpick inserted into the center comes out clean. (Makes 18 medium muffins.)

Hike Information

Local Information

Davidian Brothers Farm: Northborough; (508) 393-3444; www.davidianbros.com. Fresh produce, jarred goods, homemade bakery and deli.

Northborough online: www.northborough.com

Local Events/Attractions

Apple and pumpkin picking in autumn. To find the closest spot for picking, visit the Massachusetts Association of Roadside Stands: www.massfarmstands.com.

Local Outdoor Retailers

New England Backpacker Inc.: Worcester; (508) 853-9407; www.newenglandback packer.com

Recreational Equipment Inc. (REI): Framingham; (508) 270-6325; www.rei.com

Begin the hike by heading east on the wide Mentzer Trail.

20 Upton State Forest

Well-marked dirt trails lead you past lady's slipper flowers and lichen-crusted boulders to Dean Pond, a great place to stop for lunch. Return to your car on the Mammoth Rock Trail, scrambling between more boulders as you pass through the flat, thickly wooded forest. Hunting is permitted here in season, so take care if you're hiking here in the fall.

Start: From main parking lot at park headquarters, off Westboro Road
Distance: 4.3-mile loop
Hiking time: About 2 hours
Difficulty: Easy, due to moderate elevation change and well-kept trails
Trail surface: Broad carriage roads and narrow dirt trails
Best season: Summer
Land status: MA Department of Conservation and Recreation

Nearest town: Upton
Other trail users: Mountain bikers, equestrians
Canine compatibility: Dogs permitted
Schedule: Open year-round, sunrise to sunset
Fees and permits: None
Maps: USGS Milford, MA
Trail contact: Upton State Forest Headquarters, Upton; www.mass.gov/eea/agencies/dcr/massparks/region-central/upton-state-forest.html

Finding the trailhead: From Framingham, take I-495 south to exit 21B, for West Main Street and Upton. Turn right to drive west on West Main Street, which changes its name to Hopkinton Road as it crosses the county line from Middlesex into Worcester. In 3.5 miles from the interstate, make a hairpin right turn onto Westboro Road (just after passing Pratt Pond on the left). At 5.5 miles, turn right onto Southboro Street (called Spring Street on maps) at the state park sign. Take the middle fork at a junction, following the dirt CCC Way road to the parking lot. *DeLorme: Massachusetts Atlas & Gazetteer:* Page 51 C19. GPS: N42 12.559' / W71 36.375'

The Hike

This little-known, 2,660-acre forest in the Blackstone River Valley is a favorite for mountain bikers, but most of your loop is along narrow twisting trails that discourage much bicycle traffic. The thick woodland is laced with boulders dropped by the melting glaciers of the last ice age. And the low-lying marshland between the boulders encourages flowers like the pink lady's slipper, a member of the orchid family, which grows a single drooping flower on a tall stalk between May and June. Overhead the canopy is dominated by tall white pines, with maple and chestnut saplings below. A wide carriage road leads through quiet trees to Dean Pond in a little more than a mile, and even on a

Middle Road leads north from Dean Pond through thick forest.

sunny weekend, you can enjoy it without crowds. There's not much elevation change on this hike, but you climb gently to the Hawk Trail as you leave the pond and then follow the Mammoth Rock Trail past enormous glacial boulders. At the end of the hike, you follow the paved Southboro Road downhill past swampland and to your car.

This land was originally a seasonal hunting ground for the Nipmuc tribe, who joined with other Native Americans in King Philip's War (1675–1676) to discourage settlement here through the end of the seventeenth century. The town of Upton was incorporated in 1735, not as a usual settlement of Massachusetts's wild, western lands, but cobbled together from the borders of four surrounding towns: Hopkinton, Mendon, Sutton, and Uxbridge. Since they had settled so close to other populated areas, Upton's subsistence farmers had an easy means to supplement their agricultural income—bootmaking. After more than a century of this home-based, cottage business, changing times forced them to find a new industry, and they quickly adapted their skills to making straw hats. By 1837 William Knowlton had built a successful hat factory, which remains on the National Register of Historic Places today, although it shut down around 1970 and the building (134 Main St.) now contains apartments. At the beginning of the twentieth century, farmers began to convert their land from agriculture to dairy, poultry, flowers, and woodland.

Upton straddles the Narragansett Bay watershed—where the West and Blackstone Rivers drain into Rhode Island—and the Concord River watershed, where water flows into the Merrimack River and finally into the Gulf of Maine. Upton's local water sources include Warren Brook, Center Brook, and the Mill River, all historic sites of mills during the region's agricultural heyday.

Modern Upton shares its loyalties with northern Rhode Island and central Massachusetts, with proximity to I-495, Framingham, and Worcester. A great cultural resource is the Blackstone River Theater, in Cumberland, Rhode Island, with folk music performances scheduled from June through December, and Irish step dancing classes available for those who need to brush up on their skills. Also, Waters Farm, in nearby Sutton, hosts year-round events such as a horse-drawn Sleigh Rally in February; the hitch, harness, and driving clinic in July; an apple crisp bake-off each September; Waters Farm Days in October; and Christmas in Historic Sutton.

Miles and Directions

0.0 Start at the map kiosk in the parking lot and walk through the metal gate onto CCC Way, a broad carriage road with marshland on either side. (**Note:** The mosquitoes can be thick here in summer months.)

0.2 Turn right onto Park Road at a fork and pass by junctions with the smaller Middle Road Connector Trail, Whistling Cave Trail, and Nuthatch Trail.

1.2 Turn left at a fork onto Dean Pond Road.

1.6 Follow the trail in a sweeping left curve as you reach Dean Pond, a beautiful place for a drink and a snack. Leave the pond by following the same wide path, passing the sign To Parking Lot via Loop Trail.

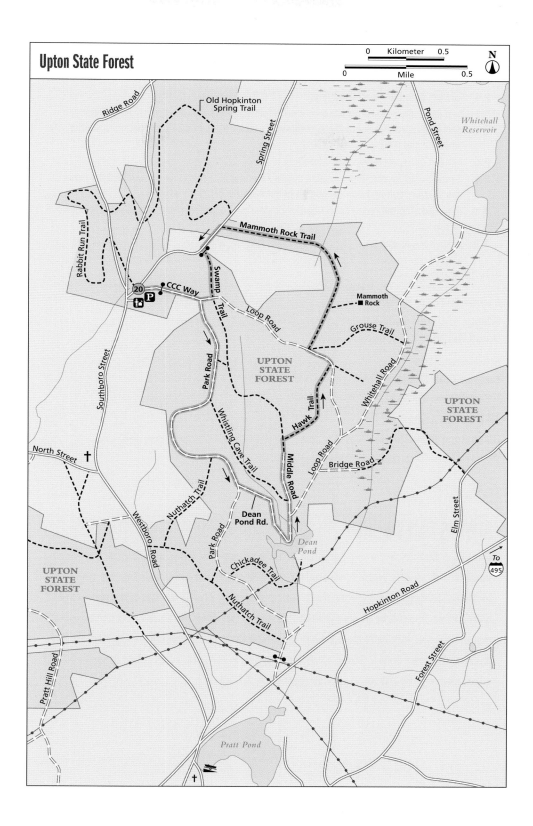

Upton State Forest

Ridge Road

Old Hopkinton
Spring Trail

Spring Street

Pond Street

Whitehall
Reservoir

Rabbit Run Trail

Mammoth Rock Trail

Swamp Trail

20

CCC Way

Loop Road

Mammoth
Rock

Grouse Trail

Park Road

UPTON
STATE
FOREST

Whitehall Road

UPTON
STATE
FOREST

Southboro Street

Whistling Cave Trail

Hawk Trail

North Street †

Nuthatch Trail

Middle Road

Loop Road

Bridge Road

Elm Street

Westboro Road

Park Road

Dean
Pond Rd.

Dean
Pond

To
495

UPTON
STATE
FOREST

Chickadee Trail

Nuthatch Trail

Hopkinton Road

Forest Street

Pratt Hill Road

Pratt Pond

†

0   Kilometer   0.5

0   Mile   0.5

N

1.7	Turn left at a fork onto Middle Road.
2.1	Turn right at a fork onto the narrower Hawk Trail.
2.4	Turn left onto the broad Loop Road.
2.7	Turn right onto the narrow Mammoth Rock Trail, following it past a house-size boulder and over several wooden footbridges. (**Bailout:** Continue straight on Loop Road for a shorter return to your car.)
3.6	Turn left onto paved Southboro Road.
3.8	Turn left onto Swamp Trail, crossing through a metal gate back into the woods. Take either fork at a junction and pass through a beautiful grove of tall white pines.
4.1	Turn right onto the broad Loop Road, soon passing a junction with the familiar Park Road on the left.
4.3	Arrive back at your car.

Hike Information

Local Information

Friends of Upton State Forest: Upton; www.friendsofuptonstateforest.org
Upton website: www.upton.ma.us

Restaurants

Country Club Sooper: Upton; (508) 529-3161
Upton House of Pizza: Upton; (508) 529-6666

Other Resources

Blackstone River Theater: Cumberland; (401) 725-9272; www.riverfolk.org
Waters Farm: Sutton; www.watersfarm.com

ALWAYS TIME TO SHOP ...

The Upton Country Store and Antique Center is a shop that looks as if it hasn't changed much in forty or fifty years. From crumbly, old *Life* magazines to lampshades, tea sets, and furniture, it seems to have a little of everything—including a candy bar and cold soda to revive a tired hiker. Reach it by turning left onto Westboro Road from the state forest and crossing the intersection with West Main Street/Hopkinton Road at 2.1 miles. After the intersection the road is called School Street. Then turn right onto MA 140 North (Main Street) at 2.9 miles, reaching the Antique Center on your left at 3.1 miles.

21 Douglas State Forest

This 4,640-acre forest sits at the corner of Massachusetts, Connecticut, and Rhode Island. Far from being just a flat, sandy floodplain, the land includes the cedar swamp and basin marsh ecosystems, as well as the rare Atlantic white cedar habitat. This loop tours the shore of Whitin Reservoir in the forest's northern end.

Start: From the dirt parking lot at the trailhead off MA 16
Distance: 3.8-mile loop
Hiking time: About 2 hours
Difficulty: Easy, with broad trails and little elevation change
Trail surface: Broad, two-track dirt paths
Best season: Summer
Land status: MA Department of Conservation and Recreation
Nearest town: Webster

Other trail users: Mountain bikers, cross-country skiers, equestrians
Canine compatibility: Dogs permitted
Schedule: Open year-round; picnic area at main entrance open 10 a.m. to 8 p.m.
Fees and permits: None
Maps: USGS Webster, MA
Trail contact: MA Department of Conservation and Recreation, Douglas; (508) 476-7872; www.mass.gov/eea/agencies/dcr/massparks/region-central/douglas-state-forest.html

Finding the trailhead: From Worcester, take I-395 south to exit 2, for Webster Center and Douglas. Turn left to drive east on MA 16 (aka Webster Street) for 4.1 miles, then pull into a dirt parking lot on your right, marked with a trailhead sign and map kiosk. *DeLorme: Massachusetts Atlas & Gazetteer:* Page 50 L8. GPS: N42 03.356' / W71 47.192'

The Hike

The wetlands that cover this sandy forest provide far more diversity than a visitor would guess. But this richness was no secret to the Native Americans who have left signs of their stay here from up to 6,000 years ago. When the pilgrims arrived in America, these people were known as the Nipmuc Tribe. European settlers used the land initially for logging, brickmaking, charcoaling, granite quarrying, and harvesting ice from Wallum Lake. The land was bought by the state in 1934 for the Civilian Conservation Corps, who cleared land for the beach and trails we see today.

Although this hike is in the northern end of the park, perhaps the best way to appreciate Douglas State Forest is to do a tiny, second loop—the Cedar Swamp Trail. The trail is a red-blazed, 0.7-mile, self-guided nature loop that begins at the nature center, located on Wallum Lake near the park's main entrance. An attraction of this trail is the frequent sprouts of the American chestnut, once the most common tree in the entire northeast, but tragically killed off in three quick decades by a blight mistakenly imported from Asia in 1904. The species still creates seedlings that grow to maturity, but as soon as they stretch beyond 15 or 20 feet tall, cracks develop in

Head north into Douglas State Forest on the broad Schmidt Trail.

their bark, and the blight quickly kills them. Other attractions are the granite quarry worked from 1893 to 1906, glacial "erratic" boulders, and the Atlantic white-cedar swamp. Retreating glaciers 15,000 years ago left "kettle-hole" ponds where enormous chunks of buried ice intersected the water table. Ponds formed when they melted, and as the climate warmed, the cedar quickly established itself here. Seventeenth-century European settlers used the cedar tree for house building since it is lightweight and water resistant.

The hike begins at a trailhead off MA 16, away from the crowds of the nature center, picnic tables, and boat launching ramp. It heads north, parallel to the long-distance Midstate Trail, then curves along the shore of Whitin Reservoir. A shaded peninsula at the northwestern tip of the reservoir makes for a beautiful spot to stop for lunch and linger by the shore. With boulders scattered among the hemlocks in these marshy, sandy woods, the forest has a beauty that doesn't demand mountaintop vistas.

Since the British-born Samuel Slater settled it as a mill town in 1812, nearby Webster has been valued most for its abundant freshwater, particularly Lake Manchaug (see sidebar). Slater founded villages to house entire families who would work

LAKE MANCHAUG

Webster's 5-mile-long, 1,442-acre Lake Chaubunagungamaug was named by the local Nipmuc tribe of Native Americans. History ordains that the lake was neutral territory, so local tribes including the Narragansett, Pequot, and Mohegan often met here. Tradition dictates that the name means "you fish on your side, I fish on mine, nobody fishes in the middle," but a more accurate translation is likely "the fishing place at the boundaries and neutral meeting grounds." Modern locals simply call it Lake Manchaug. Today you can even buy a T-shirt bearing the lake's name at www.websterlakegifts.com.

The Nipmuc were among the Algonquian tribes who first lived in central New England, and were the Native Americans who first met the European settlers in the 1600s. Nipmuc translates as "freshwater people" since they made their villages near water throughout their Nipnet territory, which ranged "from the present day Vermont and New Hampshire borders, through Worcester County in Massachusetts, into northern Rhode Island, and into northeastern Connecticut as far south as Plainfield," according to the Nipmuc Indian Association of Connecticut, based in Thompson, Connecticut. For more information on this tribe, check out www.nativetech.org/Nipmuc.

on his water-powered textile mills. This was later known as the Rhode Island System. The town of Webster was founded in 1832, and textile and shoe industries thrived here when the railroad arrived in 1840. Within the park, Whitin Reservoir and Wallum Lake are also vast water sources and popular destinations for fishing and other recreation. Mountain bikers like this location because of its more than 30 miles of wide trails and dirt roads. Pick up a free trail map at park headquarters.

Miles and Directions

0.0 Start at the small, dirt parking lot off MA 16, cross the paved highway, and step through a metal gate, heading north on the broad, sandy Schmidt Trail.

0.4 Go left at a T intersection onto the Ridge Trail and soon cross two wooden bridges over streams.

0.7 Go right at a four-way intersection, onto the narrower Reservoir Loop.

0.8 Bear left at a fork to begin a gentle climb. (*Note:* The alternative leads only to a nearby gravel pit.)

1.5 Reach Wallis Pond (visible through trees to your right) and the stonework dam where its waters drain into the reservoir. (*FYI:* The tannin-rich cedars have stained this water red, which fades to a pale yellow in the turbulence.) Instead of crossing the dam, turn left, crossing through a stone wall and following the water downstream. Soon begin to trace the shore of Whitin Reservoir on your right.

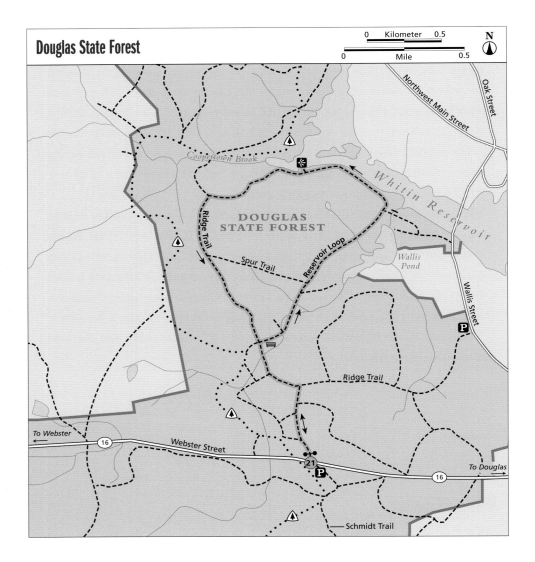

DOUGLAS
STATE FOREST

Coopertown Brook

Whitin Reservoir

Northwest Main Street

Oak Street

Ridge Trail

Spur Trail

Reservoir Loop

Wallis Pond

Wallis Street

Ridge Trail

To Webster

16

Webster Street

21

To Douglas

16

Schmidt Trail

2.0 Turn right at a fork for a quick spur to visit a gorgeous, hemlock-shaded peninsula, with wide water views. Then return to the shoreline trail and turn right, continuing along the westward path as it bears away from the water's edge.

2.5 Turn left onto the broad, sandy Ridge Trail, beginning your southward trek home.

2.8 Continue straight as a trail branches left.

3.1 Go straight through a familiar, four-way intersection, and in 100 yards, cross the pair of wooden bridges.

3.4 Turn right onto Schmidt Trail, the broad, flat carriage path you came in on.

3.8 Pass through the metal gate and cross paved MA 16 to arrive back at your car.

Wallis Pond is popular with hikers, photographers, and fishermen.

Hike Information

Local Information
Webster website: www.webster-ma.gov
Appalachian Mountain Club: www.outdoors.org

Restaurants
As you return, drive west 3 miles on MA 16 and reach a small mall on the left that includes:
Apollo Pizza: Webster, (508) 943-1215
Honey Farms Mini Market: Webster, (508) 949-0793

Organizations
The Midstate Trail homepage: www.midstatetrail.org. The Midstate Trail begins in Douglas State Forest and runs 92 miles northward, connecting with New Hampshire's Wapack Trail on the northern border of Massachusetts.

Western Massachusetts

Farther from the ocean, Massachusetts's western mountains stand tall. The state's tallest mountain—Mount Greylock—and the surrounding Berkshire Hills boast tracts of deep forest filled with the state's major wildlife, and through it all runs the long-distance Appalachian Trail, on its way from Georgia to Maine.

In fact, these mountains are much older than the Taconics, sitting just to their west. They are part of the ancient Appalachian mountain chain, which stretches south from Vermont's Green Mountains and New Hampshire's White Mountains. And even this far west, there was once an inland sea depositing limestone, which, in some places, later changed to marble.

Sounds peaceful, but the beginning of this mighty mountain chain was a car wreck. Geologists tell us that plate tectonics have rammed North America into Africa three times, beginning with the Taconic orogeny 450 million years ago. That enormous impact forced the Berkshire and Taconic Mountains far into the air, with later collisions sparking volcanic activity and leaving parts of African land stuck on our coast.

So Massachusetts is dominated by Wachusett in its center, and Greylock to the west. This is no coincidence—both peaks are monadnocks, super-tough chunks of mountain that stand alone, since their brothers have long since eroded away. The layout was the same when those early European settlers arrived; they found the Berkshires mighty inconvenient, standing as a major block to their western expansion. Building a train tunnel through the mountain range was one solution, but the engineers nearly got more than they bargained for—see the hike in Savoy Mountain State Forest for more tales of this struggle.

Even today our modern autos must zigzag painstakingly along MA 2 as the road winds slowly over Whitcomb Summit. Other hikes that visit these steep peaks include Chester-Blandford State Forest, Mohawk Trail State Forest, Monroe State Forest, October Mountain State Forest, and Pittsfield State Forest.

◀ *Explore the banks of the Westfield River on a short spur from the Red Trail (hike 22).*

22 Robinson State Park

This out-and-back hike skirts the steep bluffs above the Westfield River, providing a surprising amount of solitude for a park just 7 miles from downtown Springfield. But it's bigger than it looks—Robinson has over 800 acres, including more than 5 miles of river frontage.

Start: From the grassy parking lot off River Road, 0.3 mile from the park's North Street entrance

Distance: 2.9 miles out and back

Hiking time: About 1.5 hours

Difficulty: Easy

Trail surface: Hard-packed dirt trails and paved roads

Best season: Summer

Land status: MA Department of Conservation and Recreation

Nearest town: Agawam

Other trail users: Mountain bikers

Canine compatibility: Dogs permitted

Schedule: Open 10 a.m. to 6 p.m. Sunday through Thursday, until 8 p.m. in summer

Fees and permits: Parking fee required at front gate

Maps: USGS West Springfield, MA

Trail contact: Robinson State Park, Agawam; (413) 786-2877; www.mass.gov/eea/agencies/dcr/massparks/region-west/robinson-state-park.html

Finding the trailhead: From Holyoke, take I-91 south to exit 3 and cross the bridge over the Connecticut River onto MA 57 West toward Agawam. Turn right at the Main Street/West Springfield exit and follow Main Street for 2 miles, turning right onto North Street at a large intersection near a car dealership. At 3 miles, turn right at a sign for the park entrance. Follow River Road through the park, and at 4.1 miles, park on the shoulder of the road at Robinson Pond. *DeLorme: Massachusetts Atlas & Gazetteer:* Page 46 J16. GPS: N42 05.467' / W72 40.169'

The Hike

The Westfield River drains the creeks and brooks of the Berkshires into the Connecticut River at Springfield. This hike traces the southern bank of the river along some of its last 5 miles, touring through a mixed hemlock, maple, beech, and birch woodland punctuated by rhododendrons and fiddlehead ferns, and by several timber stands of white pine.

Agawam is perhaps best known as the home of the Six Flags New England amusement park, and crowds at Robinson can be thick, especially when they're seeking a place to swim on a hot summer day. It gets much quieter once you get out on the trails, but you still have to keep an eye out for a few joggers and speeding mountain bikes. The steep bluffs are dissected by power lines and shadowed by the active railroad track on the opposite bank. The park also includes a 17-acre island west of the falls at the Mittineague dam, but this hike does not visit it. (Mittineague, which is Indian for "the place of falling waters," is a neighborhood in the adjacent town of

The lush land flanking River Road makes this spot a great retreat from the nearby city of Springfield.

West Springfield.) Overall, this urban park offers unexpected solitude and sweeping river views, without the elevation change or long drive of more remote spots.

A large winter storm in 2012 brought down trees across the state, obscuring many trails and erasing blazes here. But a walk along the paved River Road still offers pretty vistas over the water. Cool down after the hike at Robinson Beach, a sandy bank of the pond by your parking spot that offers lifeguards, safe swimming areas, picnic tables, and porta-potties.

The Westfield was Massachusetts's first river to gain federal protection under the 1968 Wild and Scenic Rivers Act, and is today watched over by the Westfield River Watershed Association. Founded in 1952, the group offers ecology education and speakers, as well as publishing a canoe guide and monitoring the salmon restoration program in these waters. The river drains an area of 517 square miles, including seventy-eight lakes and ponds within the Westfield River basin, forty-eight of which have an area of 10 acres or more. The river is also a major source of drinking water for the Springfield region.

An effort to restore Atlantic salmon to the Connecticut River basin is underway, in a joint project between the states of Vermont, New Hampshire, Connecticut, and Massachusetts, together with the US Fish and Wildlife Service. After declining throughout the nineteenth century, native Atlantic salmon disappeared from the river and its tributaries (including the Westfield River). Since 1983 this group has reintroduced the fish into the watershed. These anadromous fish are born in freshwater, mature in the open ocean, and return to their freshwater home rivers to spawn.

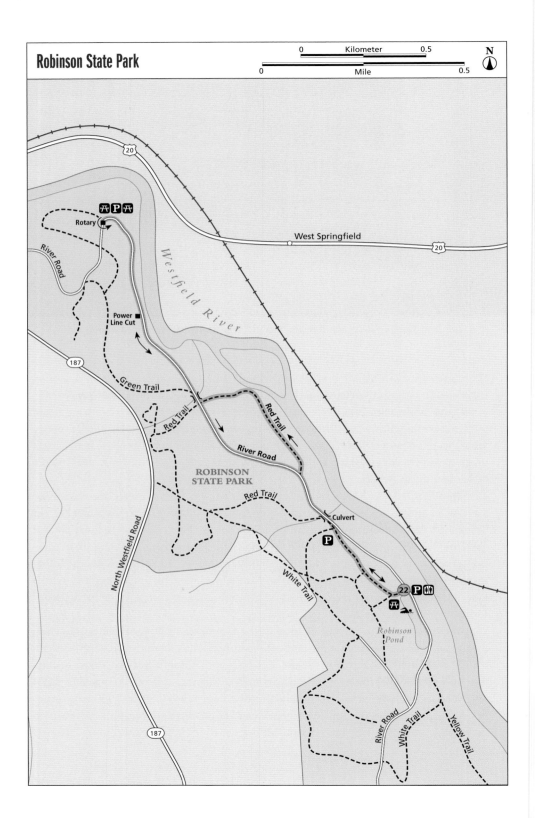

Robinson State Park

0   Kilometer   0.5

0   Mile   0.5

N

West Springfield

20

Westfield River

River Road

Rotary

187

Power
Line Cut

Green Trail

Red Trail

Red Trail

River Road

ROBINSON
STATE PARK

Red Trail

Culvert

P

North Westfield Road

White Trail

22   P

Robinson
Pond

River Road

White Trail

Yellow Trail

187

Superman, Batman, and Bugs Bunny are the attractions at Six Flags New England. The park launched three new roller coasters and a free-fall ride in 2000, and is still expanding. These coasters are not your average ride—the Superman Ride of Steel drags its passengers twenty stories into the air, drops them for 10 seconds of weightlessness, and flings them along the track at speeds up to 80 mph.

Springfield also hosts the Basketball Hall of Fame, stocked with history exhibits, interactive games, live clinics, and shooting contests.

Miles and Directions

0.0 Start at Robinson Pond and walk north on paved River Road, passing through a metal gate and keeping the river on your right.

0.4 Cross a stream in a culvert beneath the road, marked by guardrail posts.

0.5 Turn right onto the Red Trail, an unblazed footpath marked by two wooden posts.

0.8 The trail touches the banks of the river on your right, with a short spur for those who want to scramble down to the water's edge.

0.9 Turn right, back onto paved River Road, and immediately cross a stone bridge that was built by the Civilian Conservation Corps (CCC). (***Bailout:*** A left here would take you directly back to your car.)

1.2 Pass by a power-line cut with beautiful views of the river to your right and several short spur trails that lead to the muddy riverbank a few yards away.

1.5 Reach a rotary in a small field and turn for home, heading back south on River Road.

1.8 Pass by the power-line cut.

2.1 Cross the stone CCC bridge and continue south on River Road.

2.5 Cross the culvert stream.

2.9 Arrive back at your car.

Hike Information

Local Information

Agawam website: www.agawam.ma.us

Local Events/Attractions

Basketball Hall of Fame: Springfield; (413) 781-6500; www.hoophall.com
Six Flags New England: Springfield; (413) 786-9300; www2.sixflags.com/newengland. The city of Springfield is a 7-mile drive, just on the other side of the Connecticut River.

Other Resources

Westfield River Watershed Association: Westfield; www.westfieldriver.org. Offers educational programs, speakers, and newsletters, as well as a canoe guide to the river.

Local Outdoor Retailers

Sam's Outdoor Outfitters: Hadley; (413) 582-9820; www.samsoutfitters.com

23 Rattlesnake Knob

This modest loop climbs through forested trails to the saddle between Mount Norwottuck (the highest peak of the Holyoke Range) and Long Mountain, reaching
two stirring outlooks at Rattlesnake Knob. While you won't see many rattlers here,
the region is rich with cultural and natural history, including a museum of dinosaur
footprints.

Start: From the trailhead off Bachelor Street,
south of Notch Visitor Center
Distance: 4.9-mile loop
Hiking time: About 2.5 hours
Difficulty: Moderate, due to climbing
Trail surface: Broad, dirt trails
Best season: Fall
Land status: MA Department of Conservation
and Recreation
Nearest town: Amherst
Other trail users: Mountain bikers
Canine compatibility: Dogs permitted

Schedule: Open year-round
Fees and permits: None
Maps: USGS Mount Holyoke, MA
Trail contacts: Skinner State Park, Hadley;
(413) 586-0350; www.mass.gov/eea/
agencies/dcr/massparks/region-west/skinner
-state-park-generic.html. Mount Holyoke Range
State Park-Notch Visitor Center, Amherst; (413)
253-2883; www.mass.gov/eea/agencies/dcr/
massparks/region-west/mount-holyoke-range
-state-park.html

Finding the trailhead: From Springfield, take I-91 north to exit 19, for Northampton and
Amherst. From the exit, turn right to follow MA 9 east, soon crossing the Connecticut River. At 0.5
mile, turn right onto Bay Road, following signs for MA 47 South. At 2.3 miles, turn left to remain
on Bay Road and leave MA 47. At 5.2 miles, pass Atkins Farms Country Market and turn right
onto MA 116 southbound, passing the park visitor center at 6.4 miles (stop here for maps and
restrooms if you like). Turn left onto Amherst Street at 7.5 miles, following a sign for US 202 and
Granby. At 7.9 miles, turn left onto Bachelor Street, and at 8.6 miles, park at a dirt lot with a
trailhead kiosk. *DeLorme: Massachusetts Atlas & Gazetteer:* Page 35 M24. GPS: N42 16.940' /
W72 31.236'

The Hike

The short drive from I-91 to the trailhead provides stunning views of the Holyoke
Range as you go up Bay Road. Pass pastures full of cows and fields full of pumpkins,
corn, apples, and Christmas trees. From Rattlesnake Knob you can hear the cattle
mooing when the wind is right.

This hike is entirely in the town of Granby, except for the knob itself, just across
the town line into Amherst. The colored shapes on trees are not trail blazes, but refer
to the difficulty of cross-country ski slopes: green is easy, blue intermediate, and black
expert. Together, Holyoke Range State Park and Skinner State Park include 2,936
acres along the mountain ridge.

Views from the open ledge at Rattlesnake Knob are stirring in any weather.

Ever since it was settled in 1727 and incorporated in 1768, the town of Granby has struggled to establish agriculture on the shoulders of the Holyoke Range, and to establish industry with its scarce water supply. The earliest residents overcame these hurdles by the early nineteenth century by growing grains, hops, pumpkins, and turnips, even opening several distilleries to use any surplus grain. They added to their income through dairy farming and by producing buttons and hats. Despite their determined efforts, dairy farming was all that remained by 1875. Today an enormous milk bottle housing a dairy bar acts as a town landmark.

Nearby Hadley claims to have the most farmland acreage of any town in the Pioneer Valley (Connecticut River Valley). And these folks take their "pioneer" title seriously, claiming to be one of the oldest settlements in the state (founded in 1659).

Amherst, another local town, has moved on completely from its agricultural beginnings, to embrace its current main industry—education. As the home of UMass–Amherst and Amherst and Hampshire Colleges, this town sees its population whiplash between 35,000 in the academic year to less than 25,000 in the summer.

If you're hungry for culture after your walk in the woods, this is the place to be for museums and learning (see contact info below). Amherst College alone offers a Center for Russian Culture, poet Emily Dickinson's homestead, the Folger Shakespeare Library, Mead Art Museum, and the Pratt Museum of Natural History, featuring fossils, minerals, and dinosaur tracks.

Yes, dinosaurs once stomped around the Connecticut River Valley, leaving footprints in the then-soft sedimentary and sandstone rocks. The museum's ichnology department (the study of tracks) holds more than 1,100 slabs of stone dating to the Jurassic age (about 200 million years ago). A dinosaur called Anomocpus once passed through Turner's Falls, and a famous series of tracks called Noah's Raven were discovered in 1802 in South Hadley, the first dinosaur evidence in North America. There is also an extensive archaeology collection of local Native American relics.

And if your tastes run more to the literary, stop by Emily Dickinson's home, found at 280 Main St. in Amherst (contact info below). It's open for tours from March through mid-December. There's even an annual walk through town on the anniversary of her death, May 15, 1886, and a birthday party every December 8.

So, will you find many rattlesnakes in the woods as the name of the hike implies? Probably not. Although they were widespread in colonial times, Massachusetts's rattlesnakes are so rare today they are scarcely ever seen by people. In fact, the timber rattler is an endangered species in the state, and there are none at all in Maine, Rhode Island, central New Hampshire, most of Vermont, or Long Island. Instead, the most pressing danger on a muggy summer day is mosquitoes—pack plenty of bug dope and a long-sleeved shirt.

Miles and Directions

0.0 Start at a brown metal gate off Bachelor Street, walking up the sandy two-track path past a trailhead kiosk.

0.2 Continue straight on the broad, main path at intersection #216, where the Roller Coaster Trail branches left, and soon bear right again at an unmarked fork.

0.3 Turn right onto the Upper Access Trail at intersection #218 and cross a stream on a footbridge.

1.0 Pass by a rusted car hulk on your left, and then pass several junctions with smaller paths.

1.2 Continue on the main trail past a sign for the Technical Trail (a mountain bike path) on your left, and soon past intersection #242.

1.6 Follow the broad, main path—now called Southside Trail and marked with blue blazes—past junctions #229 and #227.

2.0 Continue on the main drag through intersection #210 as your blazes change to the white tags of the Metacomet-Monadnock (M-M) Trail.

2.2 Turn left with the white blazes at intersection #209 onto a narrow, steep footpath.

2.3 Turn right for a quick spur trail to Rattlesnake Knob at intersection #208, reaching the vista in 100 yards. Soak in the awesome view, retrace your steps, and turn right as you reach the same junction to begin your southbound return.

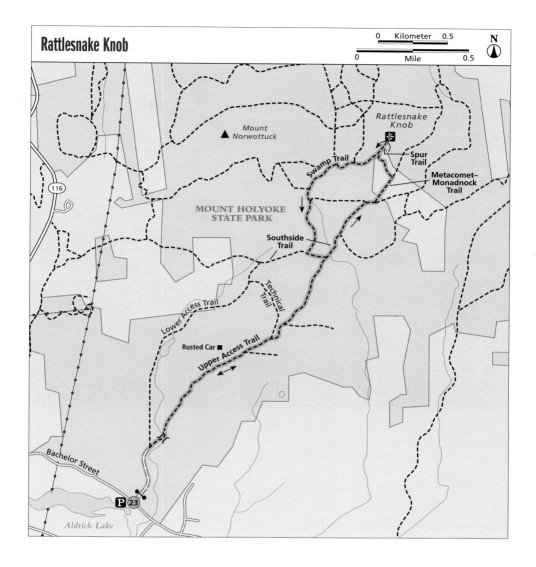

Rattlesnake Knob

0   Kilometer   0.5

0   Mile   0.5

N

Rattlesnake Knob

▲ *Mount Norwottuck*

Swamp Trail

Spur Trail

Metacomet–Monadnock Trail

MOUNT HOLYOKE STATE PARK

Southside Trail

Technical Trail

Lower Access Trail

Rusted Car ■

Upper Access Trail

Bachelor Street

P 23

Aldrich Lake

2.6   Turn left at intersection #207, then left again onto the red-blazed Swamp Trail at intersection #206 in a rambling descent.

3.2   Turn left onto the Southside Trail at intersection #228 and then right onto the familiar Upper Access Trail at intersection #229, following signs for the B. Street Gate to retrace your steps back toward your car.

3.9   Again pass by the rusted car.

4.7   Pass the junction with the Roller Coaster Trail at intersection #216.

4.9   Arrive back at your car.

A toad explores the Mt. Holyoke Range on Upper Access Trail.

Hike Information

Local Information

Amherst website: www.amherstma.gov
Mount Holyoke Range historical timeline: www.chronos-historical.org/mtholyoke/
Virtual tour of Skinner State Park: www.chronos-historical.org/skinner/

Local Events/Attractions

Museums of Amherst College: www.amherst.edu/museums
Emily Dickinson Homestead: Amherst; (413) 542-8161; www.emilydickinsonmuseum.org
Christmas tree farms in western Massachusetts: www.pickyourownchristmastree.org/MAxmaswest.php

MASSACHUSETTS'S FARMS

There are 7,700 farms in Massachusetts, which cover 520,000 acres of open space in the form of scenic and productive farmland, according to agriculture researchers at UMass Amherst. More than 80 percent of these farms are family owned. All together the farms totaled $489 million of agricultural cash receipts in 2007.

Check www.mass.gov/agr/massgrown/pyo.htm for a list of pick-your-own (PYO) farms for fruits and vegetables. The online database offers a searchable list of farms with maps, addresses, hours, and directions. It even offers tips on the best time of year to pick strawberries (June), blueberries (July to September), peaches (July to September), apples (August to November), and pumpkins (September to October). The Massachusetts Department of Agricultural Resources also publishes guides and statistics for traveling the state to buy locally grown produce. County by county, it offers information on education programs, farmers' markets, healthy school lunches, pesticide licensing, composting centers, and land preservation. The numbers show that Bay State farmers rank among the nation's top ten states for production of cranberries, wild blueberries, squash, maple syrup, and raspberries. Look a little farther down the list, and Massachusetts is in the top twenty for apples, pumpkins, organic foods, pears, highbush blueberries, strawberries, greenhouse veggies, sweet corn, and broccoli.

For further information, there's plenty on the web. Try www.berkshiregrown.com.

Restaurants
Atkins Farms Country Market: Amherst; (413) 253-9528; www.atkinsfarms.com. Serves breakfast and lunch, but can be very crowded on weekends.

Other Resources
Amherst History Museum: Amherst; www.amhersthistory.org
Hitchcock Center for the Environment: Amherst; (413) 256-6006; www.hitchcock center.org

24 Skinner State Park

The Holyoke Range, including Skinner State Park and the adjacent Holyoke Range State Park, is one of the only east–west mountain ranges in the country—most others run north–south. This hike traverses two of the peaks in the range on a steep, rocky trail, then drops down to the valley floor to loop back on a flat dirt path that circles a small reservoir.

Start: From Notch Visitor Center
Distance: 4.7-mile loop
Hiking time: About 3 hours
Difficulty: Difficult, due to steep, rocky sections
Trail surface: Steep and rocky path in first half, flat dirt trail in second half
Best season: Summer
Land status: MA Department of Conservation and Recreation
Nearest town: Northampton

Other trail users: Mountain bikers, cross-country skiers, equestrians
Canine compatibility: Dogs permitted
Schedule: Open year-round; visitor center open 9 a.m. to 5 p.m. daily
Fees and permits: None
Maps: USGS Mount Holyoke, MA
Trail contact: Skinner State Park, Hadley; (413) 586-0350; www.mass.gov/eea/agencies/dcr/massparks/region-west/skinner-state-park-generic.html

Finding the trailhead: From Springfield, take I-91 north to exit 19, for Northampton and Amherst. From the exit, turn right to follow MA 9 east, soon crossing the Connecticut River. At 0.5 mile, turn right onto Bay Road, following signs for MA 47 South. At 2.3 miles, turn left to remain on Bay Road and leave MA 47. At 5.2 miles, pass Atkins Farms Country Market and turn right onto MA 116 southbound, reaching the Notch Visitor Center at 6.4 miles. *DeLorme: Massachusetts Atlas & Gazetteer:* Page 35 L24. GPS: N42 18.304' / W72 31.685'

The Hike

The loop begins with a steep climb to Bare Mountain and provides splendid views along the ridgeline to Mount Hitchcock. The trail then drops quickly to the cool valley floor and soon reaches a small reservoir, created by the military to support a nearby, now-defunct, underground command center. Today the reservoir is filled with enormous bullfrogs and bright-orange koy fish. The trail soon reaches the fenced-in former military compound, now converted into a library for Amherst College. This post–Cold War renovation stands in stark contrast to the millennia of occupation by Native Americans, from the Nonotuck to the Algonquin, who first arrived more than 6,000 years ago and were known locally as the Norwottuck.

In 1821 the hotel atop Mount Holyoke was America's first summit house, and in 1854 the train to reach it was the state's first mountain tram. Original proprietors John and Fannie French offered accommodations including a bowling alley. Throughout its heyday from 1861 to 1894, details like this placed the Summit House

A commanding view from the summit of Mount Hitchcock.

among the region's premier attractions, alongside Mount Greylock's Bascom Lodge. A silk manufacturer named Joseph Allen Skinner donated this land to the state in 1940, and today the park is larger than 3,000 acres. The visitor center is packed with information on the human and natural history, as well as providing restrooms and maps. And you can still tour the Summit House.

For hundreds of years the Pioneer Valley has been a farming community, and much of that heritage is intact in the layout of the towns here. Hadley boasts that its square-mile town common is the largest in New England, and says it has the most farmland acreage of any town in the valley. It offers the Porter-Phelps Huntington House (built in 1752) and Hadley Farm Museum to illustrate this history. But perhaps Hadley's best claim to fame is as the birthplace of broom-making, ever since they first mechanized the process in 1797 and became one of the leading growers of broomcorn. Of course the famous five-college area (Smith, Amherst, Mount Holyoke, Hampshire, and UMass-Amherst) offers countless attractions, so check with those institutions for further opportunities.

In the fall the peaks are favorite spots to watch the annual bird migrations, such as broad-winged and red-tailed hawks and kestrels. But in the moist spring months, the air can be thick with annoying midges and blackflies. The mountains have two basic habitats: oak–hickory forests on south-facing slopes, and a mix of hemlock, white pine, birch, beech, and maple on the northern slopes. The south-side habitat usually occurs much farther south, and the north-side trees are usually found farther north in New England. But the range's odd orientation (it was formed glacially, not tectonically) provides the unique exposure to support both.

Together, Holyoke Range State Park and Skinner State Park contain 2,936 acres along the spine of the mountain range, which rises nearly 1,000 feet above the surrounding valley floor. Friends of the Mount Holyoke Range is a group that organizes hikes and supports wilderness preservation in the area. Ask at the visitors center for dates and contacts. There is even an annual 5k (3.1-mile) footrace to the summit of Mount Holyoke each September.

Miles and Directions

0.0 Start at the Notch Visitor Center. Cross MA 116 and turn right, briefly heading north on the paved road.

0.1 Turn left onto the white-blazed Metacomet-Monadnock (M-M) Trail and begin a steep climb up a series of switchbacks across slopes of loose, rocky scree.

0.5 Reach the top of Bare Mountain, with views of a sprawling gravel quarry at the base of Mount Norwottock, the campuses of Amherst and Hampshire Colleges, and the parking lot where your car sits.

0.6 Pass by a fenced-in radio tower as you continue to follow the white blazes along a ridgeline. You'll soon drop into a cool, shaded saddle between the two peaks.

1.3 Reach the top of Mount Hitchcock with its concrete foundations for a former fire tower and super views of the Connecticut River. Continue to follow the white blazes as you begin a descent through rocky, rolling terrain.

1.8 Pass by a left turn for the blue-blazed Low Place Trail at intersection #105, then immediately bear right onto the blue-blazed Parker Trail at intersection #104.

2.0 Turn right onto the yellow-blazed Northside Trail at intersection #141.

2.3 Bear right at a fork past a junction with the red-blazed College Trail at intersection #142 and continue to follow yellow blazes.

3.4 Turn right at a large, open intersection as you reach the largest Hadley Reservoir, and follow a broad path south into the woods. (**Note:** A left turn here would take you to the reservoir shore in 50 yards, while continuing straight would bring you to Bay Road in 200 yards.)

3.6 Reach a smaller reservoir and bear left along its shoreline at intersection #147. Soon bear left again at intersection #148 and begin a gentle ascent.

4.2 Reach the fenced Amherst College library property with its concrete bunkers and bear left, following the fence line toward the compound's entrance.

4.4 Turn left onto the paved Military Road, soon passing a state forest fire station.

4.6 Turn right onto MA 116 and head south.

4.7 Arrive back at the Notch Visitor Center and your car.

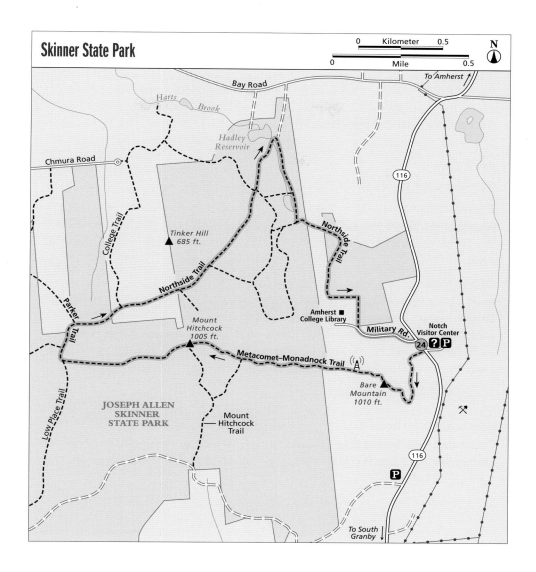

Skinner State Park

Hike Information

Local Information

Town of Hadley website: www.hadleyma.org
Northampton's homepage: www.northamptonma.gov
Mount Holyoke Range historical timeline: www.chronos–historical.org/mtholyoke/
Virtual tour of Skinner State Park: www.chronos–historical.org/skinner/

Local Events/Attractions

Atkins Farms Country Market and Apple Orchard: Amherst; (413) 253-9528; www .atkinsfarms.com. As you leave the visitor center, follow MA 116 north for 1 mile to reach the market and its shelves of fresh food, farmers' market produce in season, ice cream, and cider donuts.

Eric Carle Museum of Picture Book Art: Amherst; (413) 658-1100; www.carlemuseum .org. A fun museum and bookstore inspired by the beloved children's book author.

Hike Tours

Available at the visitor center

Organizations

Friends of the Mount Holyoke Range: South Hadley, MA; (413) 538-9914; www.mass .gov/eea/agencies/dcr/massparks/region-west/mount-holyoke-range-state-park .html

Other Resources

Notch Visitor Center: (413) 253-2883

Summit House (atop Mount Holyoke): (413) 586-0350

Guide to the Common Spring Wild Flowers of the Mount Holyoke Range: http://efg .cs.umb.edu/holyoke/. An online photographic guide to local flora, produced by researchers at UMass Amherst.

Local Outdoor Retailers

There are several along Russell Street, which is MA 9, just west of its intersection with MA 116:

Competitive Edge Ski and Bike: Holyoke; (413) 538-7662; www.compedgeskibike.com

Eastern Mountain Sports (EMS): Hadley; (413) 584-3554; www.emsonline.com

25 Chester-Blandford State Forest

The Westfield River begins as three streams draining the eastern slope of the Berkshire Hills, and then flows into the Connecticut River at Agawam. State highways and railroads run parallel along its length, including US 20, which leads you here. This hike begins with a steep climb to the cliffs above, with their soaring views up and down the river valley. The hike then traverses around these cliffs, called Observation Hill, before descending to the foot of a waterfall where Sanderson Brook flows into the Westfield River.

Start: From Sanderson Brook Road off US 20
Distance: 7.1 miles out and back
Hiking time: About 3 hours
Difficulty: Moderate, due to some very steep sections of trail
Trail surface: Short steep section is a narrow dirt trail; majority of the hike is on broad gravel roads
Best season: Fall
Land status: MA Department of Conservation and Recreation
Nearest town: Chester

Other trail users: Mountain bikers, ATV riders (although land is posted for no motorized vehicles)
Canine compatibility: Dogs permitted
Schedule: Open year-round
Fees and permits: None
Maps: USGS Chester, MA and Blandford, MA
Trail contact: Chester-Blandford State Forest headquarters, Chester; (413) 354-6347; www .mass.gov/eea/agencies/dcr/massparks/ region-west/chester-blandford-state-forest .html

Finding the trailhead: From Westfield, take US 20 west from its junction with MA 10 and US 202, passing its junction with MA 23 West at 5.6 miles and its junction with MA 112 North at 11.6 miles. Pass roads for the park headquarters and campsites, then turn left at 15.7 miles into a small dirt lot for Sanderson Brook Falls, immediately opposite the Bannish Lumber Yard. *DeLorme: Massachusetts Atlas & Gazetteer:* Page 45 28A. GPS: N42 15.359' / W72 56.827'

The Hike

The hike climbs Sanderson Brook Road, a wide, gravel trail that rises steeply past a popular local swimming hole and reaches all the way to the ridgeline above. Along the way it passes by the H. Newman Marsh Memorial Trail, named for the man (1924–1996) who helped develop the Jacob's Ladder Trail Scenic Byway. The byway is known today as US 20, but it has been used since the days when Mahican and Woronoake Native American tribes used it to travel between the Connecticut and Hudson River valleys. Jacob's Ladder itself is a 2,100-foot-high mountain ridge about a half-hour's drive west.

A Civilian Conservation Corps crew working in this forest first cleared the Newman Marsh Trail as a firebreak in the 1930s. About 100 men lived in a camp nearby,

Sanderson Brook Road settles to a modest pitch after dropping sharply from the ridgeline.

where they built two bridges and the Sanderson Brook Road, cut timber, planted trees, and exterminated the gypsy moths that were killing those trees. This hike sticks to the main paths, passing huge boulders of quartz surrounded by rhododendron, pine, and maple as it follows Observation Hill Road to a broad overlook with views up and down the valley.

This land contains so much quartz and mica that it often seems there must be shards of glass in the soil at your feet. Indeed, mining used to be the local business—removing mica, emery, and corundum (a mineral found in rubies and sapphires but more commonly used as an abrasive) from these hills. And in the wet summer months, there are enormous mushrooms splashing color—orange, red, silver, white, black, and scarlet—throughout the forest floor.

The nearby town of Chester enjoyed busy industry from the 1930s to 1960s with its emery mill, granite quarrying, and stone carving. Today only the small emery mill remains, so the town must search for a new economic engine. One candidate is the Bannish Lumber Company, located just across the street from the trailhead. Other businesses include tourism, blueberry and produce farms, and maple sugaring. But one of the most promising developments is the Chester Theatre Company, founded in 1990 as the "Miniature Theatre of Chester" and located in the town hall. This summer-stock theater plays contemporary, professional works by such famed playwrights as South African Athol Fugard. There are matinee performances at 2 p.m. on Thursday and Sunday in season. The company takes particular pride in creating touring versions of its works, having transferred seventeen of its productions to other venues in the last fifteen years. The group has also recently launched an educational

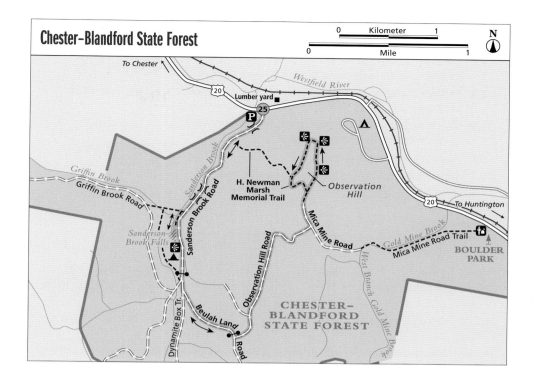

outreach program for young actors, including a play about adolescent bullying that is performed at many regional schools, and an after-school playwriting program that pairs middle-school playwrights with professional actors, directors, and designers.

Miles and Directions

0.0 Start at your car and walk southward up the broad, gravel Sanderson Brook Road, following signs for Sanderson Brook Falls.

0.2 Pass by the junction with the Newman Marsh Trail on the left.

0.6 Cross a metal bridge, and another one in 100 yards.

0.9 Turn right onto the Sanderson Falls Trail for a short spur on a narrow footpath to the falls, then return to the main path.

1.1 Turn right onto Sanderson Brook Road to continue uphill. (**Bailout:** Turn left to return to your car for a 2-mile total.)

1.4 Pass through a metal gate and stay on the main road, passing junctions with Griffin Brook Road and Dynamite Box Trail to the right. Sanderson Brook Road becomes quite steep.

2.0 Fork left through a metal gate onto Observation Hill Road, just past a junction with Beulah Land Road to the right. Follow the main road as it flattens out and traces the wooded ridgeline.

3.0 Turn left at a T intersection onto Mica Mine Road, which soon narrows to a blue-blazed footpath—part of the Newman Marsh Trail.

3.7 Reach a terrific vista over the valley floor, then follow the blue blazes to complete this overlook loop and begin your return.

4.2 Continue southward as the trail broadens again to become Mica Mine Road, and soon turn right onto Observation Hill Road, at the T intersection.

5.3 Turn right through the metal gate to begin your descent, passing the junction with Beulah Land Road.

5.9 Walk through another metal gate, continuing straight downhill past the junctions with Dynamite Box Trail and Griffin Brook Road.

6.2 Pass by the waterfall spur trail.

6.4 Cross the metal bridge, and another one in 100 yards.

7.1 Arrive back at your car.

Hike Information

Local Information

Jacob's Ladder Trail Scenic Byway Inc.: Huntington; www.jacobsladderscenicbyway .org. The 33-mile stretch of US 20 between Westfield and Lee is nicknamed The Jacob's Ladder Trail. The path was first blazed by the Mahican and Woronoake Native American tribes, then expanded in 1910 as one of the first highways built for automobiles.

Western Massachusetts Scenic Byways: www.bywayswestmass.com/byways/. Prepared by the state Department of Transportation (MassDOT), this site offers maps and details on seven special routes, including Mount Greylock, Jacob's Ladder, Route 116, Route 112, Connecticut River, Mohawk Trail, and Route 122.

Local Events/Attractions

The Berkshire Web: Pittsfield; (413) 442-7805; www.berkshireweb.com. Information on regional weather, maps, shopping, restaurants, and hotels.

Accommodations

Lee Lodging Association: Lee; www.leelodging.org
Lee Chamber of Commerce: Lee; (413) 243-0852; www.leechamber.org

Organizations

Chester Theatre Company: Chester; (413) 354-7771; http://chestertheatre.org. The theater is located at the Chester Town Hall, on Middlefield Street, just off US 20.

Other Resources

Pioneer Valley Hiking Club: West Springfield; http://pioneervalleyhikingclub.org
Hidden Hills (western MA) website: www.hidden-hills.com

Local Outdoor Retailers

Sam's Outdoor Outfitters: Hadley; (413) 582-9820; www.samsoutfitters.com

26 October Mountain State Forest

This hike follows the long-distance Appalachian Trail over Becket (2,200 feet) and Walling (2,220 feet) Mountains, then drops down to the shore of Finerty Pond, illustrating the variety of this enormous forest. It then tracks the Cordonier Trail southward through low-lying forest lands, looping back to the Appalachian Trail for a short backtrack to your car.

Start: From the trailhead on US 20, near Greenwater Pond
Distance: 6.7-mile loop
Hiking time: About 3.5 hours
Difficulty: Difficult, due to distance and steep climbs
Trail surface: Steep dirt trails and broad two-track carriage roads
Best season: Fall
Land status: MA Department of Conservation and Recreation
Nearest town: Lee
Other trail users: Mountain bikers, dirt bikers and ATVs, snowmobilers

Canine compatibility: Dogs permitted
Schedule: Open year-round
Fees and permits: None
Maps: USGS East Lee, MA
Trail contacts: October Mountain State Forest Headquarters, Lee; (413) 243-1778; www .mass.gov/eea/agencies/dcr/massparks/ region-west/october-mountain-state-forest -generic.html. Appalachian Trail website (information on the Appalachian Trail in Massachusetts); www.mass.gov/eea/agencies/dcr/ massparks/region-west/appalachian-trail.html

Finding the trailhead: From Lee, at the intersection of US 20 and the Mass Pike (exit 2), drive east. At 4.2 miles, turn right onto a small jug handle road and park. This rest area is just past the intersection of US 20 and Becket Road, and bears a historical marker sign for the town of Lee and Jacob's Ladder Trail (today called Route 20). *DeLorme: Massachusetts Atlas & Gazetteer:* Page 33 L17. GPS: N42 17.582' / W73 09.700'

The Hike

Named for George Washington's top aide, General Charles Lee, the town of Lee was settled as an agriculture and lumber village in 1760, adding textile and paper mills along the Housatonic River by 1806. The demand for its textiles soon declined, but Lee claimed twenty-five paper mills by 1857. And at one point the local Smith Paper Company was the largest in the world, fueled by the region's seemingly endless forests. But, of course, the lumber supply was soon exhausted, and the mills were destroyed by a series of floods, with the largest in 1886. Still, the region rebounded, prospering through its marble quarries. Discovered by builders in 1852, premium Lee Marble was reputed to be the hardest in the world.

Today's Berkshires specialize in tourism, and boast of Tanglewood, the summer home of the Boston Symphony Orchestra, as well as outdoor theater and outlet malls.

The deep woods of October Mountain State Forest remain far away from all of this. It is the largest state forest in Massachusetts, containing over 16,000 acres and nearly 10 miles of the 2,100-mile Appalachian Trail, on which this loop begins.

October Mountain stands between the Taconic Range and the Green Mountains, and this altitude and distance inland combine to present a very different ecosystem from coastal Massachusetts. One sign of this is the mountain maple, which covers the slopes of Becket Mountain. The familiar five-lobed maple leaf appears to have just three lobes on this small tree, although the remaining pieces are visible if you look closely. Hop hornbeam also grows here on the mountain slopes, with hemlock dominating in the lowlands. In the lower, swampy land, puddles on the trail are filled with frogs in the spring, and toads can be found traveling between water sources.

But the balance of animals was once much different. The forest began as the estate of William C. Whitney, Grover Cleveland's secretary of the navy. Whitney used it for hunting and kept it stocked with buffalo, elk, black-tailed and Virginia deer, moose, pheasants, grouse, quail, Belgian hares, and angora sheep. Local lore says that Herman Melville was the first to dub it October Mountain, during the time he lived at Arrowhead, in Pittsfield.

Today the forest is so large that, in addition to Lee, it spreads into three towns: Becket, Lenox, and Washington. These towns were so tough to settle that the largest industry in eighteenth-century Washington was charcoal making; the residents' only way to make a living was to burn the trees around them. And in 1798, times were so hard in Becket that the townspeople repealed their compulsory church tax, making all religious contributions voluntary—a practice that soon spread across the entire country.

Modern Becket and Lenox are well-known artistic centers, fly-fishing meccas, and popular spots for vacationers with second homes. In fact, Lenox was called the inland Newport in the nineteenth century, with its mansions called Berkshire cottages. If you're sleeping here, there is a fifty-site campground in the section of forest in Lee. But be careful not to pollute; the forest is the watershed for drinking water in Pittsfield and Lee, and also drains into the Housatonic and Westfield Rivers.

Miles and Directions

0.0 Start at the jug handle rest area and follow US 20 east, crossing from Lee into Becket.

0.2 Turn left at a sign for the Appalachian Trail and follow the AT's white blazes steeply uphill on the north side of the highway.

0.4 Cross an intersection with a blue-blazed vehicle trail marked S.A.M. (Snowmobile Association of Massachusetts), and soon pass under a power line.

Finerty Pond sits at the foot of Walling Mountain.

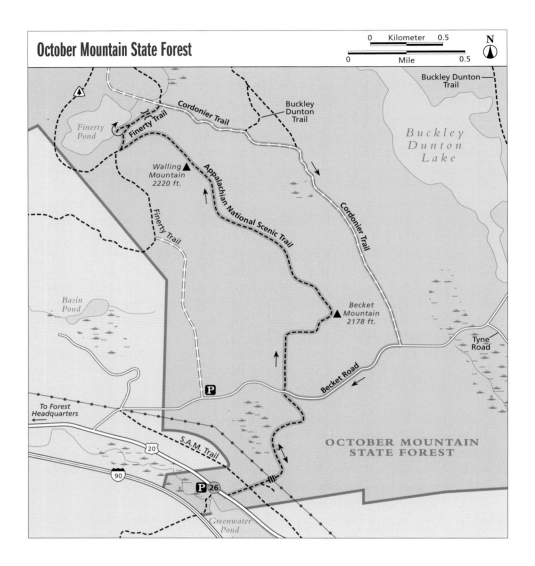

October Mountain State Forest

0   Kilometer   0.5

0   Mile   0.5

N

Buckley Dunton Trail

Cordonier Trail

Buckley Dunton Trail

Finerty Pond

Finerty Trail

Buckley Dunton Lake

Walling Mountain 2220 ft.

Appalachian National Scenic Trail

Finerty Trail

Cordonier Trail

Basin Pond

Becket Mountain 2178 ft.

Tyne Road

To Forest Headquarters

P

Becket Road

S.A.M. Trail

20

OCTOBER MOUNTAIN STATE FOREST

90

P 26

Greenwater Pond

1.1   Cross the paved Becket Road (may be called Yokum Pond Road or Tyne Road on maps), picking up the white AT blazes on the other side.

1.6   Reach the top of Becket Mountain, a wooded plateau marked by an AT logbook in a wooden box and four concrete foundations that once anchored a tower. There is also a USGS survey marker in the bedrock, and no shortage of mosquitoes. Continue to follow the AT along this ridge, soon dropping steeply downhill.

3.0   Turn right at an intersection at the bottom of a pitch onto the broad, orange-blazed Finerty Trail, leaving the narrow, white-blazed Appalachian Trail. In 50 yards, turn left for a spur trail to the shore of Finerty Pond. After enjoying the waters, backtrack on the spur trail and turn left to continue heading east on the Finerty Trail, with the pond on your left.

3.4 Turn right onto the Cordonier Trail. This broad, orange-blazed ATV trail is deeply rutted in places.

3.8 Take a right fork to stay on the Cordonier Trail. (***Note:*** A left here would lead to the Finerty Pond Trail and Buckey Dunton Trail.)

5.0 Turn right onto the paved Becket Road (aka Yokum Pond Road) and head gently downhill.

5.6 Turn left onto the familiar, white-blazed Appalachian Trail, retracing your steps from the beginning of the hike. (***Note:*** Watch for a metal storm drain in the pavement to find this junction.)

6.1 Cross under the power line.

6.5 Turn right onto paved US 20, heading west.

6.7 Arrive back at your car.

Hike Information

Local Events/Attractions

Lee website: www.leechamber.org

Herman Melville Homestead: Pittsfield; (413) 442-1793; www.mobydick.org

Accommodations

Bucksteep Manor: Washington; (413) 623-5535; www.bucksteepmanor.com

Restaurants

Locker Room Sports Pub: Lee; (413) 243-2662; www.townoflee.com/business_pages/lockerroom/index.asp

The Grind: Lee; (413) 243-2033

Other Resources

Lee Chamber of Commerce: Lee; www.leechamber.org. Lists restaurants, lodging, special events, etc.

Berkshire arts and entertainment website: www.newberkshire.com

Local Outdoor Retailers

Berkshire Bike and Board: Great Barrington; (413) 528-5555; http://berkshirebikeandboard.com

27 Pittsfield State Forest

This out-and-back hike follows the Taconic Crest Trail, a quiet, long-distance hiking trail that stretches back and forth across the New York border for 35 miles. Nearby sections of the Shaker Trail pass by dozens of historic foundations, mills, carriage roads, and holy sites.

Start: From the trailhead in the rest stop parking area on US 20 about a mile east of the New York state line
Distance: 3.4 miles out and back
Hiking time: About 2 hours
Difficulty: Moderate, since the dirt trail can be deeply rutted in places and demands a lot of scrambling
Trail surface: Narrow dirt hiking path
Best season: Fall
Land status: MA Department of Conservation and Recreation

Nearest town: Pittsfield
Other trail users: Hikers
Canine compatibility: Dogs permitted
Schedule: Open year-round
Fees and permits: None
Maps: USGS Pittsfield West, MA
Trail contact: Pittsfield State Forest, Pittsfield; (413) 442-8992; www.mass.gov/eea/agencies/dcr/massparks/region-west/pittsfield-state-forest-generic.html

Finding the trailhead: From Pittsfield, drive west on US 20 (aka Housatonic Street) from its intersection with US 7. Pass a junction with MA 41 South at 4.1 miles and then the Hancock Shaker Village. Turn right at 6.5 miles into a small rest stop off the north side of US 20, and park on the side of the paved crescent road. *DeLorme: Massachusetts Atlas & Gazetteer:* Page 32 D4. GPS: N42 26.227' / W73 22.461'

The Hike

This hike follows the long-distance Taconic Crest Trail through thick forest for a visit to the quiet Twin Pond, then back again. A quiet, idyllic path, it is very faint at times, though always clearly blazed. Beginning at the trailhead on US 20, the entire trail stretches 35 miles along the ridgeline of the Taconic Range, dancing along Massachusetts's borders with New York and Vermont. In the northern part of the state forest, the trail makes a stop at the Berry Pond campsite, which at 2,150 feet is said to be the highest pond in the state. Farther north the trail ends at NY 346, in Petersborough, New York.

Other paths launching from this busy trailhead on US 20 include the multiuse Griffin Trail and Taconic Skyline Trail, often heavily rutted with the tracks of ATV and dirt bike riders.

These woods hold vernal pools packed with frogs as well as garter snakes and eastern red-backed salamanders. But the brightest coloring surely belongs to the red eft, a neon-orange salamander that lives under rotting logs. The eft is an immature form

Twin Pond is the halfway mark for this out-and-back hike.

of the eastern newt, which begins life as a larva in a stream, spends two to three years as an eft, and then returns to the water as a mature aquatic newt.

Another attraction in the forest is Holy Mount—the center of the Shakers' philosophy of hard work and pure thoughts. With only the most primitive tools, they began working a marble quarry in this park in 1785, and inhabited the nearby village from as early as 1790. They used the quarried stone to help build a carding and fulling mill (for wool), a gristmill, and a sawmill, all located along the banks of Shaker Brook. Learn far more about this fascinating culture at the nearby Hancock Shaker Village (details below).

In more recent years this park housed a very different group of hard-working people. A camp of President Franklin D. Roosevelt's Civilian Conservation Corps (CCC) lived here from 1933 to 1941. At their peak in the state, Massachusetts had fifty-one camps employing 10,000 men. They set up campsites, practiced forest management, and did fire hazard reduction, pest control, wildlife enhancement, and recreational development.

Pittsfield also has a proud literary history, beginning with Herman Melville's residence, Arrowhead. Now a museum and National Historic Landmark, this building where the writer lived from 1850 to 1862 is open for tours. Melville's wealthy father bought land here in 1816, but later went bankrupt and died shortly thereafter, leaving him to search for work. The young man drifted through jobs as a bank teller, fur store clerk, and Pittsfield schoolteacher, before heading west for a surveying job and then to sea with the merchant marine. Finally, he sailed on a whaling ship out of Cape Cod. This was the beginning of his adventures island-hopping through the South Pacific. He worked as a bowling pin setter in Hawaii and then joined the US Navy

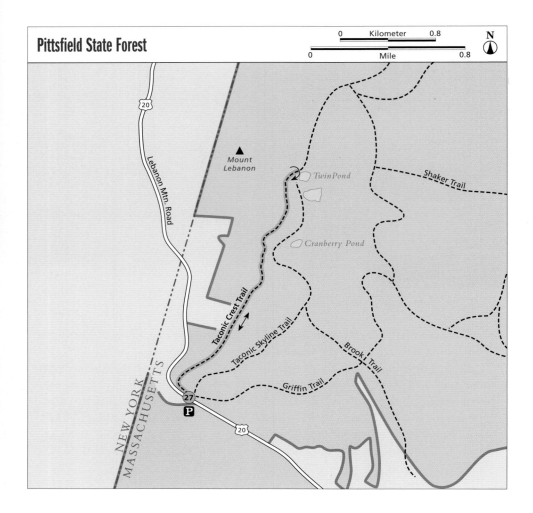

until finally coming home to New England. Bursting with stories, sights, and sounds, he visited the family farm in 1850 and fell in love with the region. In the company of other literary Berkshire residents like Nathaniel Hawthorne and Oliver Wendell Holmes, he wrote *Moby Dick* at Arrowhead.

Miles and Directions

0.0 Start at the western end of the rest stop on US 20 and head north through a chain-link fence onto the Taconic Crest Trail, a quiet footpath well blazed with white diamonds on blue plaques.

1.1 Turn left at a T intersection, then immediately right, to continue following the white-on-blue blazes.

Follow the white-on-blue diamond blazes to head north along the Massachusetts–New York border.

1.7 Reach the shore of Twin Pond, a lovely spot for a rest and a snack, then turn to retrace your steps along the Taconic Crest Trail southbound.

2.2 Turn left and quickly right to follow trail blazes through the zigzag.

3.4 Arrive back at your car.

Hike Information

Local Events/Attractions

Herman Melville Homestead: (413) 442-1793; www.mobydick.org

Organizations

Hiking the Taconic Range: www.taconichiking.com/taconic-crest-trail-north.php. A website loaded with information and photographs of dozens of peaks, ponds and points of interest along the trail.

CITY OF PEACE

You pass Hancock Shaker Village on your way to the trailhead from the east. The Shakers called this commune their "City of Peace" and lived here from 1790 to 1960.

The Shakers, whose full name is the United Society of Believers in Christ's Second Appearing, emigrated from England to America in 1774 and established their first community in nearby Albany, New York. Their leader, Ann Lee, attracted so many followers that there were nineteen Shaker communities by 1830, located in Connecticut, Indiana, Kentucky, Maine, Massachusetts, New Hampshire, New York, and Ohio. Today only one Shaker community remains, at Sabbathday Lake, Maine.

Shakers held all property in common and practiced pacifism, celibacy, and equality and separation of the sexes. The City of Peace is now a 1,200-acre "living history museum," with activities at any time of year, including hikes through the nearby woods, visits to Holy Mount and Shaker Mountain, sleigh rides, archaeology, crafts and livestock shows, antiques shows, barn dances, auctions, harvest dinners, and a Christmas celebration.

For more information, phone (413) 443-0188 or (800) 817-1137, or check http://hancockshakervillage.org. Open daily except holidays.

New England Mountain Biking Association: www.nemba.org/ridingzone/p_Pittsfield_State_Forest.html. This group sometimes has useful information on the region, such as weather reports and trail conditions.

Hancock Shaker Village: http://hancockshakervillage.org; (413) 443-0188.

Other Resources

The Berkshire Web: www.berkshireweb.com/sports/parks/pittsfieldstate.html. Information on the park's recreational opportunities, natural history, and culture.

Local Outdoor Retailers

Plaine's Bike, Ski, and Snowboard: Pittsfield; (413) 499-0294; www.plaines.com
Arcadian Shop Outdoor Specialty Store: Lenox; (413) 637-3010; www.arcadian.com
Berkshire Outfitters: Adams (on MA 8 between Adams and Cheshire); (413) 743-5900; www.berkshireoutfitters.com

28 Savoy Mountain State Forest

This loop follows a two-track multiuse trail through northern hardwood forests for a visit to Tannery Falls, then climbs the quiet Ross Brook Trail to Balanced Rock before cruising back on a gravel road. You can swim in the state forest at either North Pond or South Pond, though there is a lifeguard only at the former.

Start: From the Burnett Road parking lot, near New State Road
Distance: 5.2-mile loop
Hiking time: About 3 hours
Difficulty: Difficult, due to length and steepness
Trail surface: Wide, packed dirt, all-use trails
Best season: Summer
Land status: MA Department of Conservation and Recreation
Nearest town: North Adams

Other trail users: Mountain bikers, ATV and dirt bikers, snowmobilers, cross-country skiers
Canine compatibility: Dogs permitted
Schedule: Open year-round
Fees and permits: None
Maps: USGS Cheshire, MA
Trail contact: Savoy Mountain State Forest Headquarters, Florida; (413) 663-8469; www.mass.gov/eea/agencies/dcr/massparks/region-west/savoy-mt-state-forest-generic.html

Finding the trailhead: From North Adams, take MA 8 south to Adams and turn left onto MA 116 South. From this intersection, pass a junction with MA 8A South at 6.6 miles and turn left onto Center Road at 7.1 miles. Turn right at 9.1 miles onto paved New State Road, which soon turns to dirt. Turn left at a T intersection onto Burnett Road at 11.6 miles, then immediately turn right into a large dirt parking lot.

If you're coming from MA 2 in Florida, drive south on Central Shaft Road past forest headquarters and North Pond. Follow this street, now called Florida Road, to a left turn onto Burnett Road and another left into the dirt lot at the intersection of Burnett and New State Roads, 5.7 miles from the highway. *DeLorme: Massachusetts Atlas & Gazetteer:* Page 21 H24. GPS: N42 37.567' / W73 02.070'

The Hike

The Hoosac Range is a watershed between the Connecticut and Deerfield Rivers to the east and the Hoosic River and Berkshire Range to the west. MA 2 goes through switchback contortions as it scales these heights, culminating in the hotel and restaurant at Whitcomb Summit (on MA 2 just west of this hike).

This range is the site of one of the great engineering feats of the nineteenth century, the Hoosac Tunnel, carved through the mountain by the Boston & Maine Railroad so trains could pass from the steep-walled Deerfield River gorge to North Adams. At 4.8 miles it was the longest tunnel in North America when the first train passed through in 1875, pulling twenty-two carloads of grain. Though the tunnel is fully 26

feet wide by 22 feet tall, air is precious underground. So the workers relied on ventilation pumps driven by Deerfield River waterwheels, and a series of vertical airshafts that were drilled through 1,000 feet of rock. In the end its plans were so precise that when the workers tunneling from each end met in the center, they were less than an inch off-target.

But the achievement came at great cost. The construction depended on the first commercial use of the famously powerful and unstable explosive nitroglycerine, and 196 workers were killed over the twenty years it took to build, earning it the nickname the Bloody Pit. This loop through the 10,500-acre state forest passes two points of interest: Tannery Falls to the east and Balanced Rock (along your return path). You begin by following the Tannery Trail through northern hardwood forests typical of the eastern slopes of the Hoosac Range, dropping down to Tannery Falls. The falls are a series of plunges, cascades, and slides dropping from 20 to 60 feet as Ross Brook and Parker Brook drain into Tannery Brook on its way to the Deerfield River. You return uphill along the Ross Brook Trail and then Tannery Road to close the loop.

As a consequence of being open to vehicles, the Tannery Trail is deeply rutted, with wide mud puddles that create even wider trails as hikers and bikers swerve around them. Try to be sensitive to this trend and skirt the puddles closely to avoid making the trails even worse. There is some silver lining to the erosion, since in spring and summer these ruts are vernal pools, filled with mating frogs and salamanders. Another consequence of all this standing water is to create a tremendous population of hungry mosquitoes, so be sure to bring your favorite bug dope.

If you're staying here overnight, there are forty-five campsites at South Pond, available from May to October. And at the forest's interpretive center, there are guided hikes, natural and cultural history walks, slide shows, games, and exhibits.

Miles and Directions

0.0 Start at the large dirt parking lot on Burnett Road and walk south on New State Road.

0.1 Cross the road bridge over Gulf Brook.

0.2 Turn left onto dirt Tannery Road (no street sign) and immediately left again onto Tannery Trail, a broad multiuse path that runs eastbound, parallel to Gulf Brook on your left.

2.4 Turn left onto dirt Tannery Road, cross a road bridge over Ross Brook, and turn left into a dirt parking lot. Pass through the lot for a spur trail to Tannery Falls, then retrace your steps to the road.

2.6 Cross Tannery Road opposite the parking lot entrance to begin the blue-blazed Ross Brook Trail. Cross a wooden footbridge and head west alongside the pretty brook close on your right side.

◄ *This teetering glacial erratic located near Lewis Hill is known as Balanced Rock.*

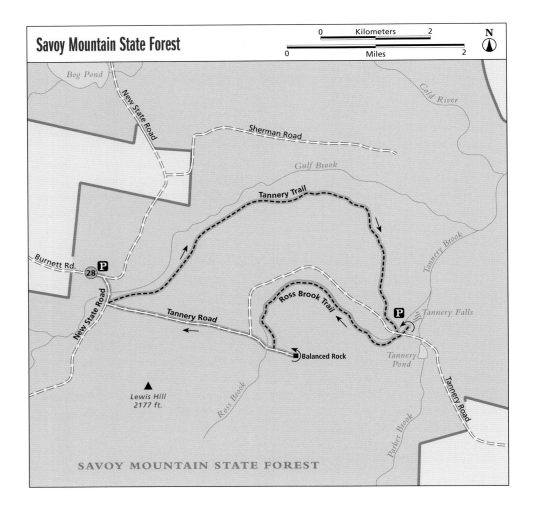

Savoy Mountain State Forest

3.8 Turn left onto the gravel Spur Road (not named on map) for a spur trail to Balanced Rock, a large boulder propped improbably on one corner. Then retrace your steps, soon passing the junction with Ross Brook Trail.

4.2 Turn left uphill onto Tannery Road. (***Note:*** A right here would take you back to Tannery Falls.)

4.9 Pass the familiar junction with Tannery Trail and immediately turn right onto New State Road.

5.1 Cross the road bridge over Gulf Brook.

5.2 Arrive back at your car.

STORY OF A HEADSTONE

A cemetery along the Lewis Hill Trail tells the sad tale of forty-five years in the Dunham family, early homesteaders who expressed their grief in poetry on the headstones here.

The oldest named grave belongs to James Cornell, who died November 3, 1819, aged sixty-four years. The next is young Alfred J., son of Bradish and Candance Dunham, who died February 1, 1843, aged three months. His headstone bears this couplet: "Short below has been thy stay/So fade the joys of earth away."

A young couple shares the next tombstone: Charles R. Dunham died September 2, 1854, aged twenty-nine years; and his wife, Caroline M., died August 1, 1853, aged twenty-six years. The stone describes their passing thusly: "In hope they lived, in hope they died/They had no fear of death or grave/Their bodies mouldering side by side/Their spirits gone to God, who gains."

The patriarch himself, Bradish Dunham, died March 18, 1862, aged sixty-seven years. And his wife, Candance, died September 5, 1864, also at sixty-seven.

Hike Information

Local Information

Waterfall fans come from afar to view Tannery Falls, and there is plenty of information at sites such as the **World Waterfall Database:** www.worldwaterfalldatabase.com/waterfall/Tannery-Falls-7418/ and **Waterfalls of the Northeastern U.S.:** www.northeastwaterfalls.com/waterfall.php?num=651&p=0.
Mohawk Trail and Savoy Mountain State Forest website: www.berkshireweb.com/mohawktrail; **Mohawk Trail website:** www.mohawktrail.com

Local Events/Attractions

Mass MoCA (Museum of Contemporary Art): North Adams; (413) 664-4481; www.massmoca.org or www.berkshireweb.com/mohawktrail/massmoca.html. Open daily from 10 a.m. to 6 p.m.; admission fee for adults.
North Adams website: www.northadams.com. Loaded with local news and events.

Accommodations

Whitcomb Summit Retreat: Florida; (413) 664-0007; www.whitcombsummitretreat.net. Located "at the highest point on the Mohawk Trail, 2,240 feet," there are forty-five campsites and three log cabins in the state forest.

Local Outdoor Retailers

Nature's Closet: Williamstown; (413) 458-7909; http://naturescloset.net
The Gear Den: Williamstown; (413) 359-0786; www.thegearden.com
Berkshire Outfitters: Adams; (413) 743-5900; www.berkshireoutfitters.com

29 Mohawk Trail State Forest

This out-and-back hike traces a traverse along the shoulder of Hawks Mountain (1,880 feet) to an exposed cliff that offers gorgeous views of the Deerfield River Valley. If you want to do some extra exploring after this short hike, pick up a map at the park headquarters (on the north side of MA 2, 0.7 mile east of here) and walk along the gorgeous Thumper Mountain Trail and Nature Trail on the banks of the Deerfield River.

Start: From the picnic table area
Distance: 2.4 miles out and back
Hiking time: About 1.5 hours
Difficulty: Moderate, due to steepness
Trail surface: Narrow dirt trail
Best season: Summer
Land status: MA Department of Conservation and Recreation
Nearest town: North Adams
Other trail users: Hikers only
Canine compatibility: Dogs permitted

Schedule: Open year-round; no restricted hours for trails, but picnic area is posted as 9:30 a.m. to 7:30 p.m.
Fees and permits: None to hike; parking fee at picnic area
Maps: USGS Rowe, MA
Trail contact: Mohawk Trail State Forest, Charlemont; (413) 339-5504; www.mass.gov/eea/agencies/dcr/massparks/region-west/mohawk-trail-state-forest.html

Finding the trailhead: From Greenfield, drive west on MA 2. Pass the intersection of MA 2 with MA 8A North in Charlemont, and pass by the main entrance to Mohawk Trail State Forest at 4.1 miles. At 4.9 miles, park in a small dirt lot on the right, immediately after a sign on MA 2 reading LEAVING PIONEER VALLEY. This modest spot offers picnic tables, restrooms, and a swimming hole in the nearby river. *DeLorme: Massachusetts Atlas & Gazetteer:* Page 21 G29. GPS: N42 38.537' / W72 56.962'

The Hike

You know you're graduating from the Pioneer Valley to the Berkshire Hills when the road signs along MA 2 begin to read WARNING: BEAR CROSSING. And indeed, hikers picking up trail maps at the park headquarters here are also given pamphlets asking them to store food carefully and not to feed the bears. The literature also warns that bears are active in daylight hours and "typically inhabit wooded wetlands, swamps, and mixed hardwood conifer forest with a dense understory adjacent to water sources." Never surprise a bear, and in an encounter, make loud noises until it goes away.

Cool your feet in the Cold River after a hot hike to the ridgeline. ▶

MA 2 is also known as the Mohawk Trail, after the famous Native American tribe that first blazed this path. The paved automobile road was completed in 1914, constructed for a total cost of $368,000 in an effort to connect the state highway system from Boston to New York, and the west beyond. This short, 12-mile section was the most challenging section to build, since it had to climb over Hoosac Mountain from Florida, near the Deerfield River, to North Adams. The task was made more difficult because the mountain is not a monolith, but has two ridges—Whitcomb Summit to the east and Perry's Pass to the west—with an elevated valley in between. The railroad also needed to cross this range, but it did so 1,200 feet underground, through the Hoosac Tunnel.

On the north side of MA 2, there are restrooms and telephones at the picnic area where you parked, and a swimming hole in the Cold River, a tributary of the Deerfield River. Also, at forest headquarters there are five cabins and fifty-six tent sites. But this hike follows the Totem Trail for a quick tour of the forest's quiet, south side. The trail follows a gorgeous, fern-lined traverse along the slope, passing frequent animal scat and tracks. From your observation post on the shoulder of Hawks Mountain, it is easy to watch the lines of tiny cars below, carrying their canoes and kayaks to the Deerfield River. This is a popular spot for whitewater paddling, not only because of the beauty of the countryside, but also because the nearby hydroelectric power station stages daily releases of floodwater, creating predictable rapids.

Nearby outfitters like Zoar Outdoor rent all the gear and instruction you need to play in these waters from April through October. Zoar offers whitewater rafting, canoeing, and kayaking trips, as well as rock climbing expeditions. A favorite stretch for paddlers of all stripes is the unimpeded length of the Deerfield River that runs 17 miles from Fife Brook Dam in Florida to the Number 4 dam in Buckland. Of course, the reason this water is so popular with boaters is the regular release schedule. According to Zoar, ten hydroelectric dams have operated on the river since 1974, all pumping out power for insatiable New England. You can check the US Geological Survey's website to see how high any Massachusetts river is running, with real-time reports. See http://waterdata.usgs.gov/ma/nwis/rt for a state map with links to river-by-river listings.

Miles and Directions

0.0 Start at the dirt lot on the shoulder of MA 2 and walk east along the highway.

0.1 Turn right and cross the highway to head south on the Totem Trail, located at a road sign for the Pioneer Valley boundary and a stone monument with a plaque reading MOHAWK TRAIL STATE FOREST, ESTABLISHED 1921.

0.2 Bear left as soon as you enter the woods, crossing a streambed below a brown, wooden pump house and following blue blazes gently uphill, roughly parallel to MA 2 below you on the left.

1.2 Emerge onto a rock outcropping with a terrific view of the river below. The trail ends here, so turn around and retrace your steps downhill.

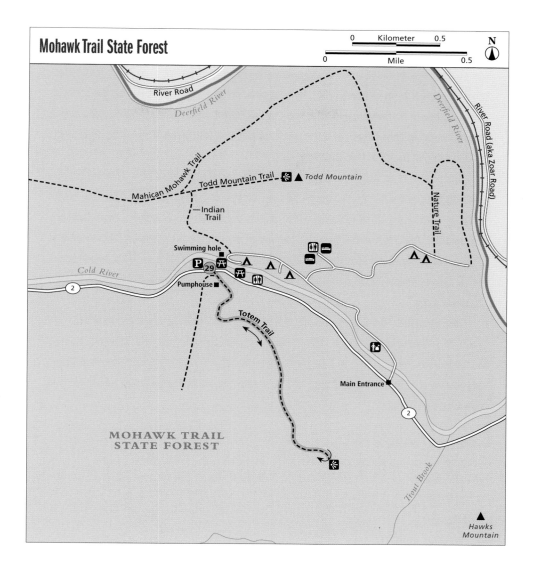

Mohawk Trail State Forest

River Road
Deerfield River
Deerfield River
River Road (aka Zoar Road)

Mahican Mohawk Trail
Todd Mountain Trail ▲ Todd Mountain

Indian Trail

Nature Trail

Swimming hole
🅿 29 ⛱
Cold River
Pumphouse ■

2

Totem Trail

MOHAWK TRAIL
STATE FOREST

Main Entrance

2

Trout Brook

▲
*Hawks
Mountain*

2.2 Cross the stream below the pump house and turn left onto MA 2 westbound.

2.4 Carefully cross the highway to arrive back at your car.

Hike Information

Local Information

Mohawk Trail region online: North Adams; (866) 743-8127; www.mohawktrail.com
Mohawk Trail website: www.berkshireweb.com/mohawktrail/index.html or www
.berkshireweb.com/mohawktrail/mtsf.html

MASS MOCA

The Massachusetts Museum of Contemporary Art—known everywhere as Mass MoCA—features displays like *Tree Logic* (1999), by Australian artist Natalie Jeremijenko. The arrangement consists of six flame maple trees hung upside down from a latticework of cables strung between eight 35-foot telephone poles. Their root balls are encased in stainless steel planters and watered by a drip irrigation system.

Open since May 1999, the museum is an enormous renovation of a 13-acre, twenty-seven-building mill complex. The buildings were first purchased in 1872 for a dye and textile company, then sold in 1940 to an electrical component manufacturer, which went out of business in 1985. Today it's on the National Register of Historic Places. Mass MoCA is located at 87 Marshall St. in North Adams and is open daily from 10 a.m. to 6 p.m., with an admission fee for adults. Phone (413) 664-4481 for more information, or check the website at www.massmoca.org.

Two other local museums include the Sterling and Francine Clark Art Institute, 225 South St., Williamstown, (413) 458-2303, www.clarkart.edu; and the Williams College Museum of Art, 15 Lawrence Hall Dr., Williamstown, (413) 597-2429, http://wcma.williams.edu. Hours at both are from 10 a.m. to 5 p.m. daily except Wednesday; free admission and wheelchair accessible.

Accommodations

The state forest has many campsites for rent from mid–April through mid-October, and cabins year-round. Leashed pets are allowed. For rates and rules, visit the park headquarters.

Restaurants

Williamstown website: www.williamstownchamber.com. Listings for lodging, dining, culture, and shopping.

Organizations

Zoar Outdoor: Charlemont; (800) 532-7483; www.zoaroutdoor.com

Local Outdoor Retailers

Nature's Closet: Williamstown; (413) 458-7909; http://naturescloset.net
The Gear Den: Williamstown; (413) 359-0786; www.thegearden.com
Berkshire Outfitters: Adams; (413) 743-5900; www.berkshireoutfitters.com

30 Monroe State Forest

From stone-age natives to a 4.8-mile train tunnel to a nuclear power plant, this region has been home to all stages of humanity. This varied loop climbs to the wooded peak of Spruce Mountain, with some beautiful views to the south along power-line cuts. It then descends to Hunt Hill for an optional side trip to a stone balcony outlook over the Deerfield River Valley, and completes the loop with a flat hike along the dirt Raycroft Road.

Start: From the trailhead at the junction of Main Road and North Road
Distance: 5.7-mile loop
Hiking time: About 3 hours
Difficulty: Moderate, with some scrambling uphill pitches
Trail surface: Half scrambling uphill pitches and half flat, broad, two-track trails
Best season: Fall
Land status: MA Department of Conservation and Recreation
Nearest town: North Adams

Other trail users: 4-wheel-drive vehicles on Raycroft Road, mountain bikers on trail sections
Canine compatibility: Dogs permitted
Schedule: Open year-round
Fees and permits: None
Maps: USGS Rowe, MA
Trail contact: Monroe State Forest, Charlemont; (413) 339-5504; www.mass.gov/eea/agencies/dcr/massparks/region-west/monroe-state-forest-generic.html

Finding the trailhead: From Greenfield, drive west on MA 2. Pass the intersection of MA 2 with MA 8A North in Charlemont, and at 5 miles, wind up a steep mountain road. At the top, pass the Whitcomb Summit Retreat at 11.5 miles, and at 12.3 miles, turn right onto Tilda Hill Road at the Florida Volunteer Fire Department. At 16.3 miles, turn right at a trailhead sign onto Raycroft Road (called South Road on some maps), just opposite dirt North Road. Park on the shoulder of the dirt road there.

From North Adams, drive east on MA 2 until you reach the Golden Eagle restaurant at the hairpin turn. Drive 2.5 miles past the restaurant and turn left onto Tilda Hill Road at the Florida Volunteer Fire Department. At 6.6 miles, turn right at a trailhead sign onto Raycroft Road (called South Road on some maps), just opposite North Road. Park on the shoulder of the dirt road there. *DeLorme: Massachusetts Atlas & Gazetteer:* Page 21 B26. GPS: N42 43.229' / W72 59.428'

The Hike

As you drive west on MA 2 from Charlemont, you'll leave the Pioneer Valley and climb a roller-coaster-steep mountain pass through the Hoosac Range, with rocky cliffs so high your car radio loses reception. A series of hotels and souvenir shops boast 50-mile views from observation towers along the hairpin switchbacks, culminating at the 2,240-foot Whitcomb Summit.

The view from Spruce Mountain includes the reservoir for a hydroelectric dam and the ski slopes in nearby Charlemont.

Monroe State Forest is 4,321 acres of woodland that borders Vermont on its northern edge and nestles in a bend of the Deerfield River on its southern end. The classic northern hardwood forest contains mostly birch, beech, and maple, with a smattering of hemlock, spruce, and fir. Moose prints and droppings are common, and grouse may leap up from the brush underfoot, sounding like helicopters as they frantically beat their wings. And keep an eye out for wild turkeys, which had disappeared from the region until the state released thirty-seven birds in the Berkshires in 1972. By 1986 there were 5,000 birds, and it seems like there are many more today.

Trails were once well-marked with blue paint blazes, but these are fading and peeling off trees, so keep a close eye on your path. There are two lean-tos and many tent sites along Dunbar Brook in the park's lower, eastern half if you're looking for an overnight spot. But the park is known for its aggressive mosquito population, so be sure to bring plenty of bug dope. The falls in Dunbar Creek at the trailhead are a popular swimming hole and may be just what you need to cool off after this loop.

Colonial settlement began here in 1750, but natives had been fishing and hunting here since 400 BC. At a settlement where Fife Brook joins the Deerfield River, they left behind flaked scraping knives and spear points made from quartzite, schist, and chert. There have been three major engineering marvels in the years since then: the Hoosac railroad tunnel in 1875, Yankee Nuclear Power Station in 1961, and the

LOCAL POWER SUPPLIES

This region is home to two major power plants—a hydroelectric dam and a decommissioned nuclear power plant.

The Bear Swamp Pumped Storage Facility produces 600 megawatts of power by switching water between the upper and lower reservoirs daily. Run by a partnership of Brookfield and Emera, the plant fills the upper pond by night, when electricity is cheap, then releases it by day to fulfill demand. The water cascades 770 feet through tunnels within the mountain, driving two turbines. A second plant is built into the Fife Brook Dam itself, driving a comparatively small 10-megawatt station from the flow of the Deerfield River

To reach the underground Bear Swamp Visitor Center from the trailhead, turn right onto Main Road and head west. At 1.6 miles, stay on Main Road by bearing right at an intersection with Davis Road. At 2 miles, turn right onto Kingsley Hill Road, bearing left at 2.4 miles. After a very steep descent, turn right at 3.3 miles onto River Road. Turn left at 5.8 miles into the lot. The visitor center is open Friday, Saturday, and Sunday from May 1 to Columbus Day weekend. Call (802) 423-7015, ext. 640, for more information, or check www.emera.com/en/home/bearswamp.aspx.

The Yankee Rowe Nuclear Power Station was the third nuclear power plant built in the country, and the first built in New England. It operated from 1961 to 1992 and was dismantled in 2007, with various parts shipped to secure storage sites around the country. Most of the sprawling, riverside site has been restored today, with only a 2-acre plot remaining for the storage of spent fuel. The plant was owned and operated by a consortium of eleven power companies in Maine, Massachusetts, New Hampshire, and Vermont. For more information, check out www.yankeerowe.com.

Bear Swamp "pumped storage" hydroelectric plant. The railroad tunnel is scarcely used anymore. The nuclear plant, called Yankee Rowe, shut down in 1992, and was decommissioned in 2007. The hydro plant is located underground in the hollowed-out mountain under the Bear Swamp Upper Reservoir, high above the river's eastern bank.

Despite its name, the town of Florida is actually one of the coldest in the state. It had a boom time in the second half of the nineteenth century while the railroad tunnel was being constructed. This boom took its toll, as all but the most inaccessible sections of Monroe State Forest were cleared for agriculture in the nineteenth century and have since been harvested at least once for timber. But the town's modern economy is based more on its natural splendors, specifically fly fishing. The section

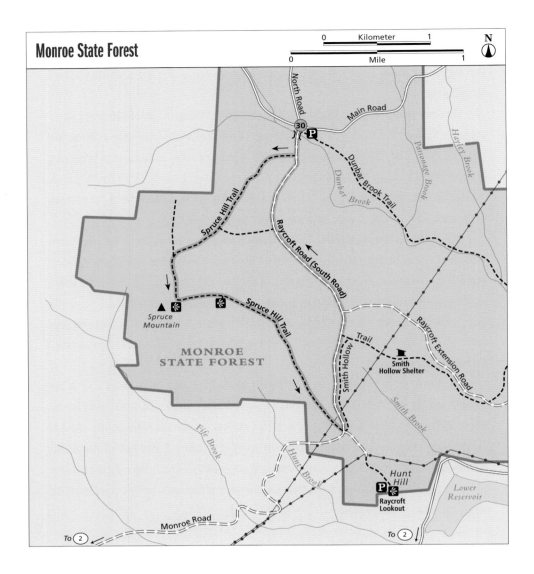

Monroe State Forest

0 Kilometer 1

0 Mile 1

N

North Road

Main Road

30
P

Dunbar Brook Trail

Dunbar Brook

Parsonage Brook

Hayley Brook

Spruce Hill Trail

Raycroft Road (South Road)

Spruce Hill Trail

Spruce Mountain

MONROE STATE FOREST

Raycroft Extension Road

Trail

Smith Hollow Trail

Smith Hollow Shelter

Smith Brook

Fife Brook

Hunt Brook

Hunt Hill

Raycroft Lookout

Lower Reservoir

Monroe Road

To 2

To 2

of the Deerfield River that runs through here is famed for its brown, rainbow, and brook trout. Its neighbor Monroe, named for President James Monroe, was even slower to develop. Hindered by its mountainous terrain and lack of water, it relied on dairy farming. Likewise, the tunnel brought prosperity here. Modern hydroelectric plants in the Deerfield River continued the trend, and today the region also is relying increasingly on the charms of its natural beauty. Canoes and kayaks on cartops in the summer months reveal that whitewater junkies don't mind river dams, as long as they know when the water releases will create killer rapids.

Miles and Directions

0.0 Start at the map kiosk at the trailhead on Main Road and follow the dirt Raycroft Road south, crossing a bridge over Dunbar Brook. On the other side, follow the road uphill into the forest.

0.3 Turn right onto the Spruce Hill Trail, a narrow, blue-blazed path leading steeply uphill. This junction comes just before the road takes a sharp right bend.

1.5 Continue straight on the blue-blazed hiking trail as it intersects an ATV trail marked with red diamond placards. The path can be overgrown here in lush summer months, but is well blazed.

2.0 Reach Spruce Mountain, marked only by a small clearing and a fire circle. It's a wooded summit, but for a grand view of surrounding peaks, walk 20 yards to a granite outcropping to your right. Then return to the trail and follow blue blazes southeast.

3.5 Cross a power line, with great views to either side.

3.6 Turn left onto dirt Raycroft Road as you emerge from the woods at a three-way intersection. (**Side trip:** Continue straight here for a 0.5-mile spur to the Raycroft Outlook, a stone balcony built by CCC workers, with views of the Hoosac and Green Mountains.)

3.7 Pass under the power line again for an easy, downhill, northbound cruise toward your car.

4.2 Pass by junctions with the blue-blazed Smith Hollow Trail, then the rough, dirt Raycroft Extension Road, both to your right.

5.5 Pass by your original turn onto the Spruce Hill Trail, leading uphill to your left.

5.7 Cross Dunbar Brook on the wooden bridge and arrive back at your car.

Hike Information

Local Information

Mohawk Trail region website: www.mohawktrail.com

The Berkshire Web: www.berkshireweb.com/sports/parks/

Accommodations

Whitcomb Summit Retreat: Florida; (413) 664-0007; www.whitcombsummitretreat .net. Located "at the highest point on the Mohawk Trail, 2,240 feet," there are forty-five campsites and three log cabins in the state forest.

Restaurants

North Adams regional website: www.northadams.com. Dining, events, and news.

Other Resources

Great Outdoor Recreation Pages (GORP): www.gorp.com/parks-guide/mohawk-trail -outdoor-pp2-guide-cid401887.html

Local Outdoor Retailers

Nature's Closet: Williamstown; (413) 458-7909; http://naturescloset.net

The Gear Den: Williamstown; (413) 359-0786; www.thegearden.com

Berkshire Outfitters: Adams; (413) 743-5900; www.berkshireoutfitters.com

Midstate Trail

How do you get from Rhode Island to New Hampshire?

If you're in Massachusetts's Worcester County, you can walk from state to state on the 92-mile Midstate Trail, completed in 1985. And there's no reason to stop once you get there—it connects on its northern end to the Wapack Trail, heading 21 miles to North Pack Mountain in Greenfield, New Hampshire; and it connects on its southern end to a planned 63-mile hiking trail to the Rhode Island seashore.

In between, the trail tours natural wonders like the autumnal hawk migration over Mount Wachusett, the path's highest point. And it passes man-made sights like the Barre Falls Dam, a flood control project, not a hydroelectric plant. There's plenty of peaceful walking, though of course a long-distance trail must follow some paved roads to cross an entire state. The Midstate Trail depends on a great variety of landholders, including federal land at the dams, Audubon and Boy Scout preserves, wildlife management areas and state forests, and dozens of generous private property owners.

Please be respectful when passing near private homes. Leash your dog and keep your voice down, for the future of the trail depends on their largesse.

The Midstate Trail is well blazed with yellow triangles nailed to trees at head height. Since it is a conglomeration of independently maintained sections, always remember that the trail is subject to change according to erosion, traffic, seasons, private property rights, etc. This guide gives the main landmarks and distances, but it is up to you to bring a map and compass, and to carefully follow the blazes. If you're camping overnight on the trail, there are five designated shelters: Douglas State Forest, Moose Hill, Buck Hill, Long Pond, and Muddy Pond.

There are two important guides to have if you're hiking the Midstate Trail: the Appalachian Mountain Club's *Midstate Trail Guide,* fifth edition (a 55-page pamphlet) and the AMC's *Massachusetts and Rhode Island Trail Guide,* seventh edition (a 370-page book, though just 9 pages cover this trail). Both publications include maps. Note, however, that both these guides are written for the southbound hiker, so you may have to extrapolate some distances and directions. To buy either guidebook, check the trail group's website at www.midstatetrail.org, or contact the AMC at 5 Joy St., Boston, MA, 02108; (617) 523-0636. You could also phone the AMC's Worcester Chapter at (508) 797-9744. Always hike with a map; for the Midstate Trail, I rely on DeLorme's *Massachusetts Atlas and Gazetteer.*

The Ware River twists through countryside near the
Providence & Worcester Railroad line (hike 36). ▼

31 Midstate Trail Northbound

Day One

Cedar and hemlock trees fill this swampy, sandy land, which drains through many streams into nearby ponds and reservoirs. The trail follows wide, flat paths as it crosses MA 16 and ends at the village of West Sutton.

Start: From Southwest Main Street, in Douglas State Forest
Distance: 7.8 miles one way
Hiking time: About 3.5 hours
Difficulty: Easy and mostly flat
Trail surface: Broad, sandy, two-track dirt paths
Best season: Spring
Nearest town: Webster
Other trail users: Mountain bikers, cross-country skiers, equestrians

Canine compatibility: Dog friendly
Schedule: Open year-round; picnic area at main entrance open 10 a.m. to 8 p.m.
Fees and permits: None
Maps: USGS Webster, MA
Trail contact: MA Department of Conservation and Recreation, Douglas; (508) 476-7872; www.mass.gov/eea/agencies/dcr/massparks/region-central/douglas-state-forest.html or www.mass.gov/eea/images/dcr/parks/trail maps/midstatetrailmap.gif

Finding the trailhead: From Worcester, take I-395 south to exit 2, for Webster Center and Douglas. Turn right to drive east on MA 16 (aka Webster Street) for 5 miles, then turn right onto Cedar Street at signs for the forest entrance. At 5.8 miles, turn right onto Southwest Main Street and park on the shoulder of the road at 7.1 miles at a wooden Midstate Trail sign. To find more facilities, you could continue 1 mile farther south on Cedar Street until you reach the park's main entrance and nature center, located on Wallum Lake Road. There are picnic tables, map kiosks, park rangers, and a boat launching ramp here. Beginning your hike at the main entrance would add 1.5 miles to these directions. *DeLorme: Massachusetts Atlas & Gazetteer:* Page 50 M8. GPS: N42 02.348' / W71 47.021'

The Hike

The sandy flats of southern Massachusetts don't provide the climbs or views of the mountainous north, but Douglas State Forest offers more solitude than you'll find anywhere else on the trail.

Douglas State Forest is a 5,000-acre plot wedged into the corner of three state borders—Massachusetts, Connecticut, and Rhode Island. The 92-mile Midstate Trail

Just 2 miles from the Connecticut and Rhode Island state lines, the Midstate Trail heads north across Massachusetts.

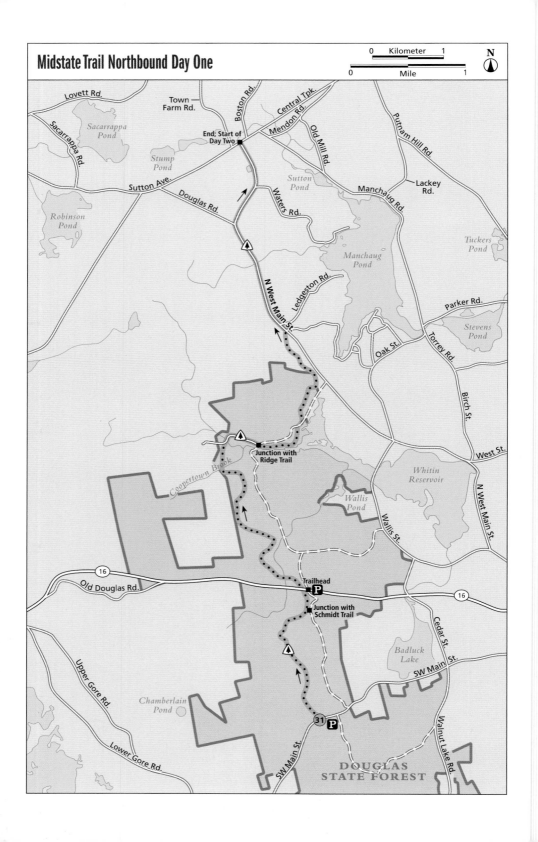

Midstate Trail Northbound Day One

0 ___ Kilometer ___ 1

0 ___ Mile ___ 1

N

Lovett Rd.

Town — Farm Rd.

Boston Rd.

Central Tpk.

Sacarrappa Rd.

Sacarrappa Pond

Mendon Rd.

Old Mill Rd.

Putnam Hill Rd.

Stump Pond

End; Start of Day Two

Sutton Pond

Manchaug Rd.

Lackey Rd.

Sutton Ave.

Douglas Rd.

Waters Rd.

Robinson Pond

Tuckers Pond

N West Main St.

Ledgeston Rd.

Manchaug Pond

Oak St.

Parker Rd.

Stevens Pond

Torrey Rd.

Coopertown Brook

Birch St.

West St.

Junction with Ridge Trail

Whitin Reservoir

Wallis Pond

N West Main St.

16

Old Douglas Rd.

Wallis St.

Trailhead P

16

Junction with Schmidt Trail

Upper Gore Rd.

Cedar St.

Badluck Lake

SW Main St.

Chamberlain Pond

31 P

Walnut Lake Rd.

Lower Gore Rd.

SW Main St.

DOUGLAS STATE FOREST

begins its northward trek here, at a granite monument on the border between Massachusetts and Rhode Island.

But this hike begins just north of the line, since there is no parking area directly at the trail's southern terminus. It rolls through deciduous forests and gentle hills scattered with large boulders. If you'd like to start this long-distance trail with one foot in Rhode Island, you can hike the 3.5 miles southbound first, then double back.

For another perspective on the region, the hike to Whitin Reservoir, also in Douglas State Forest, circles through the park's northern end, above MA 16.

Miles and Directions

0.0 Start on Southwest Main Street and head north, following the yellow triangles.

1.4 Turn left with the yellow blazes, passing a junction with the wide, sandy Schmidt Trail.

1.6 Cross the paved MA 16 (aka Webster Street). (**FYI:** This is the same trailhead as the Douglas State Forest loop.

4.1 Cross the wide, sandy Ridge Trail in a large intersection, following yellow blazes north as Coopertown Brook on your right flows toward Whitin Reservoir.

4.6 Turn right onto the broad Ridge Trail, and in 50 yards, turn left to leave it again, returning to the narrow Midstate Trail as you depart state forest land.

5.1 Merge onto a rocky road and pass behind a series of private homes.

5.8 Turn left onto the paved Northwest Main Street, at its intersection with Lakeshore Drive.

6.9 Turn right at a fork onto Douglas Road. (**Note:** Be careful, the left fork is also called Douglas Road.)

7.3 Pass by Waters Road on your right.

7.8 Reach Central Turnpike (aka Sutton Avenue) at West Sutton.

Hike Information

Local Information

Midstate Trail information on this park: www.midstatetrail.org/douglas.html

Organizations

Midstate Trail Association: www.midstatetrail.org

32 Midstate Trail Northbound

Day Two

Pass by corn fields, river basins, and a flood control dam on flat trails before switching to a section of paved roads and finishing at a tunnel crossing under US 20.

Start: From Central Turnpike in West Sutton
Distance: 10.6 miles one way
Hiking time: About 4 hours
Difficulty: Easy, with minimal elevation change
Trail surface: Mixture of dirt, gravel, and paved roads
Best season: Summer
Nearest town: Webster

Other trail users: Nonmotorized use only: mountain bikers, cross-country skiers, equestrians
Canine compatibility: Dog friendly
Schedule: Open year-round
Fees and permits: None
Maps: USGS Webster, MA
Trail contact: Midstate Trail Association, www .midstate trail.org

Finding the trailhead: From Worcester, take I-395 south to exit 4A, for Sutton, and drive east on Sutton Avenue. The road's name soon changes to Central Turnpike, and at 3.2 miles, reach West Sutton, where you'll park near a junction with Town Farm Road. *DeLorme: Massachusetts Atlas & Gazetteer:* Page 50 I8. GPS: N42 06.917' / W71 47.879'

The Hike

This stretch of the Midstate Trail is fairly urban, crossing I-395, coming through the town of Oxford, and passing through the French River basin near a large rock quarry.

The trail also twists through the US Army Corps of Engineers' Hodges Village Dam property; 1,200 acres filled with upland hardwoods, red oak, white oak, and hickory. The federal government manages the land for flood control, wildlife habitat, forest production, watershed protection, and outdoor recreation. In the autumn, hunting is allowed on this land, but only on the west side of the French River.

The nearby Buffumville Lake Project is a double reservoir resulting from the flood control dams. Bisected by Putnam Road, the north pond is 265 acres and the south 186 acres. Both are shallow, averaging about 6 feet deep.

Corn fields and grain silos blanket the hills along Town Farm Road.

Miles and Directions

0.0 Start at the intersection of Douglas Road and Central Turnpike in West Sutton. Head north on the paved Town Farm Road, climbing steeply to a hillside dotted with silos and blanketed with corn fields.

1.0 Turn left onto a dirt road, heading west into the woods along a border with the Merrill Pond Wildlife Management Area to the right.

2.2 Cross an earthen dam above Sacarrappa Pond to your left.

2.4 Cross through a cable gate onto paved Lovett Road.

3.1 Turn right onto Brown Road, heading north as you climb past farms, fields, and cattle.

4.4 Turn left onto Dana Road, heading west.

4.8 Pass under I-395 and cross over railroad tracks.

5.2 Turn right onto MA 12 (aka Main Street) in the town of Oxford, then immediately turn left onto Rocky Hill Road, heading west.

5.8 As the pavement ends, fork right to pass through a yellow metal gate onto a wide dirt trail. (*Note:* the gate on the left leads to the dam projects.)

6.4 Cross a metal footbridge over the French River and wind between a marsh to your left and a rock quarry to your right.

7.5 Follow a dirt road through a yellow metal gate onto the paved Old Charlton Road.

8.4 Turn left onto Turner Road, then pass over the Little River as it flows southward toward Buffumville Lake.

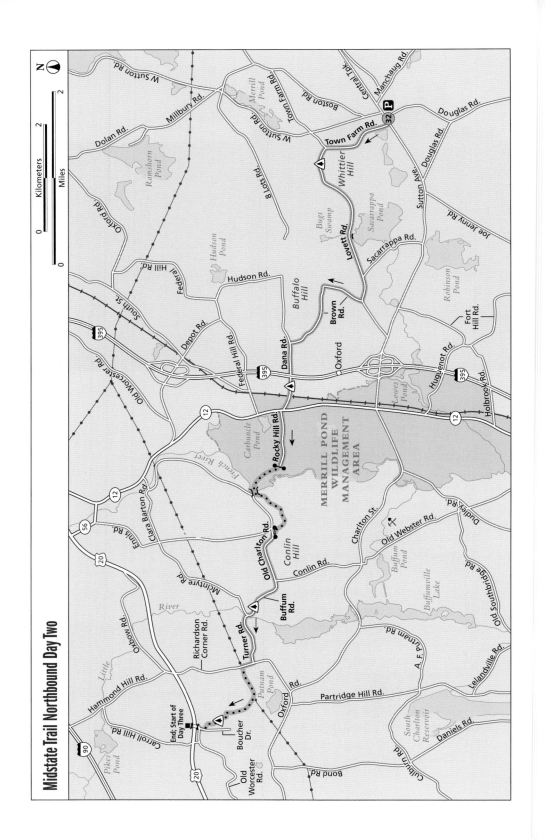

Midstate Trail Northbound Day Two

9.0 Turn right at a T intersection onto Richardson Corner Road.

9.1 Turn left onto a footpath, following a power line along a dirt trail.

10.3 Turn right onto the paved Boucher Drive, then immediately left onto a wooded path.

10.6 Cross under US 20 through a narrow, concrete, 50-yard drainage tunnel under a stone abutment, to reach the end of this segment at 10.6 miles.

Hike Information

Local Information

Buffumville Lake and Hodges Village Dam: Charlton; (508) 248-5697; www.nae.usace .army.mil/Missions/Recreation/HodgesVillageDam.aspx

Local Outdoor Retailers

New England Backpacker: Worcester; (508) 853-9407; www.newenglandbackpacker.com

Bolio Sporting Goods: Milford; (508) 634-3938; http://boliosportinggoods.com

Bert's Outdoor Store: Webster; (508) 943-3335

The trail crosses US 20 by burrowing through a 50-yard-long, concrete drainage tunnel.

33 Midstate Trail Northbound

Day Three

The region is full of swamps and streams, all draining toward Quabbin Reservoir just to the west. This trail section crosses the Mass Pike before passing quieter spots including an orchard, a pond, and a bird sanctuary.

Start: From US 20 near Charlton
Distance: 11.3 miles one way
Hiking time: About 4 hours
Difficulty: Moderate, alternating between swampland and rolling hills
Trail surface: Variable, including narrow hiking paths, broad logging roads, gravel, and pavement
Best season: Summer
Nearest town: Charlton
Other trail users: Snowmobilers, cross-country skiers

Canine compatibility: Dog friendly
Schedule: Open year-round
Fees and permits: None
Maps: USGS Worcester South, MA
Trail contacts: Burncoat Pond Wildlife Sanctuary, Spencer; (978) 464-2712; www .massaudubon.org/Nature_Connection/ Sanctuaries/Burncoat_Pond/. Spencer State Forest, Spencer; (508) 886-6333; www.mass .gov/eea/agencies/dcr/massparks/region -central/spencer-state-forest.html

Finding the trailhead: From Worcester, take US 20 west. Cross MA 56 in North Oxford, and in 3 miles, turn left at a light onto Old Worcester Road. At mile 3.1, turn left again and park on the shoulder at a junction with Boucher Drive. *DeLorme: Massachusetts Atlas & Gazetteer:* Page 49 G29. GPS: N42 08.836' / W71 56.203'

The Hike

This section of trail alternates between pavement and swampland as it winds between ponds and crosses two major state highways.

Beginning on US 20 between the rural neighborhoods of Charlton and Richardson Corners, it crosses the busy Mass Pike (I-90), then returns to more rural surroundings in the Four Chimneys Wildlife Management Area. Continuing northward, it crosses briefly through 965-acre Spencer State Forest, passing just west of Stiles Reservoir, and just north of Burncoat Pond. This section finally passes through Audubon land before reaching MA 9.

Burncoat Pond is the heart of a 220-acre bird sanctuary.

Miles and Directions

0.0 Start at the north end of the drainage tunnel under US 20 and turn left, walking west and parallel to US 20 close on your left.

0.4 Turn right onto paved Carroll Hill Road, then turn left onto an unmarked dirt road, heading uphill between two private homes.

0.8 Turn right along a clear-cut for a natural gas pipeline.

1.7 Turn right onto paved Northside Road, which soon passes over the Mass Turnpike (I-90).

2.2 Turn right at a stop sign onto paved Stafford Street, and in 50 yards, turn left onto a footpath. Climb past an orchard on your left and reenter the woods at the top of the hill.

3.0 Bear right onto paved Cemetery Road, then turn right at the bottom of a hill onto Gould Road, passing Wee Laddie Pond to your left.

3.4 Cross a railroad overpass and follow the yellow blazes straight ahead, onto the dirt Wheelock Road.

4.1 Continue walking north as the street becomes paved, then turn left onto a woods trail that leads into the Four Chimneys Wildlife Management Area.

5.4 Pass through a small dirt parking lot and metal gate and turn left onto paved Borkum Road.

5.8 Turn left onto the paved Clark Road, heading west. In 100 yards, turn right onto paved East Charlton Road, heading north past several junctions with local streets.

7.0 Turn right onto Ash Street, and in 100 yards, turn right again onto a dirt path crossing a field between two private homes.

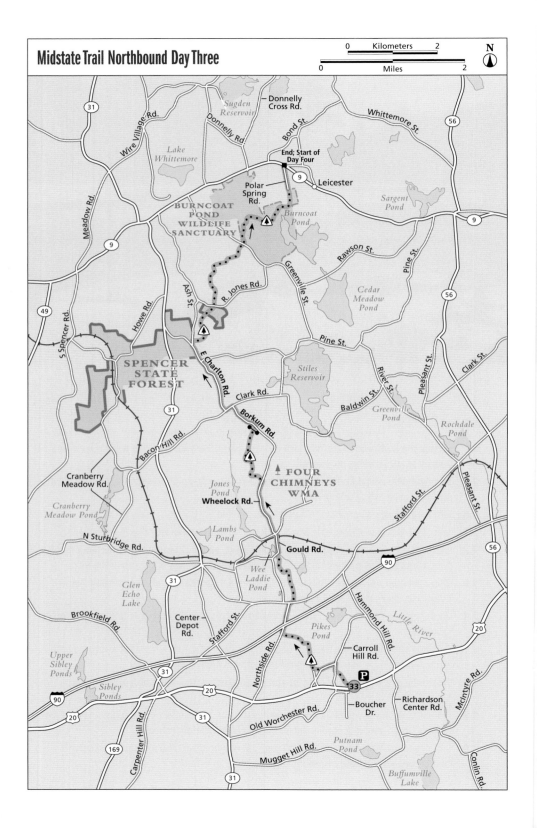

7.9 Cross the paved R. Jones Road.

9.1 Turn right onto paved Candlewood Drive, passing by a housing development.

9.3 Turn right onto paved Greenville Street, then in 50 yards, turn left onto a woods path.

10.1 Enter Mass Audubon's Burncoat Pond Wildlife Sanctuary.

10.9 Pass the Audubon entrance kiosk to leave the sanctuary and follow yellow blazes onto the dirt Polar Spring Road.

11.3 Reach MA 9 at the parking lot for a driving range between Spencer and Leicester.

Hike Information

Local Outdoor Retailers

New England Backpacker: Worcester; (508) 853-9407; www.newenglandbackpacker.com

Hay bales sit in the winter sun near Spencer State Forest.

34 Midstate Trail Northbound

Day Four

This marshy land is dotted with glacial features like moraines and erratics, as the trail provides expansive views over large reservoirs and solitary hilltops.

Start: From the junction of MA 9 and Polar Spring Road, just east of Tafts Corner
Distance: 8.6 miles one way
Hiking time: About 4 hours
Difficulty: Difficult, with many rolling hills and stream crossings
Trail surface: Alternating between marshy footpaths, steep hilltop scrambles, and gravel and paved roads
Best season: Summer
Nearest town: Spencer
Other trail users: Various
Canine compatibility: Dog friendly
Schedule: Open year-round

Fees and permits: None
Maps: USGS Worcester North, MA
Trail contacts: Moose Hill Wildlife Management Area; www.mass.gov/eea/docs/dfg/dfw/habitat/maps-wma/central/moosehillwma.pdf; Worcester County 4-H Center, Worcester; (508) 831-1223; http://worcestercounty4-h.org. Camp Marshall, Spencer; (508) 885-4891; www.campmarshall.net. Treasure Valley Scout Reservation, Worcester; (508) 752-3769; http://mohegancouncilbsa.doubleknot.com/treasure-valley-scout-reservation/29747

Finding the trailhead: From Worcester, go west on MA 9. Pass a junction with MA 56 in Leicester, and at 2.6 miles, turn left onto the dirt Polar Spring Road, adjacent to a golf driving range. *DeLorme: Massachusetts Atlas & Gazetteer:* Page 37 O28. GPS: N42 15.364' / W71 57.297'

The Hike

Passing through a patchwork quilt of public land, you curve between ponds and reservoirs, passing a rural airport, an overnight shelter, a 4-H campground, and a Boy Scout reservation.

The section starts on MA 9 at its intersection with Polar Spring Road, between Spencer and Leicester. You first pass though the 632-acre Moose Hill Wildlife Management Area and over Moose Hill itself, with great views of Sugden (aka Moose Hill) Reservoir. Pass just east of Spencer Airport, and then pass an overnight lean-to called the Buck Hill shelter. Walk by the horse barns, corrals, and summer campgrounds of the Worcester County 4-H Center before walking through the Boy Scouts' Treasure Valley Scout Reservation, maintained by Troop 126 in Leicester. Finally, reach the shores of 89-acre Browning Pond (maximum depth 42 feet).

Walk the ridge of Shaw Brook Dam, a huge earthen berm.

Miles and Directions

0.0 Start on the dirt Polar Spring Road and cross MA 9 to head north along the edge of an open field used by a plant nursery.

0.4 Cross paved Bond Street.

1.0 Cross paved Moose Hill Road (aka Howard Hurley Road).

1.2 Cross the top of the large, earthen Shaw Brook Dam creating Moose Hill Pond to your right. This site is just east of the larger Sugden Reservoir.

1.5 Pass through a metal gate and turn right onto Moose Hill Road (aka Donnelly Cross Road).

1.8 Turn left onto a dirt footpath and climb uphill into the Moose Hill Wildlife Management Area.

2.1 Curve around a private home and cross over the top of Moose Hill, an open hilltop with terrific views to all sides.

4.0 Cross paved Paxton Road, just north of the tiny Spencer Airport.

5.2 Cross Turkey Hill Brook on a concrete bridge, then continue climbing.

5.7 Pass by the Buck Hill shelter, a lean-to with a fire pit, just below the hilltop.

6.6 Turn right onto paved McCormick Road, passing by the Worcester County 4-H Center and Camp Marshall, and in 100 yards, turn left to reenter the woods on a narrow path.

7.6 Cross MA 31 (aka North Spencer Road) and turn left onto Browning Pond Road.

7.7 Turn right onto a hiking path, entering the Treasure Valley Scout Reservation.

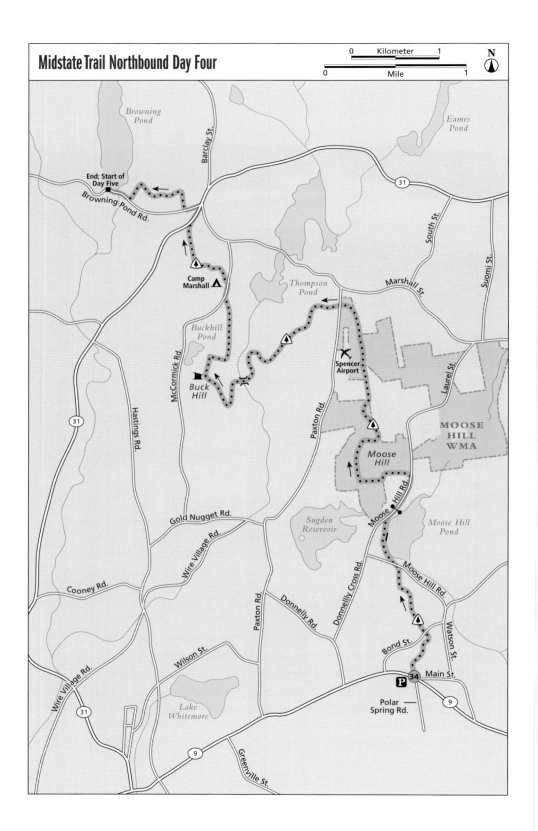

Midstate Trail Northbound Day Four

Kilometer

Mile

N

8.3 Turn left onto dirt Browning Pond Circle, and in 100 yards, turn right onto paved Browning Pond Road.

8.6 Turn right onto a woods trail, just on the southern shore of Browning Pond.

Hike Information

Accommodations

Spencer Country Inn: 500 Main St., Spencer; (508) 885-9036; www.spencercountry inn.com

An abandoned barn stands near the Moose Hill Wildlife Management Area.

35 Midstate Trail Northbound

Day Five

Wind past low-lying ponds and marshlands and pass through a state forest and a state park as you reach the halfway point of this long-distance trail before finishing at a flood control dam.

Start: From the southern tip of Browning Pond, in North Spencer
Distance: 11.5 miles one way
Hiking time: About 4 hours
Difficulty: Easy and flat
Trail surface: Wide dirt paths and roads
Best season: Summer
Nearest town: Worcester
Other trail users: Various
Canine compatibility: Dog friendly
Schedule: Barre Falls Dam park hours are sunrise to sunset
Fees and permits: None

Maps: USGS Worcester North, MA
Trail contacts: Ware River Watershed, Rutland; (508) 882-3636; www.mass.gov/eea/ agencies/dcr/massparks/region-central/ ware-river-watershed.html. Rutland State Park, Rutland; (508) 886-6333; www.mass.gov/ eea/agencies/dcr/massparks/region-central/ rutland-state-park.html. Mass Central Rail Trail, Florence; (413) 575-2277; www.masscentral railtrail.org/home.html. Barre Falls Dam, Hubbardston; (978) 318-8111; www.nae.usace .army.mil/Missions/Recreation/BarreFallsDam .aspx

Finding the trailhead: From Worcester, go west on MA 9. Pass a junction with MA 56 in Leicester, then turn right onto MA 31 North (aka Pleasant Street) in Spencer. The name changes to North Spencer Road. At 5.1 miles, turn left onto Browning Pond Road. At 6 miles, park in a small dirt lot on the right, at the southern tip of Browning Pond. *DeLorme: Massachusetts Atlas & Gazetteer:* Page 37 L26. GPS: N42 18.489' / W71 59.916'

The Hike

This hike begins at the southern end of Browning Pond in North Spencer, passes the enormous erratic known as Samson's Pebble, then reaches the midpoint of the Midstate Trail. From here there are 46 trail miles to reach either the Rhode Island or New Hampshire borders. Next you pass the Long Pond lean-to shelter, proceed into 300-acre Rutland State Park, skirt the western edge of Blood Swamp, and finally reach Barre Falls Dam.

Long Pond actually comprises three ponds—an 81-acre southern pond with a maximum depth of 25 feet, a much shallower middle pond (just a couple of feet deep), and the 30-acre north pond, which is shallow and weedy like the middle one—bisected by MA 122. The Mass Division of Fisheries and Wildlife recently

Pine Plain Road runs toward the Barre Falls Dam.

counted thirteen species of fish in these ponds: largemouth and smallmouth bass, chain pickerel, yellow perch, white perch, black crappie, bluegill, pumpkinseed, rock-bass, brown bullheads, white suckers, golden shiners, and rainbow trout (stocked).

Miles and Directions

0.0 Start on Browning Pond Road, pass through a metal gate, and head into the woods, keeping the pond on your right. In 100 yards, turn left onto a smaller path and begin to climb.

0.6 Crest the top of the hill and enter Oakham State Forest.

1.2 Pass by Sampson's Pebble, an enormous boulder dropped here by retreating glaciers.

2.9 Cross under a power line.

3.5 Pass a sign for the midpoint of the Midstate Trail, then immediately cross dirt East Hill Road.

3.9 Reach Long Pond and trace its western shore, keeping the water on your right and climbing steeply.

4.8 At the top of the hill, pass an overnight lean-to with a fire circle.

5.3 Cross paved Crawford Road.

5.8 Cross busy MA 122 (aka Barre Paxton Road) and pass through a yellow metal gate in a dirt parking lot on the other side, entering the Ware River Watershed and Rutland State Park.

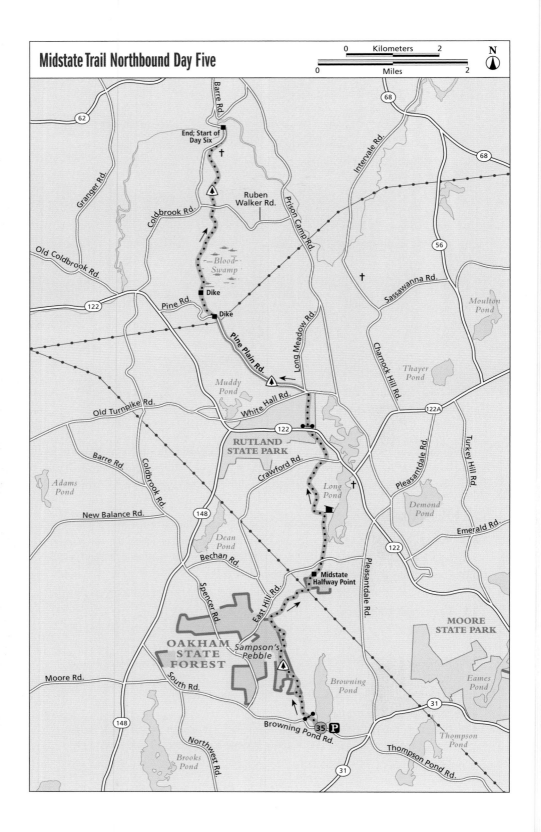

Kilometers

Miles

N

62

68

68

Barre Rd.

End; Start of
Day Six

†

Granger Rd.

Coldbrook Rd.

Ruben
Walker Rd.

Intervale Rd.

56

Old Coldbrook Rd.

*Blood-
Swamp*

Prison Camp Rd.

†

Sassawanna Rd.

*Moulton
Pond*

122

Pine Rd.

Dike

Dike

Pine Plain Rd.

Long Meadow Rd.

Charnock Hill Rd.

*Thayer
Pond*

*Muddy
Pond*

White Hall Rd.

Old Turnpike Rd.

122

122A

**RUTLAND
STATE PARK**

Turkey Hill Rd.

Pleasantdale Rd.

*Adams
Pond*

Barre Rd.

Coldbrook Rd.

Crawford Rd.

*Long
Pond*

†

*Demond
Pond*

Emerald Rd.

New Balance Rd.

148

*Dean
Pond*

122

Bechan Rd.

Midstate
Halfway Point

Pleasantdale Rd.

**MOORE
STATE PARK**

Spencer Rd.

East Hill Rd.

**OAKHAM
STATE
FOREST**

*Sampson's
Pebble*

*Browning
Pond*

*Eames
Pond*

Moore Rd.

South Rd.

31

Browning Pond Rd.

35

P

*Thompson
Pond*

148

Northwest Rd.

*Brooks
Pond*

Thompson Pond Rd.

31

5.9 Cross the Ware River Trail (part of the long-distance Mass Central Rail Trail) onto a smaller path.

6.4 Reach a large, dirt intersection, cross White Hall Road, and head northwest on the broad, straight Pine Plains Road. Long Meadow Road also heads north from this junction.

7.6 Fork right at a metal gate to stay on Pine Plains Road, then pass under a power line.

8.2 Pass a large, gravel flood control dam (Dike #3) on the right.

8.7 Pass another gravel dam (Dike #2, with paved Wood Road running along its ridge) on your left.

9.4 Pass close by Blood Swamp, keeping the water on your right.

10.2 Cross dirt Ruben Walker Road.

11.2 Merge right onto the dirt Coldbrook Road (soon becomes paved).

11.5 Reach Barre Falls Dam, with its picnic tables, parking lot, and restrooms.

Hike Information

Local Outdoor Retailers

New England Backpacker: Worcester; (508) 853-9407; www.newenglandbackpacker.com

Pass the halfway point of the Midstate Trail just south of Rutland State Park.

Day Six

Forested trails follow winding riverbanks as this section crosses MA 56 and MA 68 before ending the day at a bird sanctuary.

Start: From Barre Falls Dam
Distance: 11.8 miles one way
Hiking time: About 4 hours
Difficulty: Moderate, with narrow scrambly trails but without much elevation change
Trail surface: Dirt footpaths
Best season: Summer
Nearest town: Hubbardston
Other trail users: Mountain bikers, snowmobilers
Canine compatibility: Dog friendly

Schedule: Both Barre Falls Dam and Mass Audubon park hours are sunrise to sunset
Fees and permits: None
Maps: USGS Sterling, MA
Trail contacts: Barre Falls Dam, Hubbardston; (978) 318-8111; www.nae.usace.army.mil/ Missions/Recreation/BarreFallsDam.aspx. Wachusett Meadow Wildlife Sanctuary, Princeton; (978) 464-2712; www.massaudubon .org/Nature_Connection/Sanctuaries/Wachusett_Meadow/index.php

Finding the trailhead: From Leominster, follow MA 2 west to exit 22, for Gardner and Hubbardston. Circle a rotary to follow MA 68 South. Shortly after passing through Hubbardston, turn right at a flashing yellow light onto MA 62 West (aka Old Boston Turnpike). At 2.1 miles, turn left onto Barre Road, at signs for the Barre Falls Dam Picnic Area and US Army Corps of Engineers. At 3 miles, pass the park headquarters and cross the dam. At 3.2 miles, park in a small paved lot with picnic tables and restrooms. *DeLorme: Massachusetts Atlas & Gazetteer:* Page 37 E24. GPS: N42 25.634' / W72 01.422'

The Hike

This hike begins along the Ware River, then wanders through thick forest in somewhat higher ground. This is a tricky section of trail since it includes a large zigzag, heading south for nearly a mile even as you continue to move north overall. The route continues on dirt roads to Audubon's Wachusett Meadow Wildlife Sanctuary in Princeton.

Barre Falls Dam is a flood control reservoir for the Ware River. With normal water levels the river flows right through it, so there is no lake visible. The US Army Corps of Engineers completed it in 1958 at a cost of about $2 million. Its 885-foot length and 62-foot height could hold back almost eight billion gallons of floodwater.

Today there are many bluebird boxes in the floodplain below the dam. The trailhead parking area at the dam has restrooms, roofed picnic tables, and a map kiosk.

Hikers cross the Ware River on a footbridge just east of Hubbardston State Forest.

But be careful; there is hunting in these woods from the Saturday after Columbus Day to the Saturday after Thanksgiving. Also, a deep snowpack can linger in these woods long into March, making the trail impassable unless you have snowshoes or backcountry skis. After crossing Davis Street, you'll cross the busy MA 68, then skirt the southern edge of the 875-acre Savage Hill Wildlife Management Area. The hike ends just before Wachusett Meadow Wildlife Sanctuary, where you cannot take your dog. But you'll see plenty of animals, both those living naturally in the sanctuary, and also the herd of sheep that often graze around sanctuary headquarters. There are restrooms, trail maps, and a natural history center at Wachusett Meadow. And the Audubon sanctuary organizes hawk watching during the annual fall migration.

Miles and Directions

0.0 Start from the paved lot on the eastern side of Barre Falls Dam.

0.1 Cross the dam, passing a three-story concrete tower and the white park office building, and then a bridge over a concrete-walled spillway. Turn right immediately after the bridge, leaving the pavement and picking up the yellow Midstate Trail blazes as you wind down a grassy trail below the towering dam on your right.

0.5 Pass through a metal gate onto the dirt Tracy Road, with the Ware River close on your right.

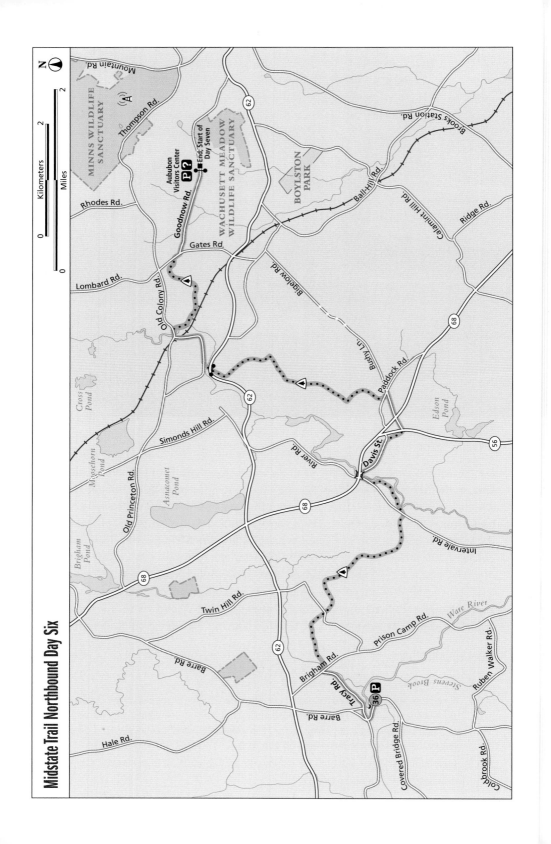

Midstate Trail Northbound Day Six

1.1 Turn right at a T intersection onto dirt Brigham Road, cross a wooden automobile bridge over the river, and turn left on the other side.

4.0 Cross the paved Intervale Road.

4.7 Turn right onto Intervale Road, and in 100 yards, turn right again onto MA 68. Cross a bridge over the Ware River and turn right once again, onto the paved, uphill Davis Street.

5.4 Turn right off the pavement onto a wide woods trail.

5.6 Cross paved MA 56 (aka Pommogussett Road) onto paved Bushy Lane.

5.8 Cross paved MA 68 (aka East County Road), continuing on Bushy Lane.

6.1 Turn left onto paved Paddock Road, and in 100 yards, turn right onto a woods trail that leads into UMass Amherst's Savage Hill Forest.

8.4 Pass through a red metal gate and turn right onto dirt Old Colony Road Extension.

8.6 Cross busy MA 62 (aka Hubbardston Road) onto paved Old Colony Road, and in 100 yards, turn right at a T intersection to continue along this road.

9.2 Cross a railroad track, then a wooden footbridge with gorgeous views of the Ware River. Turn right on the other side to reenter the woods.

10.6 Cross an open meadow through the Four Corners Town Hayfields conservation area.

10.7 Turn right onto paved Gates Road, then left onto paved Goodnow Road. This soon turns into the broad, dirt West Trail as you enter Audubon's Wachusett Meadow Wildlife Sanctuary.

11.8 Reach a metal gate at a junction with Chapman Trail. The Midstate Trail turns left to go north here, but you'll continue through the gate to end the day at the nearby sanctuary headquarters with its parking lot, restrooms, free maps, and natural history displays.

Hike Information

Local Information

Savage Hill Forest: Amherst; (413) 545-2665; http://eco.umass.edu/facilities/our -forest-properties/savage-hill-forest/

Four Corners Preservation Society: Princeton; www.fourcornerspreservationsociety.com

Local Events/Attractions

Apples, honey, and Christmas trees are for sale at homes and farms throughout this region.

Local Outdoor Retailers

Olympia Sports: Auburn; (508) 832-6032; www.olympiasports.net

37 Midstate Trail Northbound

Day Seven

Narrow dirt paths give way to steep, rocky trails as this section climbs from a bird sanctuary to Mount Wachusett and the Crow Hill Ledges before finishing the day 11.2 miles later at MA 2.

Start: From the visitor center at Wachusett Meadow Wildlife Sanctuary
Distance: 11.2 miles one way
Hiking time: About 3 hours
Difficulty: Moderate, due to some steep sections on Mount Wachusett
Trail surface: Dirt hiking trails, with some sections very rocky
Best season: Summer
Nearest town: Princeton
Other trail users: Hikers only on trails in Audubon sanctuaries; skiers and mountain bikers at Wachusett Mountain State Reservation
Canine compatibility: Pets are not allowed in Audubon's sanctuaries, where this hike begins, but there are many dogs at Wachusett Mountain State Reservation.
Schedule: Audubon sanctuary trail hours are sunrise to sunset

Fees and permits: Audubon charges an adult visitor fee.
Maps: USGS Sterling, MA
Trail contacts: Wachusett Meadow Wildlife Sanctuary, Princeton; (978) 464-2712; www.massaudubon.org/Nature_Connection/Sanctuaries/Wachusett_Meadow/index.php. Wachusett Mountain State Reservation, Princeton; (978) 464-2987; www.mass.gov/eea/agencies/dcr/massparks/region-central/wachusett-mountain-state-reservation.html. Redemption Rock, The Trustees of Reservations, Princeton; (413) 532-1631; www.thetrustees.org/places-to-visit/central-ma/redemption-rock.html. Leominster State Forest, Westminster; (978) 874-2303; www.mass.gov/eea/agencies/dcr/massparks/region-central/leominster-state-forest.html

Finding the trailhead: From Leominster, head west on MA 2 to exit 28, for Fitchburg and Princeton. Head south on MA 31 through Leominster State Forest, and at 3.9 miles, turn left at a blinking red light, continuing south on the combined MA 31 and MA 140. At 5.5 miles, turn right onto MA 31 (aka Princeton Road) at a blinking yellow light, then right again at 8.1 miles onto the combined MA 31 and MA 62 West. At 8.4 miles, bear right through the blinking yellow light at Princeton Center, to continue on MA 62 West (aka Hubbardston Road). Pass the gazebo on the town green. At 9 miles, turn right onto Goodnow Road. The wildlife sanctuary's parking lot is on the left in 1 mile. *DeLorme: Massachusetts Atlas & Gazetteer:* Page 38 C1. GPS: N42 27.352' / W71 54.521'

Binary boulders balance just south of the Wachusett ski area base lodge.

The Hike

Your reward at the middle of this hike is the sign in the parking lot at the Mount Wachusett ski area: MIDSTATE TRAIL: NEW HAMPSHIRE 23 MILES, RHODE ISLAND 69 MILES. FOLLOW THE YELLOW TRIANGLES. That sign sums up the Midstate Trail experience perfectly. Both ambitious and user friendly, the trail leads hikers carefully through woods, between parks, across roads, and around ponds, all the while heading northward to Mount Watatic and the state border just beyond.

This section of the Midstate Trail climbs from Audubon's pristine Wachusett Meadow Wildlife Sanctuary up the steep shoulders of Mount Wachusett, with its crowds, cars, and frequent festivals at the ski area's base lodge. But the mountain also has great beauty, like the garter snakes that awaken in these woods each spring, and the dozens of tall, silent windmills on the mountain's flank.

After descending to the ski area parking lot, you head north, meandering through the city of Fitchburg's watershed land, to historic Redemption Rock, a quarter-acre historic site managed by the Trustees of Reservations. It marks the spot where an early Concord settler negotiated with Native Americans for the release of a kidnapped minister's wife during King Philip's War in 1676, the bloody, last-gasp struggle by Native Americans against the pilgrims and settlers who were taking over their land.

Next the trail climbs over the steep Crow Hill Ledges of Leominster State Forest. Rock climbers love the ledges for their steep, exposed faces. And hikers love the ledges for their views of Crow Hill Pond and Crocker Pond just below, and glimpses of distant Boston far to the east. But it provides funny moments when the two meet, as hikers who stop to snack at cliff's edge can be suddenly joined by a helmeted head climbing up at their feet! This segment ends at Wyman Road, immediately off exit 26 of MA 2.

Miles and Directions

0.0 Start at the metal gate just west of the sanctuary parking lot, where the paved Goodnow Road turns to the dirt Beaver Bend Trail, and head north on Chapman Trail with the Midstate Trail's yellow blazes.

0.9 Cross the dirt Thompson Road and soon leave Audubon land.

1.7 Cross paved Westminster Road and pick up the Harrington Trail/Midstate Trail on the other side.

2.4 Cross a small wooden footbridge over West Wachusett Brook, then cross the dirt West Road and continue along Harrington/Midstate.

2.7 Cross the gravel Administration Road. Pass a junction with Semuhenna Trail, then turn right onto the Link Trail.

3.1 Turn left at a T onto the Mountain House Trail, soon crossing the paved Summit Road.

3.3 Cross a parking lot, pass by the Wachusett Mountain Summit fire tower, and pick up the yellow blazes again at a sign for Old Indian Trail as you walk past a chairlift terminal.

4.3 Cross paved Summit Road as the Midstate Trail runs along Semuhenna Trail, then Old Indian Trail again.

4.8 Cross dirt Balance Rock Road and reach a pair of stacked, car-sized boulders.

5.2 Emerge into the ski area's large parking lot and walk around its edge, keeping the base lodge buildings close on your right side.

5.4 Cross a wooden footbridge over a duck pond marked with a fountain and a flagpole and cross paved Mountain Road to a footpath in the woods.

6.4 Reach the small dirt parking lot at Redemption Rock and soon cross the paved MA 140.

6.6 Pass by a large glacial boulder on your left and continue climbing uphill, soon scaling a steep cliff and reaching an overlook with great views of Mount Wachusett.

8.1 Follow the yellow blazes in a left turn up a series of rock cliffs—Crow Hill Ledges. Turn right at the top of the cliffs and soon reach an overlook with views of Crow Hills Pond and MA 31 to the southeast, and rock climbers under your feet.

8.9 Descend from the ledges on a series of 100 steep stone steps built by the CCC.

Kilometers

0   2

Miles

0   2

N

State Rd.

140

2

2A

Willard Rd.

Turnpike Rd.

2

Main St.

Round
Meadow
Pond

Waterman
Ln.

Depot Rd.

Sawmill
Pond

31

End; Start of
Day Eight

Wachusett
Village Inn

Narrows Rd.

Stone
Hill Rd.

Notown Rd.

Meetinghouse
Pond

140

Wyman
Pond

East Rd.

Crow
Hill
Ledges

Crocker
Pond

South St.

Davis St.

Princeton Rd.

Park Rd.

140

LEOMINSTER
STATE FOREST

Rocky Pond Rd.

31

Bolton Rd.

Wachusett
Lake

Redemption
Rock

Paradise
Pond

Noyes
Pond

Balance Rock

Ski Area

P

Mare
Meadow
Reservoir

Balance Rock Rd.

Old
Indian Trail

North Rd.

Summit Rd.

Summit Rd.

WACHUSETT
MOUNTAIN STATE
RESERVATION

140

31

Lanes Rd.

W. Princeton Rd.

West Rd.

Summit
Rd. Loop

Bickford
Pond

Greene Rd.

Harrington Trail

Wachusett
Mtn. Summit

Mountain Rd.

Beaman Rd.

140

31

Rhodes Rd.

Administration
Rd.

Westminster Rd.

Mirick Rd.

31

Thompson Rd.

Chapman Trail

Goodnow   Road

37

? P

Merriam Rd.

Gates Rd.

Audubon
Visitor Center

Radford Rd.

62

62

62

WACHUSETT MEADOW
WILDLIFE SANCTUARY

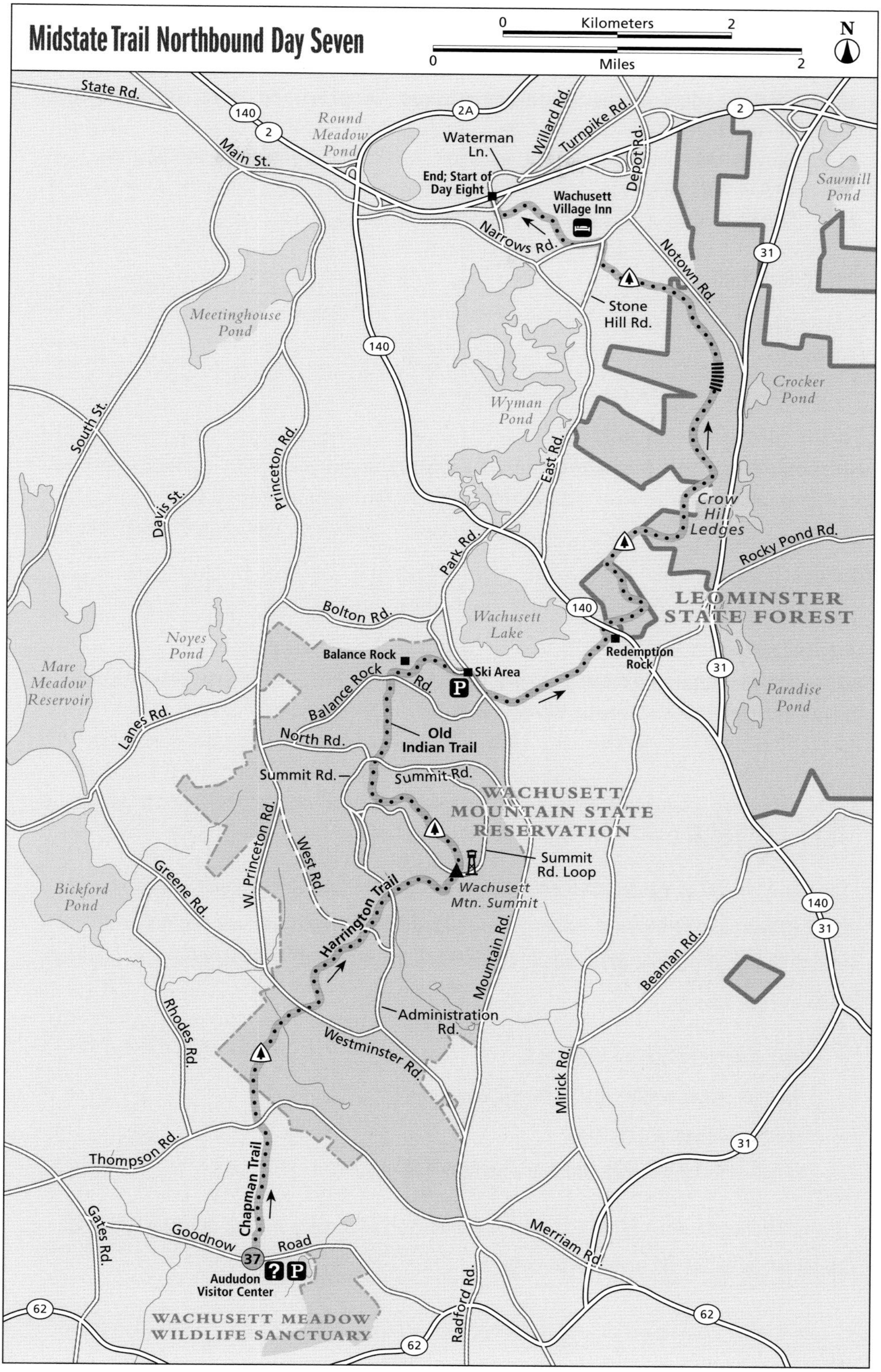

10.0 Turn right onto the paved Stone Hill Road, then cross paved Narrows Road, walk over a wooden car bridge, and turn left onto a hiking path on the other side.

10.8 Reach the paved parking lot behind the Wachusett Village Inn, skirt the left edge of the lot, and reenter woods on the other side.

11.0 Turn right onto paved Barrett Lane, left onto Village Inn Road, and right onto Waterman Lane to cross over MA 2.

11.2 Turn left onto a paved utility road just on the north side of MA 2.

Hike Information

Local Information
The Holden *Landmark:* www.thelandmark.com. A small, weekly newspaper, full of local links and information.

Local Events/Attractions
Audubon's Wachusett Meadow Wildlife Sanctuary organizes events including a bird-seed sale, fall harvest festival, bird-a-thon bird watching, and a book sale.

Accommodations
Wachusett Village Inn: Westminster; (978) 874-3783; www.wachusettvillageinn.com. Also offers sleigh rides in the winter; reservations required.

Organizations
Wachusett Mountain Ski Area: Princeton; www.wachusett.com. Hosts events and fairs year-round; check the website for scheduling.

FALL FOLIAGE

The visitor center at Wachusett Meadow explains that New England's famous foliage changes color in the autumn because leaves lose the green chlorophyll that has masked their true colors all year. As a rule of thumb, it offers the following guide to identifying trees by the color of their foliage.

> Red: blueberry, sumac, red maple
>
> Orange: sugar maple, shadbush, white oak
>
> Yellow: quaking aspen, alder
>
> Violet: viburnum maple, white ash (may also be yellow)

Mount Wachusett also has an excellent visitor center, accessible by trail or by car, on Mountain Road, near the ski area's base lodge.

38 Midstate Trail Northbound

Day Eight

This quiet section crosses open cattle pastures and hay fields, then wooded conservation land and logging roads before ending at MA 12.

Start: From the Waterman Bridge overpass, which crosses MA 2 at exit 26
Distance: 8.0 miles one way
Hiking time: About 3 hours
Difficulty: Easy, with dirt paths and no major climbing
Trail surface: Dirt footpaths winding through woods
Best season: Summer
Land status: Westminster Conservation Commission

Nearest town: Fitchburg
Other trail users: None
Canine compatibility: Trail passes close to private homes, so be careful of other dogs
Schedule: Open year-round
Fees and permits: None
Maps: USGS Fitchburg, MA
Trail contacts: AMC, Worcester Chapter, www.amcworcester.org. Midstate Trail website, www.midstatetrail.org

Finding the trailhead: From Leominster, take MA 2 west to exit 27, for Narrows Road and Depot Road. Turn left onto Narrows Road, and at 0.2 mile, turn right onto Village Inn Road. Turn left at 0.8 mile and park in the large lot behind the Wachusett Village Inn. *DeLorme: Massachusetts Atlas & Gazetteer:* Page 26 M3. GPS: N42 35.592' / W71 53.018'

The Hike

This stretch of the Midstate Trail begins and ends on busy roads, but passes through quiet woods in between. Its reward is a visit to the beautiful Muddy Pond shelter at the hike's midpoint, before it finishes on MA 12 just southeast of Ashburnham.

The Midstate Trail follows a slow and steady climb from Round Meadow Pond through wooded agricultural land, passing tractors and caged turkeys and rabbits in rural backyards. It crosses under an MBTA rail line and over the Whitman River, emerging at the main intersection in Whitmanville, which is not really a town, but the intersection of four streets: Bragg Hill Road, South Ashburnham Road, Whitmanville Road, and Oakmont Avenue.

Climb gently from the Whitman River up Bragg Hill, reaching Muddy Pond in another 1.6 miles. With a lean-to shelter (maintained by the Westminster Conservation Commission), fire pit, and gorgeous lakeside views, this is a great spot for lunch. Muddy Pond drains into Whitman Reservoir, which flows into the Whitman River and feeds Crocker Pond. The hike continues through tall trees and stone walls, ending when you cross Phillips Brook near Ashburnham.

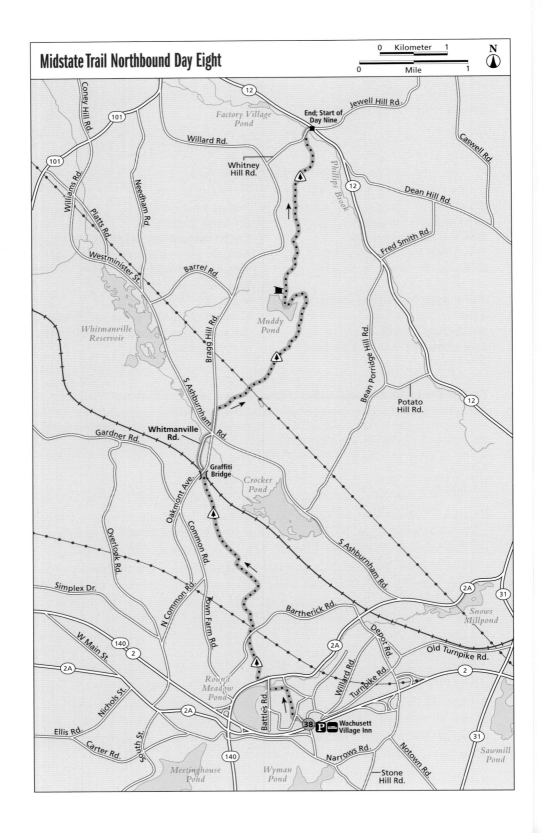

Midstate Trail Northbound Day Eight

Jewell Hill Rd.

12

Coney Hill Rd.

101

Factory Village Pond

End; Start of Day Nine

Caswell Rd.

Willard Rd.

Williams Rd.

Whitney Hill Rd.

Phillips Brook

12

Dean Hill Rd.

Needham Rd.

101

Platts Rd.

Fred Smith Rd.

Westminister St.

Barrel Rd.

Whitmanville Reservoir

Bragg Hill Rd.

Muddy Pond

Bean Porridge Hill Rd.

S Ashburnham Rd.

Potato Hill Rd.

12

Gardner Rd.

Whitmanville Rd.

Graffiti Bridge

Crocker Pond

Oakmont Ave.

S Ashburnham Rd.

Overlook Rd.

Common Rd.

2A

31

Simplex Dr.

N Common Rd.

Town Farm Rd.

Bartherick Rd.

Snows Millpond

2A

W Main St.

140

2

Round Meadow Pond

Willard Rd.

Depot Rd.

Old Turnpike Rd.

2

Turnpike Rd.

Nichols St.

2A

Battles Rd.

38

P

Wachusett Village Inn

31

Ellis Rd.

Carter Rd.

South St.

140

Meetinghouse Pond

Wyman Pond

Narrows Rd.

Notown Rd.

Stone Hill Rd.

Sawmill Pond

Muddy Pond hosts a range of animal life, including this garter snake.

Miles and Directions

0.0 Start at the paved utility road off the Waterman Bridge overpass, about 50 yards on the north side of MA2, and follow yellow blazes through a metal gate.

0.7 Turn right onto paved Battles Road, passing by Round Meadow Pond to your left.

0.8 Cross paved Merriam Road, immediately turn left onto MA 2A (aka State Road East), then turn right onto a woods path.

1.3 Cross Bartherick Road, then under a power line.

1.8 Follow a stone wall between hay fields filled with cattle. Watch for cow patties.

3.3 Turn right onto paved Oakmont Avenue, walk under the stone railroad overpass called the Graffiti Bridge, then immediately turn left onto the dead end of paved Whitmanville Road.

3.8 Cross busy South Ashburnham Road and head uphill on the paved Bragg Hill Road.

4.0 At the top of a rise, turn right onto a dirt road leading into town conservation land.

4.5 Pass under a power line as you follow a broad logging road through the woods.

5.4 Cross a stone wall as the trail narrows to a footpath.

6.0 Reach a wooden overnight shelter with its fire circle and gorgeous views of Muddy Pond.

7.9 Turn right onto dirt Whitney Hill Road.

8.0 Cross a wooden footbridge over Phillips Brook and reach MA 12 (aka Fitchburg Road).

Hike Information

Accommodations

Wachusett Village Inn: Westminster; (978) 874-3783; www.wachusettvillageinn.com

Restaurants

Mill No. 3 Farmstand: Fitchburg; (978) 345-1100; www.millno3.com. The store is on MA 31, 0.9 mile north of its intersection with MA 2A South and 0.2 mile south of its intersection with MA 12 North. It offers fresh produce, coffee, a bakery, deli sandwiches, and even Christmas trees in season.

Hike Tours

Five-star Adventures: Wachusett Village Inn, Westminster; (978) 939-7354; www.five staroutdooradventures.com

Other Resources

Montachusett Regional Vo-Tech: Fitchburg; (978) 345-9200; www.montytech.net. Website lists regional events, appearances, and performances.

◀ *A forgotten tractor sits on conservation land just north of Whitmanville.*

39 Midstate Trail Northbound

Day Nine

This final section hits a series of peaks, rolling over Mount Hunger and Fisher Hill before it crosses MA 119 and finally ascends rocky Mount Watatic.

Start: From MA 12 just southeast of Ashburnham
Distance: 8.8 miles one way
Hiking time: About 3 hours
Difficulty: Difficult, due to steep climbs and twisting trails
Trail surface: Mostly dirt, with some rocky scrambling
Best season: Summer
Nearest town: Ashburnham

Other trail users: None
Canine compatibility: Dog friendly
Schedule: Open year-round
Fees and permits: None
Maps: USGS Ashburnham, MA
Trail contacts: Friends of the Wapack Trail, West Peterborough; www.wapack.org. Nashua River Watershed Association, Groton; (978) 448-0299; www.nashuariverwatershed.org

Finding the trailhead: From Leominster, follow MA 2 west to exit 28, for Fitchburg and Princeton. Follow MA 31 North (aka Princeton Road) toward Fitchburg. At 2.1 miles, take a hairpin left turn at a stop sign in West Fitchburg, onto MA 12 North (aka Ashburnham Street). At 4.4 miles, park on the shoulder at Blackburn Village, an intersection between the dirt Whitney Hill Road on the left and Jewell Hill Road on the right. *DeLorme: Massachusetts Atlas & Gazetteer:* Page 26 H3. GPS: N42 37.549' / W71 52.913'

The Hike

After crossing Russell Hill Road, the trail climbs steeply and follows a rolling ridgeline between Brown Hill and Mount Hunger, with awesome views of Stodge Meadow Pond and surrounding hilltops to the north. These outlooks are a popular destination for hikers, so expect some company. Descending from the ridge, the trail threads between the 118-acre Winnekeag Lake and Stodge Meadow Pond, briefly tracing MA 101.

This is the last northbound leg of the 92-mile Midstate Trail, depositing the hiker on the New Hampshire line, just past the summit of Mount Watatic. At 1,832 feet in elevation, it is the second-largest mountain in Massachusetts east of the Connecticut River (Mount Wachusett is 2,006 feet). Also, Watatic is a major viewing point for the annual hawk migration every fall, so keep your eyes on the skies if you're here in season. A granite monument on the peak pays tribute to the conservation efforts that have protected this beautiful spot:

Stone cairns stand on the summit of Mount Watatic.

Other stones in other places may commemorate the histories of people and things now dead and gone. This stone marks the site of a mountain that lived, a mountain that lives on because of people who cared, people who started with nothing but a dream and the will to work for it, until the dream became as real, as solid as this stone, as sure as the ground beneath your feet, as true as this mountain on which you stand, this mountain holding you up to meet the sky.

In truth, the summit is the emotional end of the line, unless you really want to walk the extra 1.2 miles to a nondescript stone wall in the woods marking the state line and the Midstate Trail terminus.

The Friends of the Wapack Trail, another long-distance path, have posted topo maps at major intersections through these woods. The Wapack Trail heads 21 miles north from Mount Watatic to North Pack Monadnock, in Greenfield, New Hampshire, passing over the peaks of Pratt, New Ipswich, Barrett, and Temple Mountains along the way. For a history of the ski area that formerly existed on the slopes of Mount Watatic, check the New England Lost Ski Areas Project at www.nelsap.org/ma/watatic.html.

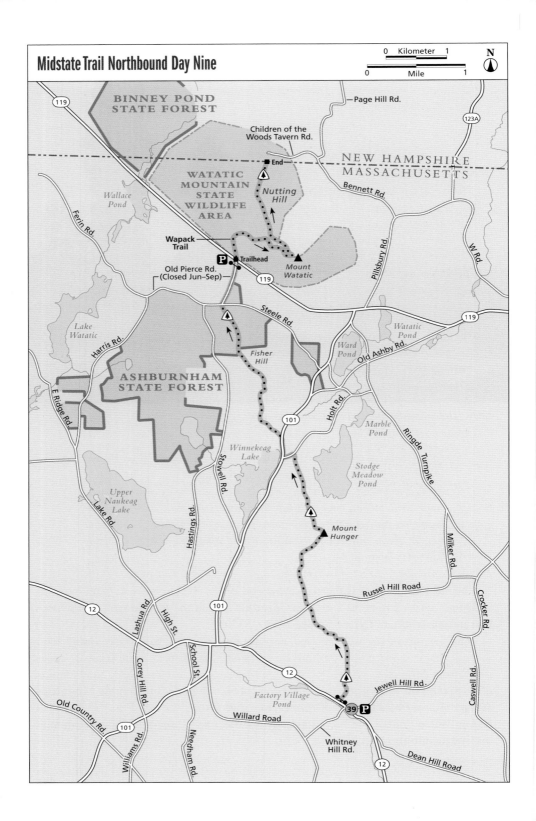

Miles and Directions

0.0 Start at the intersection of Whitney Hill Road and MA 12. Head north on MA 12, and in 100 yards, turn right onto a narrow woods trail.

1.5 Cross the paved Russell Hill Road and climb steeply.

2.5 Reach the bare rock ledges of Mount Hunger, with great views of Stodge Meadow Pond and Mount Watatic to the north. Then descend through a thick hemlock forest.

3.5 Turn left onto the paved Holt Road.

3.7 Turn right onto MA 101 (aka Ashby Road), skirting the shore of Lake Winnekeag.

3.9 Turn left onto a narrow woods trail, 50 yards north of the entrance to Camp Winnekeag. Follow the yellow blazes as you pass several other foot trails and begin to climb steeply.

4.7 Reach an open, grassy hilltop and cross over Fisher Hill, soon entering Ashburnham State Forest with its thick forest of hemlock and white pine.

5.8 Cross a logging road and turn right onto dirt Old Pierce Road, which soon becomes paved.

6.3 Cross MA 119 (aka Rindge Street) to the dirt parking lot for Mount Watatic Reservation. Pass through the metal gate and follow yellow blazes for the Midstate Trail, coinciding here with the Wapack Trail, and begin to climb.

7.5 Reach a stone cairn at the summit of Mount Watatic, with its 360-degree views and whipping winds. (**Note:** The Midstate Trail takes a hairpin left turn just *before* reaching the summit, so you must retreat slightly to continue along a wooded footpath.)

8.2 Cross the open, rocky ridgeline of Nutting Hill, following yellow blazes painted on the rock.

8.4 Turn right at a fork to leave the Mount Watatic Reservation; continue following yellow blazes and the Wapack Trail down a wide woods road.

8.7 Reach the New Hampshire border at an unremarkable stone wall. To reach the Midstate Trail's granite monument, turn left onto a narrow trail along this wall, at a sign reading MST CONNECTOR, MA ROUTE 119, 1.25 MILES.

8.8 Reach a granite block set in the wall, reading MIDSTATE TRAIL, NH-RI, 1985. Continue to follow these blue blazes for a quick return to the trailhead on MA 119.

Hike Information

Local Information

Ashburnham Lakes Coalition: www.ashburnhamlakescoalition.org

Camp Winnekeag: www.adventistcamps.org/article/22/camp-directory/camp-winnekeag. A Christian youth camp and convention center operated by the Southern New England Conference of Seventh Day Adventists.

Restaurants

Village Pizza: Ashburnham; www.ashburnhampizza.com

Other Resources

Johnny Appleseed Visitors Information Center: www.appleseed.org. This rest stop on MA 2 westbound, between exits 34 and 35, offers food, restrooms, maps, and books on natural history and Native Americans.

NURSERY RHYMES IN MASSACHUSETTS

On September 26, 1774, a boy named John Chapman was born in Leominster. He traveled the country spreading seeds, eventually earning the name Johnny Appleseed. Today he is remembered by the Johnny Appleseed Trail, which is MA 2 from its junction with I-495 in the east to its junction with I-91 in the west.

Johnny is not the only nursery rhyme hero who hailed from Massachusetts. In the early 1800s, Mary Elizabeth Sawyer was born near Sterling. Like most rural families of that era, the Sawyers kept sheep, and in 1816 Mary's father let her adopt a newborn lamb. She cared for it so well that it followed her as she walked to school that spring, so she snuck it into the classroom. The animal was quickly discovered, and someone wrote a poem about the pair— "Mary Had a Little Lamb." A replica of that original schoolhouse stands in Sudbury today.

For more information about the Johnny Appleseed Trail, phone (978) 534-2302 or check www.appleseed.org. If you're there in the fall, check the website for a list of more than twenty local orchards, and fill a sack with fresh fruits and vegetables after your hike.

Local Outdoor Retailers

Maynard Outdoor Store: Maynard; (978) 897-2133; www.maynardoutdoor.net

◄   *The Wapack Trail offers cool and shade less than a mile from the peak.*

The Art of Hiking

When standing nose to snout with a bear, you're probably not too concerned with the issue of ethical behavior in the wild. No doubt you're just wetting yourself. But let's be honest. How often are you nose to snout with a bear? For most of us a hike into the "wild" means loading up the 4-Runner with everything North Face and driving to a toileted trailhead. Sure, you can mourn how civilized we've become—how GPS units have replaced natural instinct and Gore-Tex, true grit—but the silly gadgets of civilization aside, we have plenty of reason to take pride in how we've matured. With survival now on the back burner, we've begun to reason—and it's about time—that we have a responsibility to protect, no longer just conquer, our wild places; that they, not we, are at risk. So please, do what you can. A walk in the woods is a nice opportunity to marvel at the natural world and renew your energy to preserve it. Now, in keeping with our chronic tendency to reduce everything to a list, here are some rules to remember.

Zero impact. Always leave an area just like you found it—if not better than you found it. Avoid camping in fragile areas and along the banks of streams and lakes. Use a camp stove versus building a wood fire. Pack out all your trash and extra food. Bury human waste at least 200 feet from water sources under 6 to 8 inches of topsoil. Don't bathe with soap in a lake or stream—bathe in the water without soap. Leave what you find. As a general rule, don't gather plants, animals, artifacts, or rocks. Some places, including national parks, prohibit taking anything. Know and abide by the rules and regulations of the land on which you travel.

Stay on the trail. It's true, a path anywhere leads nowhere new, but purists will just have to get over it. Paths serve an important purpose; they limit our impact on natural areas. Straying from a designated trail may seem innocent, but it can cause damage to sensitive areas—damage that may take years to recover, if it can recover at all. Even simple shortcuts can be destructive. So please, stay on the trail. Take a moment to appreciate the work that went into the creation and maintenance of a trail for your enjoyment.

Keep your dog under control. You can buy a flexi-lead that allows your dog to go exploring along the trail while allowing you the ability to reel him in should another hiker approach or should he decide to chase a rabbit. Massachusetts state parks require a 6-foot maximum leash. Always obey leash laws, and be sure to bury your dog's waste or pack it out in plastic bags.

Yield to horses. When you approach these animals on the trail, always step quietly off the trail and let them pass. If you are wearing a large backpack, it's a good idea to sit down. From a horse's perspective, a hiker wearing a large backpack is a scary trail monster, and these sensitive animals can be spooked easily.

The trail crosses open meadows at the Four Corners Town Hayfields conservation area (hike 36).

Getting into Shape

Unless you want to be sore or, worse, sustain an injury—and possibly have to shorten your trip or vacation—be sure to get in shape before a big hike. If you're terribly out of shape, start a walking program early, preferably eight weeks in advance. Start with a 15-minute walk during your lunch hour or after work and gradually increase your walking time to an hour. You should also increase your elevation gain. Walking briskly up hills strengthens your leg muscles and gets your heart rate up. If you work in a storied office building, take the stairs instead of the elevator. If you prefer going to a gym, walk the treadmill or use a Stairmaster. You can further increase your strength and endurance by walking with a loaded backpack. Stationary exercises you might consider are squats, leg lifts, sit-ups, and push-ups. Other good ways to get in shape include biking, running, aerobics, and, of course, short hikes.

Preparedness

It's been said that failing to plan means planning to fail. So do take the necessary time to plan your trip. Whether going on a short day hike or an extended backpack trip, always prepare for the worst. Traveling with an awareness and attitude of safety consciousness is the best way to prevent problems from arising in the first place. In order to remain comfortable, you need to concern yourself with the basics: water, food, and shelter. Don't go on a hike without having these bases covered. And don't go on a hike expecting to find these items in the woods.

Water. Even in frigid conditions you need at least 2 quarts of water per day to function efficiently. Add heat and taxing terrain and you can bump that figure up to 1 gallon. That's simply a base to work from—your metabolism and your level of conditioning can raise or lower that amount. Unless you know your level, assume that you need 1 gallon of water per day. Now, where do you plan on getting the water?

Preferably not from natural water sources. These sources can be loaded with intestinal disturbers, such as bacteria, viruses, and fertilizers. *Giardia lamblia,* the most common of these disturbers, is a protozoan parasite that lives part of its lifecycle as a cyst in water sources. The parasite spreads when mammals defecate in water sources. Once ingested, giardia can induce cramping, diarrhea, vomiting, and fatigue within two days to two weeks after ingestion. Giardia and other parasites are treatable. If you get sick after drinking untreated water, you may have a parasite. See a doctor immediately.

Treating water. The best and easiest solution to avoid polluted water is to carry your water with you. Depending on the nature of your hike and the duration, however, this may not be an option—seeing as 1 gallon of water weighs 8.5 pounds. In that case you'll need to look into treating water. Regardless of which method you choose, you should always carry some water with you in case of an emergency. Save this reserve until you absolutely need it.

There are three methods of treating water: boiling, chemical treatment, and filtering. If you boil water, it's recommended that you do so for 10 to 15 minutes; 20

minutes kills all disease-causing organisms including hepatitis. This is often impractical because you're forced to exhaust a great deal of your fuel supply. Giardia dies at 170° F. Since water boils at 210° F, bringing water to a boil is an easy and effective way to ensure water has reached 170° F. You can opt for chemical treatment (e.g., Potable Aqua), which will kill giardia but will not take care of other chemical pollutants. Another drawback to chemical treatments can be the unpleasant taste of the water after it's treated. You can remedy this by adding neutralizing tablets after the water has finished treatment. Another way to minimize the taste is to add powdered drink mix to the already treated water. Filters are the preferred method for treating water. Filters remove giardia, organic and inorganic contaminants, and don't leave an aftertaste. Water filters are far from perfect, as they can easily become clogged or leak if a gasket wears out. It's always a good idea to carry a backup supply of chemical treatment tablets in case your filter decides to quit on you.

Food. If we're talking about "survival," you can go days without food, as long as you have water. But we're talking about "comfort" here. Try to avoid foods that are high in sugar and fat like candy bars and potato chips. These food types are harder to digest and are low in nutritional value. Remember, the saying "you are what you eat" rings true, and if you eat junk foods, that is what you'll feel like at the end of the day. Instead, bring along foods that are easy to pack, nutritious, and high in energy (e.g., bagels, nutrition bars, dehydrated fruit, gorp, and jerky). If you are on an overnight trip, easy-to-fix dinners include rice mixes with dehydrated potatoes, corn, pasta with cheese sauce, and soup mixes. For a tasty breakfast you can fix hot oatmeal with brown sugar and reconstituted milk powder topped off with banana chips. If you like a hot drink in the morning, bring along herbal tea bags or hot chocolate. If you are a coffee junkie, you can purchase coffee that is packaged like tea bags. You can prepackage all your meals in heavy-duty resealable plastic bags to keep food from spilling in your pack. These bags can be reused to pack out trash.

Shelter. The type of shelter you choose depends less on the conditions than on your tolerance for discomfort. Shelter comes in many forms—tent, tarp, lean-to, bivy sack, cabin, cave, etc. If you're camping in the desert, a bivy sack may suffice, but if you're above the treeline and a storm is approaching, a better choice is a three- or four-season tent. Tents are the logical and most popular choice for most backpackers because they're lightweight and packable—and you can rest assured that you'll always have shelter from the elements. Before you leave on your trip, anticipate what the weather and terrain will be like, and plan for the type of shelter that will work best for your comfort level.

Finding a campsite. If there are established campsites, stick to those. If not, start looking for a campsite early—like around 3:30 or 4 p.m. Stop at the first appropriate site you see, remembering that good campsites are found and not made. Depending on the area, it could be a long time before you find another suitable location. Pitch your camp in an area that's reasonably level and clear of underbrush (which can harbor insects and conceal approaching animals). Make sure the area is at least 200 feet from fragile areas like lakeshores, meadows, and stream banks. Woody stemmed plants like kinnikinnik, blueberry, and whortleberry are easily damaged, so avoid plopping your tent on top of them. Try to avoid camping above treeline, as the tundra is fragile, and you're exposing yourself to possible high winds and lightning.

If you are camping in stormy, rainy weather, look for a rock outcrop or a shelter in the trees to keep the wind from blowing your tent all night. Be sure that you don't camp under trees with dead limbs that might break off on top of you. Also, try to find an area that has an absorbent surface, such as sandy soil or forest duff. This, in addition to camping on a surface with a slight angle, will provide better drainage. By all means, don't dig trenches to provide drainage around your tent—remember you're practicing zero-impact camping.

If you're in bear country, steer clear of creek beds or animal paths. If you see any signs of a bear's presence (e.g., scat, footprints), relocate. You'll need to find a campsite near a tall tree where you can hang your food and other items that may attract bears, such as deodorant, toothpaste, or soap. Carry a lightweight nylon rope with which to hang your food. As a rule you should hang your food at least 15 feet from the ground and 4 feet away from the tree trunk. Trees at higher elevations don't often have branches longer than 5 feet, so you may need to string rope between two trees or find a leaning snag. You can put food and other items in a waterproof stuff sack or a dry bag and tie one end of the rope to the stuff sack. To get the other end of the rope over the tree branch, tie a good-sized rock to it and gently toss the rock over the tree branch. Pull the stuff sack up until it reaches the top of the branch and tie it off securely. Don't hang your food near your tent! If possible, hang your food at least 100 feet away from your campsite. Alternatives to hanging your food are bear-proof plastic tubes and metal bear boxes. Chipmunks, ground squirrels, and pine martens will also steal your food if you don't hang it.

Lastly, think of comfort. Lie down on the ground where you intend to sleep and see if it's a good fit. Bring along an insulating pad for warmth and extra comfort. The days of using pine boughs or digging a hip depression in the ground are long gone. And for the final touch, have your tent face east. You'll appreciate the warmth of the morning sun and have a nice view to wake up to.

First Aid

If you plan to spend a lot of time outdoors hiking, spend a few hours and bucks to take a good wilderness or mountain-oriented first-aid class. You'll not only learn first-aid basics, but also how to be creative miles from nowhere. Specialized companies like Wilderness Medicine Institute (WMI) offer such courses. Check out WMI for course dates and locations at http://wmi.nols.edu.

Now we know you're tough, but get 10 miles into the woods and develop a blister, and you'll wish you had carried a first-aid kit. Face it; it's just plain good sense. Many companies produce lightweight, compact first-aid kits; just make sure yours contains at least the following:

FIRST AID

- ☐ Band-Aids
- ☐ moleskin, duct tape or athletic tape, and/or Band-Aid's Blister Relief Compeed
- ☐ various sterile gauze and dressings
- ☐ white surgical tape
- ☐ an Ace bandage
- ☐ an antihistamine
- ☐ aspirin, ibuprofen, or acetaminophen
- ☐ Betadine solution
- ☐ first-aid book
- ☐ Tums
- ☐ tweezers
- ☐ scissors
- ☐ antibacterial wipes
- ☐ triple-antibiotic ointment
- ☐ plastic gloves
- ☐ sterile cotton tip applicators
- ☐ a thermometer

Here are a few tips for dealing with and hopefully preventing certain ailments.

Sunburn. In most parts of Massachusetts, summer sun can be an intense and constant companion on hikes. It is a good idea to take along sunscreen or sunblock, protective clothing, and a wide-brimmed hat. If you do get sunburn, treat the area with aloe vera gel and protect the area from further sun exposure.

Blisters. Be prepared to take care of these hike-spoilers by carrying moleskin (a lightly padded adhesive), gauze and tape, or Band-Aids. An effective way to apply moleskin is to cut out a circle of moleskin and remove the center—like a doughnut—and place it over the blistered area. Cutting the center out will reduce the pressure applied to the sensitive skin. Other products that can help you combat blisters are Bodyglide and Second Skin. Bodyglide (888-263-9454) is applied to suspicious hot spots before a blister forms to help decrease friction to that area. Second Skin (made by Spenco) is applied to the blister after it has popped and acts as a second skin to help prevent further irritation.

Insect bites and stings. Prevention is the best approach to insect management. Massachusetts has a variety of biting insects, including mosquitoes, blackflies, ticks, deer flies, and no-see-ums. Insects are at their peak in the early summer and after wet weather. The best repellent for insects is protective clothing. Wear loose-fitting, tightly woven, light-colored clothing, as insects are attracted to darker colors. Wear long sleeves and pants tucked into socks. A hat and/or head net protects the face and head. A bandanna with insect repellent can also be worn tied around your neck. In general, having those layers available to put on if insects are troublesome is a good idea. Another preventative measure is to avoid any soaps, lotions, perfumes, or deodorants. These are all products designed to attract, not repel. A diet high in sugars can also attract insects. Being prepared can keep insects from ruining a great hiking experience.

You can treat most insect bites and stings by applying calamine lotion or hydrocortisone 1 percent cream topically and, for bites with moderate swelling, taking a pain medication such as ibuprofen or acetaminophen to reduce swelling. If you forgot to pack these items, a cold compress or a paste of mud and ashes can sometimes assuage the itching and discomfort. Remove any stingers by using tweezers or scraping the area with your fingernail or a knife blade. Don't pinch the area, as you'll only spread the venom.

Some hikers are highly sensitive to bites and stings and may have a systemic allergic reaction, called anaphylaxis, that can be life threatening. This type of reaction usually follows quickly after an exposure, minutes after a sting or bite. Signs of a systemic allergic reaction can include generalized itching, generalized skin redness, hives, swelling of the mouth, face, and neck, low blood pressure, upper and lower airway obstruction with labored breathing, and shock. The treatment for this severe type of reaction is epinephrine (Adrenaline) along with Benadryl. Epinephrine reverses the systemic reaction but does not help the ongoing allergic problem. Administration of Benadryl may prevent continued reaction to the sting, but will not reverse the cardiovascular or respiratory symptoms, which can be life threatening. If you know you're sensitive to bites and stings, carry Benadryl and a prepackaged kit of epinephrine (e.g., Anakit), which can be obtained only by prescription from your doctor.

Ticks. As you well know, ticks can carry disease, such as Rocky Mountain spotted fever and Lyme disease. The best defense is, of course, prevention. If you know you're going to be hiking through an area littered with ticks, wear long pants tucked into socks and a long-sleeved shirt. You can apply a permethrin repellent to your clothing and a DEET repellent to exposed skin. At the end of your hike, do a spot check for ticks (and insects in general). If you do find a tick, coat the insect with Vaseline or tree sap to cut off its air supply. The tick should release its hold, but if it doesn't, grab the head of the tick firmly—with a pair of tweezers if you have them—and gently pull it away from the skin with a twisting motion. Sometimes the mouthparts linger, embedded in your skin. If this happens, try to remove them with a disinfected needle. Clean the affected area with an antibacterial cleanser and then apply triple antibiotic ointment. Monitor the area for a few days. If irritation persists or a white spot develops, see a doctor for possible infection.

Poison ivy, oak, and sumac. These skin irritants can be found most anywhere in North America and come in the form of a bush or a vine, having leaflets in groups of three, five, seven, or nine. Learn how to spot the plants. The oil they secrete can cause an allergic reaction in the form of blisters, usually about 12 hours after exposure. The itchy rash can last from ten days to several weeks. The best defense against these irritants is to wear protective clothing and to apply a nonprescription product such as IvyBlock to exposed skin. This lotion is meant to guard against the effects of poison ivy/oak/sumac and can be washed off with soap and water. Washing with water immediately after contact with the plant can remove any lingering oil from your skin, as the oil is water-soluble. Should you contract a rash from any of these plants, use Benadryl or a similar product to reduce the itching. If the rash is localized, create a light Clorox/water wash or use calamine lotion to dry up the area. If the rash has spread, either tough it out or see your doctor about getting a dose of cortisone (available both orally and by injection).

Snakebites. First off, snakebites are rare in North America. Unless startled or provoked, the majority of snakes will not bite. If you're wise to their habitats and keep a careful eye on the trail, you should be just fine. If you see a snake of any kind, give it wide berth. The standard first aid for snake bites is to get to a doctor within two hours if you can. If not, squeeze out as much venom as possible and try to slow your metabolism by resting, so your kidneys can detoxify the poison faster. Snake bites are not usually life threatening, except in children, the elderly, and people with heart conditions.

Dehydration. Have you ever hiked in hot weather and had a roaring headache and felt fatigued after only a few miles? More than likely you were dehydrated. Symptoms of dehydration include fatigue, headache, and decreased coordination and judgment. When you're hiking, your body's rate of fluid loss depends on the outside temperature, humidity, altitude, and your activity level. On average a hiker walking in warm weather will lose 4 liters of fluid per day. That fluid loss is easily replaced by normal consumption of liquids and food. However, if a hiker is walking briskly in hot, dry weather and hauling a heavy pack, he or she can lose 1 to 3 liters of water per hour. It's important to always carry plenty of water and to stop often and drink fluids regularly, even if you aren't thirsty.

Heat exhaustion is the result of losing large amounts of electrolytes and often occurs if a hiker is dehydrated and has been under heavy exertion. Common symptoms of heat exhaustion include cramping, exhaustion, fatigue, lightheadedness, and nausea. You can treat heat exhaustion by getting out of the sun and drinking an electrolyte solution made up of 1 teaspoon of salt and 1 tablespoon of sugar dissolved in a liter of water. Drink this solution slowly over a period of 1 hour. Drinking plenty of fluids, more than the amount you are losing, can prevent heat exhaustion. Avoid hiking during the hottest parts of the day, and wear breathable clothing, a wide-brimmed hat, and sunglasses. Untreated, heat exhaustion can lead to heatstroke, a life-threatening condition.

Hypothermia is one of the biggest dangers in the backcountry—especially for day hikers in the summertime. That may sound strange, but imagine starting out on a hike in midsummer when it's sunny and 80 degrees. You're clad in nylon shorts and a cotton T-shirt. About halfway through your hike, the sky begins to cloud up, and in the next hour a light drizzle begins to fall and the wind starts to pick up. Before you know it, you're soaking wet and shivering—the perfect recipe for hypothermia. More advanced signs include decreased coordination, slurred speech, and blurred vision. When a victim's temperature falls below 92 degrees Fahrenheit, blood pressure and pulse plummet, possibly leading to coma and death.

To avoid hypothermia, always bring a windproof/rainproof shell, a fleece jacket, and a hat. Remember that Massachusetts temperatures can vary a lot in one day. In spring or fall, or during rainy and windy weather, packing along Capilene tights and gloves is a good idea. Learn to adjust your clothing layers based on the temperature. If you're climbing uphill at a moderate pace, you will stay warm, but when you stop for a break, you'll become cold quickly unless you add more layers of clothing.

If a hiker is showing advanced signs of hypothermia, dress him in dry clothes, including a hat and gloves. Place the victim in a sleeping bag in a tent or shelter that will provide protection from the wind and other elements. Give him warm fluids to drink, and keep him awake.

Frostbite. When the mercury dips below 32°F, your extremities begin to chill. If a persistent chill attacks a localized area, say your hands or your toes, the circulatory system reacts by cutting off blood flow to the affected area—the idea being to protect and preserve the body's overall temperature. And so it's death by attrition for the affected area. Ice crystals start to form from the water in the cells of the neglected tissue. Deprived of heat, nourishment, and now water, the tissue literally starves. This is frostbite.

Prevention is your best defense against this situation. Most prone to frostbite are your face, hands, and feet—so protect these areas well. Wool is the material of choice because it provides ample air space for insulation and draws moisture away from the skin. However, synthetic fabrics have recently made great strides in the cold-weather-clothing market. Do your research. A pair of light silk or polypro liners under your regular gloves or mittens is a good trick for keeping warm. They afford some additional warmth, but more importantly they allow you to remove your mitts for detailed work without exposing the skin. If your feet or hands start to feel cold or numb due to the elements, warm them as quickly as possible. Place cold hands under your armpits or bury them in your crotch. Carry hand and foot warmers if possible. If your feet are cold, change your socks. If there's plenty of room in your boots, add another pair of socks. Remember, though, that constricting your feet in tight boots can restrict blood flow and actually make your feet colder more quickly. Your socks need to have breathing room if they're going to be effective. Dead air provides insulation. If your face is cold, place your warm hands over your face or simply wear a head stocking (called a balaclava).

Should your skin go numb and start to appear white and waxy but is still cold and soft, chances are you've got superficial frostbite. Rewarm as quickly as possible with skin-to-skin contact. No damage should occur. Do *not* let the area get frostbitten again!

If your skin is white and waxy but dents when you press on it, you have partial-thickness frostbite. Rewarm as you would for superficial frostbite, but expect swelling and blisters to form. Don't massage the affected area, but do take ibuprofen for pain and reduction of tissue damage. If blisters form, you need to leave the backcountry.

If your skin is frozen hard like an ice cube, you have full-thickness frostbite. Don't try to thaw the area unless you can maintain the warmth. In other words, don't stop to warm up your frostbitten feet only to head back on the trail. You'll do more damage than good. Tests have shown that hikers who walked on thawed feet did more harm, and endured more pain, than hikers who left the affected areas alone. Do your best to get out of the cold entirely and seek medical attention—which usually consists of performing a rapid rewarming in warm water (104°F–108°F) for 20 to 30 minutes. Get to a doctor as soon as possible!

The overall objective in preventing both hypothermia and frostbite is to keep the body's core warm. Protect key areas where heat escapes, like the top of the head, and maintain the proper nutrition and hydration levels. Foods that are high in calories aid the body in producing heat. Never smoke or drink alcohol when you're in situations where the cold is threatening. By affecting blood flow, these activities ultimately cool the body's core temperature.

Navigation

Whether you are going on a short hike in a familiar area or planning a weeklong backpack trip, you should always be equipped with the proper navigational equipment—at the very least a detailed map and a sturdy compass. But these tools are only useful if you know how to use them. Courses and books are available, so make sure your skills are up to snuff.

Maps. There are many different types of maps available to help you find your way on the trail. Easiest to find are USDA Forest Service maps and Bureau of Land Management (BLM) maps. These maps tend to cover large areas, so be sure they are detailed enough for your particular trip. You can also obtain national park maps as well as high-quality maps from private companies and trail groups. Look for them at outdoor stores or ranger stations. Being large, these maps are best used for trip planning and driving, but not to navigate in the backcountry.

US Geological Survey (USGS) topographic maps (topos) are particularly popular with hikers—especially serious backcountry hikers. These maps contain the standard map symbols such as roads, lakes, and rivers, as well as contour lines that show the details of the trail terrain like ridges, valleys, passes, and mountain peaks. The 7.5-minute series (1 inch on the map equals approximately two-fifths of a mile on the ground) provides the closest inspection available. USGS maps are available by mail (US Geological Survey, Map Distribution Branch, PO Box 25286, Denver, CO 80225), or you can visit them online at www.usgs.gov.

If you want to check out the high-tech world of maps, you can purchase topographic maps on CD-ROM. These software-mapping programs let you select a route on your computer, print it out, and then take it with you on the trail. Some software mapping programs let you insert symbols and labels, download waypoints from a GPS unit, and export the maps to other software programs. Mapping software programs such as DeLorme's TopoUSA (www.delorme.com) and MAPTECH's Terrain Navigator (www.maptech.com) let you do all these things and more. Check out topos on websites such as www.topozone.com, too.

The art of map reading is a skill that you can develop by first practicing in an area you are familiar with. To begin, orient the map so it's lined up in the correct direction (i.e., north on the map is lined up with true north). Next, familiarize yourself with the map symbols and try to match them up with terrain features around you such as a high ridge, mountain peak, river, or lake. If you are practicing with a USGS map, notice the contour lines. On gentler terrain these contour lines are spaced farther apart, and on steeper terrain they are closer together. Pick a short loop trail and stop frequently to check your position on the map. As you practice map reading, you'll learn how to anticipate a steep section on the trail or a good place to take a rest break, etc.

Compasses. First off, the sun is not a substitute for a compass. So what kind of compass should you have? Features you should look for include a rectangular base with detailed scales, a liquid-filled protective housing, a sighting line on the mirror, luminous alignment and back-bearing arrows, a luminous north-seeking arrow, and a well-defined bezel ring.

You can learn compass basics by reading the detailed instructions included with your compass. If you want to fine-tune your compass skills, sign up for an orienteering class or purchase a book on compass reading. Once you've learned the basic skills on using a compass, remember to practice these skills before you head into the backcountry.

Because magnetic north keeps moving around the North Pole and because topo maps use true north, using a map and compass together requires making adjustments for declination (the difference between magnetic and true north). Topo maps show the declination, but if you are looking at a 1970 map, be aware that the declination has changed. To determine current declination, you can download shareware for Windows from the USGS (sorry Mac users!). Check out their website at http://geomag.usgs.gov.

Global Positioning Systems (GPS). If you are a klutz at using a compass, you may be interested in checking out the technical wizardry of the GPS device. The GPS was developed by the Pentagon and works off twenty-four NAVSTAR satellites, which were designed to guide missiles to their targets. A GPS device is a handheld unit that calculates your latitude and longitude with the easy press of a button. The Department of Defense used to scramble the satellite signals a bit to prevent civilians (and spies!) from getting extremely accurate readings, but that practice was discontinued in May 2000, and GPS units now provide nearly pinpoint accuracy (within 30 to 60 feet).

There are many different types of GPS units available, and they range in price from $100 to $400. In general, all GPS units have a display screen and keypad where you input information. In addition to acting as a compass, the unit allows you to plot your route, retrace your path, track your traveling speed, find the mileage between way-points (straight line distance), and calculate the total mileage of your route. Despite the advances in GPS technology, don't put all your trust in your GPS. Per the USGS, "GPS units do not replace basic map and compass skills." Keep in mind that these devices don't pick up signals indoors, in heavily wooded areas, or in deep valleys. And most important to remember, they run on batteries.

Pedometers. A pedometer is a handy device that can track your mileage as you hike. This device is a small, clip-on unit with a digital display that calculates your hiking distance in miles or kilometers based on your walking stride. Some units also calculate the calories you burn and your total hiking time. Pedometers are available at most large outdoor stores and range in price from $20 to $40.

Trip Planning

Planning your hiking adventure begins with letting a friend or relative know your trip itinerary so they can call for help if you don't return at your scheduled time. Your next task is to make sure you are outfitted to experience the risks and rewards of the trail. This section highlights gear and clothing you may want to take with you to get the most out of your hike.

Equipment

With the outdoor market currently flooded with products, many of which are pure gimmickry, it seems impossible to both differentiate and choose. Do I really need a tropical-fish-lined collapsible shower? (No, you don't.) The only defense against the maddening quantity of items thrust in your face is to think practically—and to do so before you go shopping. The worst buys are impulsive buys. Since most name brands will differ only slightly in quality, it's best to know what you're looking for in terms of function. Buy only what you need. You will, don't forget, be carrying what you've bought on your back. Your pack should weigh no more than 30 percent of your body weight. Here are some things to keep in mind before you go shopping.

Clothes. Clothing is your armor against Mother Nature's little surprises. Massachusetts's weather can range from blistering heat to brutal cold, and hikers should be prepared for any possibility, especially when hiking in mountainous areas. The sun may feel hot until a cloud comes along, and instantly the air temperature feels very cool.

During the summer your main consideration is protecting your skin from sunburn and having layers to adapt to changeable weather conditions. Wearing long pants and a long-sleeve shirt made out of materials such as Supplex nylon will protect your skin from the damaging rays of the sun. Avoid wearing 100 percent cotton, as it doesn't dry easily and offers no warmth when wet.

Since the weather can change from warm to chilly quickly, if you wear a T-shirt and shorts, make sure you have top and bottom "insulating" layers (see below) in your pack. Aside from keeping you warm, this layer needs to "breathe" so you stay dry while hiking. A fabric that provides insulation and dries quickly is fleece. (It's interesting to note that this one-of-a-kind fabric is made out of recycled plastic.) Purchasing a zip-up jacket or pullover made of this material is highly recommended.

Another important layer is the "shell" layer. You'll need some type of waterproof, windproof, breathable jacket that'll fit over all your other layers. It should have a large hood that fits over a hat. You'll also need a good pair of rain pants made from a similar waterproof, breathable fabric. A fabric that easily fits the bill is Gore-Tex. However, while a quality Gore-Tex jacket can range in price from $100 to $450, you should know that there are more affordable fabrics out there that work just as well.

Now that you've learned the basics of layering, you can't forget to protect your hands and face. In cold, windy, rainy, or snowy weather, you'll need a hat made of wool or fleece and insulated, waterproof gloves that will keep your hands warm and toasty. Buying a pair of light silk or polypro liners to wear under your regular gloves or mittens is a good idea. They'll allow you to remove your outer gloves for detailed work without exposing the skin. Even in summer a light winter hat and gloves can really help too. Remember, over 50 percent of body heat is lost through the head, so if your extremities are cold, put on that hat! Carry packages of hand and foot warmers if you plan to be above treeline, in case it gets really cold or snowy.

A handy item for those hot canyon or plains hikes is the neck cooler. You have to soak it in water for about 20 minutes, but then it stays damp and helps cool your body through your neck. Even wrapping a wet bandanna around your neck will help cool your body.

For winter hiking or snowshoeing, you'll need an additional lower "wicking" layer of long underwear that keeps perspiration away from your skin. Wearing long underwear made from synthetic fibers such as Capilene, Coolmax, or Thermax is an excellent choice. These fabrics wick moisture away from the skin and draw it toward the next layer of clothing where it then evaporates. Avoid wearing long underwear made of cotton, as it is slow to dry and keeps moisture next to your skin.

Footwear. If you have any extra money to spend on your trip, put that money into boots or trail shoes. Poor-fitting boots will bring a hike to a halt faster than anything else. To avoid this annoyance, buy boots that provide support and are lightweight and flexible. When you purchase footwear, go to an outdoor store that specializes in backpacking and camping equipment. Knowledgeable salespeople can really help you find the right boot and the right fit for the type of hiking/backpacking you want to do. A lightweight hiking boot that can be waterproofed is usually adequate for most day hikes and short backpacks. Trail running shoes provide a little extra cushion and are made in a high-top style that many people wear for hiking. These running shoes are lighter, more flexible, and more breathable than hiking boots. Sturdier boots may be your best bet for rugged trails and multiday backpacks. If you know you'll be hiking in wet weather or crossing streams or muddy areas often, purchase boots or shoes with a Gore-Tex liner, which will help keep your feet dry. Especially during spring and early summer when trails are muddy or snowy, make sure you wear waterproofed boots for maximum dryness. Walking around mud holes and snow damages wet ground and makes a bigger muddy mess. Get muddy! It's easier to clean your boots than repair damaged vegetation.

When buying boots, be sure to wear the same type of socks you'll be wearing on the trail. If the boots you're buying are for heavy-duty or cold-weather hiking, try the boots on while wearing two pairs of socks. Speaking of socks, a good sock combination is to wear a thinner sock made of wool or polypro/nylon covered by a heavier outer sock made of wool or a wool/acrylic blend. The inner sock protects the foot from the rubbing effects of the outer sock and prevents blisters. SmartWool or Thorlos are excellent choices for an outer sock.

Many outdoor stores have some type of ramp to simulate hiking uphill and downhill. Be sure to take advantage of this test, as toe-jamming boot fronts can be very painful and debilitating on a downhill trek.

Once you've purchased your footwear, be sure to break them in before you hit the trail. New footwear is often stiff and needs to be stretched and molded to your foot. A little leather conditioner such as Lexol can help the break-in process without major destruction to your feet in the process.

Hiking poles. Hiking with poles brings interesting comments ranging from "There's no snow now" to "Wow! I wish I had a pair of those on this trail!" Hiking poles help with balance and, more importantly, take pressure off your knees. The ones with shock absorbers are easier on your elbows and your knees. Some poles even come with a camera attachment to be used as a monopod. And heaven forbid you meet a moose, bear, or unfriendly dog, those poles will make you look a lot bigger.

Packs. No matter what type of hiking you do, you'll need a pack of some sort to carry the basic trail essentials. There are a variety of backpacks on the market, but let's first discuss what you intend to use it for: day hikes or overnight trips.

If you plan on doing a day hike, a daypack should have some of the following characteristics: a padded hip belt that's at least 2 inches in diameter (avoid packs with only a small piece of nylon webbing for a hip belt); a chest strap (the chest strap helps stabilize the pack against your body); external pockets to carry water and other items that you want easy access to; an internal pocket to hold keys, a knife, a wallet, and other miscellaneous items; an external lashing system to hold a jacket; and maybe a hydration pocket for carrying a hydration system (which consists of a water bladder with an attachable drinking hose).

For short hikes some hikers like to use a fanny pack to store just a camera, food, a compass, a map, and other trail essentials. Most fanny packs have pockets for two water bottles and a padded hip belt.

If you intend to do an extended, overnight trip, there are multiple considerations. First off, you need to decide what kind of framed pack you want. There are two backpack types for backpacking: the internal frame and the external frame. An internal frame pack rests closer to your body, making it more stable and easier to balance when hiking over rough terrain. An external frame pack is just that, an aluminum frame attached to the exterior of the pack. An external frame pack is better for long backpack trips because it distributes the pack weight better, and you can carry heavier loads. It's easier to pack, and your gear is more accessible. It also offers better ventilation for your back in hot weather.

The most critical measurement for fitting a pack is torso length. The pack needs to rest evenly on your hips without sagging. A good pack will come in two or three sizes and have straps and hip belts that are adjustable according to your body size and characteristics.

When you purchase a backpack, go to an outdoor store with salespeople who are knowledgeable in how to properly fit a pack. Once the pack is fitted for you, load the pack with the amount of weight you plan on taking on the trail. The weight of the pack should be distributed evenly, and you should be able to swing your arms and walk briskly without feeling out of balance. Another good technique for evaluating a pack is to walk up and down stairs and make quick turns to the right and to the left to be sure the pack doesn't feel out of balance.

Other features that are nice to have on a backpack include a removable daypack or fanny pack, external pockets for extra water, and extra lash points to attach a jacket or other items. But remember that all these extra features add weight to the basic pack, cutting down on the amount of other stuff you can carry.

Sleeping bags and pads. Sleeping bags are rated by temperature. You can purchase a bag made of synthetic fiber such as Polarguard HV or DuPont Hollofil II, or you can buy a goose down bag. Goose down bags are more expensive, but they have a higher insulating capacity by weight and will keep their loft longer. You'll want to purchase a bag with a temperature rating that fits the time of year and conditions you are most likely to camp in. One caveat: The techno-standard for temperature ratings is far from perfect. Ratings vary from manufacturer to manufacturer, so to protect yourself you should purchase a bag rated 10 to 15 degrees below the temperature you expect to be camping in. Synthetic bags are more resistant to water than down bags, but many down bags are now made with a Gore-Tex shell that helps to repel water. Down bags are also more compressible than synthetic bags and take up less room in your pack, which is an important consideration if you are planning a multiday backpack trip. Make sure to buy a compression stuff sack for your sleeping bag to minimize the space it consumes in your backpack. Features to look for in a sleeping bag include a mummy-style shape, a hood you can cinch down around your head in cold weather, and draft tubes along the zippers that help keep heat in and drafts out. Some sleeping bags are designed specifically for a woman's anatomy.

You'll also want a sleeping pad to provide insulation and padding from the cold ground. There are different types of sleeping pads available, from the more expensive self-inflating air mattresses like Therm-a-Rest to the less expensive closed-cell foam pads (e.g., RidgeRest). Self-inflating air mattresses are usually heavier than closed-cell foam mattresses and are prone to punctures but can be repaired.

Tents. The tent is your home away from home while on the trail. It provides protection from wind, snow, rain, and insects. A three-season tent is a good choice for backpacking and can range in price from $100 to $500. These lightweight and versatile tents provide protection in all types of weather except heavy snowstorms or high winds, and range in weight from 4 to 8 pounds. Look for a tent that's easy to set up and will easily fit two people with gear. Dome-type tents usually offer more headroom and places to store gear. Other tent designs include a vestibule where you can store wet boots. Some nice-to-have items in a tent include interior pockets to store small items and lashing points to hang a clothesline. Most three-season tents also come with stakes so you can secure the tent in high winds. Before you purchase a tent, set it up and take it down a few times to be sure it is easy to handle, and sit inside the tent and make sure it has enough room for you and your gear.

Cell phones. Many hikers are carrying their cell phones into the backcountry these days in case of emergency. That's fine and good, but please know that cell phone coverage is often poor to nonexistent in valleys, canyons, and thick forest. More serious, people have started to call for help merely because they're tired or lost. Let's go back to being prepared. You are responsible for yourself in the backcountry. Use your brain to avoid problems, and if you do encounter one, first use your brain to try to correct the situation. Only use your cell phone, if it works, in cases of true emergencies.

Day Hikes

❑ daypack

❑ water and water bottles/water hydration system

❑ food and high-energy snacks

❑ first-aid kit

❑ headlamp/flashlight with extra batteries and bulbs

❑ maps and compass/GPS unit

❑ knife/multipurpose tool

❑ sunscreen and sunglasses

❑ insect repellent

❑ matches in waterproof container and fire starter

❑ insulating top and bottom layers (fleece, wool, etc.)

❑ raingear

❑ winter hat and gloves

- ☐ wide-brimmed sun hat
- ☐ extra socks
- ☐ gaiters, depending on season
- ☐ backpacker's trowel, toilet paper, and resealable plastic bags
- ☐ whistle and/or mirror
- ☐ space blanket/bag
- ☐ camera/film
- ☐ guidebook
- ☐ watch
- ☐ water treatment tablets
- ☐ premoistened hand wipes
- ☐ hand and foot warmers if hiking at higher elevations
- ☐ duct tape for repairs

Overnight Trips
(in addition to what's listed for Day Hikes)

- ☐ backpack and waterproof rain cover
- ☐ tent and ground cloth
- ☐ sleeping bag
- ☐ insulating ground pad
- ☐ collapsible water container (2- to 3-gallon capacity)
- ☐ water filter
- ☐ clothing (extra wool socks, shirt and shorts, long pants, long underwear)
- ☐ bandanna
- ☐ sandals or running shoes to wear around camp and to ford streams
- ☐ stove and fuel
- ☐ cook set/utensils and pot scrubber
- ☐ biodegradable soap
- ☐ extra resealable plastic bags
- ☐ garbage bags
- ☐ journal/pen
- ☐ permit (if required)
- ☐ repair kit (tent, stove, pack, etc.)
- ☐ waterproof stuff sacks to store gear (one for hanging food)
- ☐ nylon rope to hang food
- ☐ toiletry items
- ☐ hand towel

Hiking with children isn't a matter of how many miles you can cover or how much elevation gain you make in a day; it's about seeing and experiencing nature through their eyes.

Kids like to explore and have fun. They like to stop and point out bugs and plants, look under rocks, jump in puddles, and throw sticks. If you're taking a toddler or young child on a hike, start with a trail that you're familiar with. Trails that have interesting things for kids, like piles of leaves to play in or a small stream to wade through during the summer, will make the hike much more enjoyable for them and keep them from getting bored.

You can keep your child's attention if you have a strategy before starting on the trail. Using games is not only an effective way to keep a child's attention, but it's also a great way to teach him or her about nature. Play hide and seek, where your child is the mouse and you are the hawk. Quiz children on the names of plants and animals. If your children are old enough, let them carry their own daypack filled with snacks and water. So that you are sure to go at their pace and not yours, let them lead the way. Playing follow the leader works particularly well when you have a group of children. Have each child take a turn at being the leader. *The Kids' Outdoor Adventure Book* by Stacy Tornio and Ken Keffer (FalconGuides) offers 448 great ideas for outdoor and nature activities.

With children, a lot of clothing is key. You always want to bring extra clothing for your children no matter what the season. In the winter, have your children wear wool socks and warm layers such as long underwear, a polar fleece jacket and hat, wool mittens, and a good winter parka. It's not a bad idea to have these along in late fall and early spring as well. Good footwear is also important. A sturdy pair of high-top tennis shoes or lightweight hiking boots are the best bet for little ones. If you're hiking in the summer near a lake or stream, bring along a pair of old sneakers that your child can put on when he or she wants to go exploring in the water. Remember when you're near any type of water to always watch your child at all times. Also keep a close eye on teething toddlers who may decide a rock or a poison mushroom is an interesting item to put in their mouth.

From spring through fall you'll want your kids to wear a wide-brimmed hat to keep their face, head, and ears protected from the hot sun. Also make sure that your children wear sunscreen at all times. Choose a brand without PABA—children have sensitive skin and may have an allergic reaction to sunscreen that contains PABA. If you are hiking with children younger than six months, don't use sunscreen or insect repellent. Instead, be sure that their head, face, neck, and ears are protected from the sun with a wide-brimmed hat, and that all other skin exposed to the sun is protected with the appropriate clothing.

Remember that food is fun. Kids like snacks, so it's important to bring a lot of munchies for the trail. Stopping often for snack breaks is a fun way to keep the trail interesting. Raisins, apples, granola bars, crackers and cheese, Cheerios, and trail mix all make great snacks. If your children are old enough to carry their own backpack, fill it with treats before you leave. If your kids don't like drinking water, you can bring boxes of fruit juice.

Avoid poorly designed child-carrying packs—you don't want to break your back carrying your child. Most child-carrying backpacks designed to hold a 40-pound child will contain a large carrying pocket to hold diapers and other items. Some have an optional rain/sun hood. Tough Traveler (800-GO-TOUGH or www.toughtrav eler.com) is a company that specializes in making backpacks for carrying children and other outdoor gear for children.

Hiking with Your Dog

Bringing your furry friend with you is always more fun than leaving him behind. Our canine pals make great trail buddies because they never complain and always make good company. Hiking with your dog can be a rewarding experience, especially if you plan ahead.

Getting your dog in shape. Before you plan outdoor adventures with your dog, make sure he's in shape for the trail. A good rule of thumb is to assume that your dog will travel twice as far as you will on the trail. If you plan on doing a 5-mile hike, be sure your dog is in shape for a 10-mile hike. Getting your dog into shape takes the same discipline as getting yourself into shape, but luckily your dog can get in shape with you. Take your dog with you on your daily runs or walks. If there is a park near your house, hit a tennis ball or play Frisbee with your dog.

Swimming is also an excellent way to get your dog into shape. If there is a lake or river near where you live and your dog likes the water, have him retrieve a tennis ball or stick. Gradually build up your dog's stamina over a two- to three-month period.

Training your dog for the trail. Before you go on your first hiking adventure with your dog, be sure he has a firm grasp on the basics of canine etiquette and behavior. Make sure he can sit, lie down, stay, and come. One of the most important commands you can teach your canine pal is to "come" under any situation. It's easy for your friend's nose to lead him astray or possibly get lost. Another helpful command is the "get behind" command. When you're on a hiking trail that's narrow, you can have your dog follow behind you when other trail users approach. Nothing is more bothersome than an enthusiastic dog that runs back and forth on the trail and disrupts the peace of the trail for others. When you see other trail users approaching, give them the right of way by quietly stepping off the trail and making your dog lie down and stay until they pass. The best bet is to keep your dog on a leash to prevent injury to him and to avoid harassing other hikers, horses, and wildlife. Complaints about dogs in the backcountry are on the rise. Be a responsible dog owner to ensure you can keep taking your buddy into the backcountry with you.

Equipment. The most critical pieces of equipment you can invest in for your dog are proper identification and a sturdy leash. Flexi-leads work well for hiking because they give your dog more freedom to explore but still leave you in control. Make sure your dog has identification that includes your name and address and a number for your veterinarian. Other forms of identification for your dog include a tattoo or a microchip. You should consult your veterinarian for more information on these last two options.

The next piece of equipment you'll want to consider is a pack for your dog. By no means should you hold all of your dog's essentials in your pack—let him carry his own gear! Dogs that are in good shape and don't have physical problems can carry up to 25 percent of their own weight for multiple days.

Companies that make good-quality packs include RuffWear (888-RUFF-WEAR; www.ruffwear.com), Granite Gear (218-834-6157; www.granitegear.com), and Wolf Packs (541-482-7669; www.wolfpacks.com). Most packs are fitted by a dog's weight and girth measurement. Companies that make dog packs generally include guidelines to help you pick out the size that's right for your dog. Some characteristics to look for when purchasing a pack for your dog include a harness with two padded girth straps, a padded chest strap, leash attachments, removable saddle bags, internal water bladders, and external gear cords.

You can introduce your dog to the pack by first placing the empty pack on his back and letting him wear it around the yard. Keep an eye on him during this first introduction. He may decide to chew through the straps if you aren't watching closely. Once he learns to treat the pack as an object of fun and not a foreign enemy, fill the pack evenly on both sides with a few ounces of dog food in resealable plastic bags. Have your dog wear his pack on your daily walks for a period of two to three weeks. Each week add a little more weight to the pack until your dog will accept carrying the maximum amount of weight he can carry.

You can also purchase collapsible water and dog food bowls for your dog. Plastic storage containers also work well and double to protect your dog's food from getting wet. These bowls are lightweight and can easily be stashed into your pack or your dog's. Some dogs don't like the collapsible bowls, so see what works before heading into the backcountry. If you plan on hiking on rocky terrain or in the snow, you can purchase footwear for your dog that will protect his feet from cuts and bruises. All of these products can be purchased from RuffWear (888-RUFF-WEAR; www.ruff wear.com).

The following is a checklist of items to bring when you take your dog hiking:

❑ water bowls
❑ a comb
❑ a collar and a leash
❑ dog food
❑ a dog pack
❑ flea/tick powder

- paw protection
- water
- resealable plastic bags
- a first-aid kit that contains eye ointment, tweezers, scissors, stretchy foot wrap, gauze, antibacterial wash, sterile cotton tip applicators, antibiotic ointment, and cotton wrap

You might consider carrying contact lens saline solution for flushing any doggie wounds. For backpacking, consider bringing a pad or mat to put in your tent for your dog. Never leave your dog tied up in camp unattended. He might become a meal for a predator.

Cleaning up after your dog. Although it sounds unpleasant, use resealable plastic bags to pick up and carry out your dog's waste or bury them like human feces.

Barking dogs. Most people hike and backpack to escape the sounds of the city, including barking dogs. If your dog is a barker, best to leave him at home to avoid dogs getting any more bad raps in the backcountry.

Bears and moose. If your dog discovers and provokes a bear or a moose, and the animal starts chasing him, you'll probably be the destination of this mad chase. In bear and moose country, keep your dog on a leash for his own safety.

Lost dogs. It's not unusual for an unleashed dog to stray from its owner, only to spoil a trip while you hunt for the wayward pooch or, worse, never see him again. If your dog does not respond well to voice commands, keep him leashed for his own safety.

First aid for your dog. Your dog is just as prone—if not more prone—to getting in trouble on the trail as you are, so be prepared. Here's a rundown of the more likely misfortunes that might befall your little friend.

Bees and wasps. If a bee or wasp stings your dog, remove the stinger with a pair of tweezers and place a mudpack or a cloth dipped in cold water over the affected area.

Porcupines. One good reason to keep your dog on leash is to prevent him from getting a nose full of porcupine quills. You may be able to remove the quills with a pair of pliers, but a vet is the best person to do this nasty job because most dogs need to be sedated.

Heatstroke. Avoid hiking with your dog in really hot weather. Dogs with heatstroke will pant excessively, lie down and refuse to get up, and become lethargic and disoriented. If your dog shows any of these signs on the trail, have him lie down in the shade. If you are near a stream, pour cool water over your dog's entire body to help bring his body temperature back to normal.

Dehydration. Dogs may dehydrate faster than humans, so make sure your dog is drinking enough water.

Heartworm. Dogs get heartworms from mosquitoes that carry the disease in the prime mosquito months of July and August. Giving your dog a monthly pill prescribed by your veterinarian easily prevents this condition.

Plant pitfalls. Plant hazards include burrs, thorns, thistles, and poison ivy. If you find any burrs, foxtails, or thistles on your dog, remove them as soon as possible before they become an unmanageable mat. Thorns can pierce a dog's foot and cause a great deal of pain. If you see that your dog is lame, stop and check his feet for thorns. Dogs are immune to poison ivy but they can pick up the sticky, oily substance from the plant and transfer it to you.

Protect those paws. Be sure to keep your dog's nails trimmed so he avoids getting soft tissue or joint injuries. If your dog slows and refuses to go on, check to see that his paws aren't torn or worn. You can protect your dog's paws from trail hazards such as sharp gravel, talus, ice, snowballs, and thorns by purchasing dog boots.

Ticks and fleas. Dogs can get Rocky Mountain spotted fever from ticks, as well as other diseases, like Lyme disease. Before you hit the trail, treat your dog with a flea and tick spray or powder. You can also ask your veterinarian about a once-a-month pour-on treatment that repels fleas and ticks.

Mosquitoes and deer flies. These little flying machines can do a job on your dog's snout and ears. Best bet is to spray your dog with fly repellent for horses, to discourage both pests from bothering your dog.

Giardia. Dogs can get giardia, which results in diarrhea. It is usually not debilitating, but definitely messy.

Mushrooms. Make sure your dog doesn't sample mushrooms along the trail. They could be poisonous to him, but he doesn't know that.

Websites. A number of websites have excellent hints about hiking and backpacking with your dog. Suggested sites include: www.petmd.com or http://www.back packer.com

Dog regulations. When you and your dog are finally ready to hit the trail, keep in mind that national parks and monuments and some state parks do not allow dogs on trails. Your best bet is to hike in national forests, BLM lands, and canine-friendly state parks. Always call ahead to see what the regulations are, as they may change from time to time.

Mile Circle trail reaches the shore of Flowering Pond (hike 15).

Hike Index

About the Author

When he's not cranking out newspaper and magazine stories on deadline, Ben has been lucky to call New England his outdoor playground. He even proposed to his wife, Shannon, while they were cross-country skiing through the Vermont woods one January day. Nowadays they chase their children down ski trails, bike paths, canoe launches, and frozen ponds.

Ben's indoor education includes an economics degree from Colby College (Waterville, Maine) and a master's in journalism from Columbia University (NYC). But perhaps more important was his outdoor education, including childhood summers at Camp Chewonki (Wiscasset, Maine), and semesters at the Mountain School (Vershire, Vermont) and Sea Education Association (Woods Hole, Massachusetts).

PHOTO BY ANNIE BRANCH

Before he started earning a living in journalism, he worked outdoor jobs like commercial fishing for halibut in Alaska, running the harbor launch at a Maine yacht club, and guiding visitors around a New Mexico ranch on horseback. Those jobs pale in comparison to writing about something he loves—the hiking trails of Massachusetts.

◀ *Birdhouses on fence rails add to the natural diversity of the Borderland State Park (hike 3).*

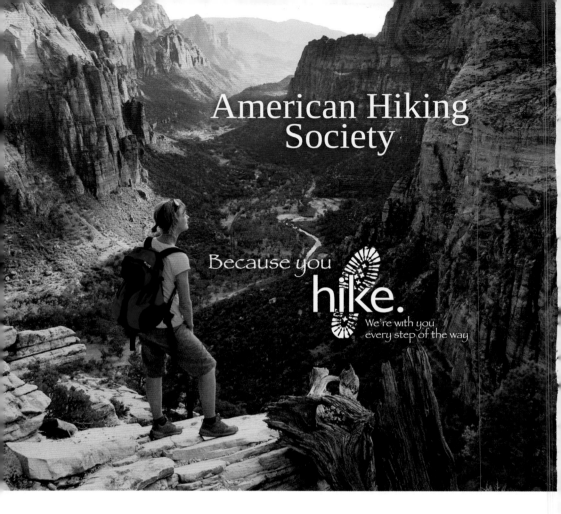

American Hiking Society

Because you **hike.**
We're with you every step of the way

As a national voice for hikers, **American Hiking Society** works every day:

- Building and maintaining hiking trails
- Educating and supporting hikers by providing information and resources
- Supporting hiking and trail organizations nationwide
- Speaking for hikers in the halls of Congress and with federal land managers

Whether you're a casual hiker or a seasoned backpacker, become a member of American Hiking Society and join the national hiking community! You'll enjoy great member benefits and help preserve the nation's hiking trails, so tomorrow's hike is even better than today's. We invite you to join us now!

American Hiking Society